ROLAND G.
HENIN

Dear Danielle Hover ...
Thank-you so very much for
your support and your
contribution to
Mentoring ....

Kindly Accept this Book
As a token of our
Appreciation for your
Efforts.
in Good Cooking ...
Always!
Enjoy! Sincerely!!

R.G. Henin, CMC
Nov. 2017

Also by Susan Crowther

The No Recipe Cookbook
The Vegetarian Chef
Lifestyles for Learning

ROLAND G.
HENIN

CERTIFIED MASTER CHEF
50 YEARS OF MENTORING
GREAT AMERICAN CHEFS

SUSAN CROWTHER

FOREWORD BY
Thomas Keller

AFTERWORD BY
Raimund Hofmeister, CMC

Skyhorse Publishing

Skyhorse Publishing books may be purchased in bulk at special discounts for sales promotion, corporate gifts, fund-raising, or educational purposes. Special editions can also be created to specifications. For details, contact the Special Sales Department, Skyhorse Publishing, 307 West 36th Street, 11th Floor, New York, NY 10018 or info@skyhorsepublishing.com.

www.skyhorsepublishing.com

10 9 8 7 6 5 4 3 2 1

Library of Congress Cataloging-in-Publication Data is available on file.

ISBN: 978-1-51072-800-4
eISBN: 978-1-51072-801-1

Cover design by Jenny Zemanek
Cover photo by Tom McCann

Printed in the United States of America

To Bill Tyler, for giving me my first dishwashing job.
To Chef Pierre Latuberne, in gratitude.

Thank you to the following chefs and colleagues of Roland Henin who contributed to the creation of this project:

Peter Afouxinedes
Larry Banares
William Bennett
Jill Bosich, CEC
Beth Brown, PCII
Edward Brown, AOS
Mary Burich
David Burke, AOS
Adolfo Calles, CCC
Nick Catlett, CEC
Mike Colameco, AOS
David Coombs
Alex Darvishi
Ron DeSantis, CMC
Kevin Doherty, PCIII, CEC
Jerry Dollar
Mark Erickson, CMC
Susan Ettesvold, CEPC
John Fisher
Andrew Friedman
Steve Giunta, CMC
Christopher Gould
Scott Green
Hartmut Handke, CMC
James Hanyzeski, CMC
Dawn Hedges, CSC
Raimund Hofmeister, CMC
Dan Hugelier, CMC
Larry Johnson, CEC

David Kellaway, CMC
Thomas Keller
Keith Keogh
Ambarish Lulay
Chris Matta
Lawrence McFadden, CMC
Kenneth McNamee
David Megenis, CMC
Steve Mengel
Ferdinand Metz, CMC
Ashley Miller
Mark Mistriner
Colin Moody, PCII, CEC
Jeffrey Mora
Lou Piuggi
Franz Popperl
Richard Rosendale, CMC
Kevin Ryan
Scott Steiner
Dan Thiessen
Brad Toles
Lynne Toles
Randy Torres, PCIII, CEC
Juan Carlos Velez
Percy Whatley, PCIII, CEC
Brian Williams
Pam Williams
Jon Wilson, CEC

Contents

The Interviews

The Executive Chef
Thomas Keller
Steve Mengel
Jerry Dollar

The General: Culinary Institute of America
David Burke
Mike Colameco
Edward Brown
Lou Piuggi
Pamela Williams

The Coach: Team USA, Culinary Olympics
Larry Banares
Jeffrey Mora
Franz Popperl
Keith Keogh
Kevin L. Ryan
Kevin Doherty
Andrew Friedman

The Director: The Art Institute of Seattle
Dan Thiessen
John Fisher
Brian Williams

The Judge: American Culinary Federation
Jill Bosich
Susan Ettesvold
Randy Torres

The Corporate Chef: Delaware North
Percy Whatley
William Bennett
Ambarish Lulay
Colin Moody
Mary Burich
Larry Johnson
Scott Green
Jon Wilson
Chris Gould
Beth Brown
Ashley Miller
Dawn Hedges; Nick Catlett; Juan Carlos Valdez; Aldofo Calles

Certified Master Chefs
Dan Hugelier
Steve Giunta
Raimund Hofmeister
Ron DeSantis
Rich Rosendale

Foreword

by Thomas Keller

In all professions without doubt, but certainly in cooking one is a student all his life.
                                                    —Fernand Point

L
ike a lot of people in our profession, I began my culinary education at a young age, and I've had many teachers along the way. But there's only one teacher I call my mentor, the person who has done more than any other to make me the chef I am today.

I first crossed paths with Master Chef Roland G. Henin in the summer of 1977. I was twenty-one and working as a cook at the Dunes Club in Narragansett, Rhode Island. Roland was executive chef. At that point in my life, what appealed to me most about cooking was the physicality of it. It required strength, stamina, and quickness. It was an exhilarating challenge, like being part of a sports team. You were always competing, either with your fellow cooks or with the orders. Very often, you were up against both.

Then, as now, I was an energetic cook. But I lacked direction. There was no broader purpose to what I did, no overarching vision. With a few words from Chef Henin, that all changed. We were in the kitchen together when Chef Henin summed it up: There is a reason that cooks cook. And that reason is to nurture people. That observation sounds so fundamental to me now. But at the time, it struck me with the force of a revelation. Yes, cooking was physical. But it was also emotional, a conduit for human connection. We cook to nurture. To make people happy. To create lasting memories around a meal. Chef Henin's words became my guiding principle, the foundation of everything I try to do.

Of course, there were many other lessons from that summer. I was the low man in the kitchen hierarchy, often tasked with the rudiments of preparing staff meals. What Chef Henin taught me about French technique could nearly fill a textbook. As patient as he was stern, he encouraged repetition and a keen attention to detail, the better to gain mastery over all the steps. To this day, I wouldn't say I've perfected hollandaise—or anything else in the kitchen—because there is no such thing as perfection. But you can strive for perfection through perseverance, and find joy in the process. Chef Henin helped me discover that joy.

Chef Henin also gave me my second cookbook (my mother gave me my first), *Ma Gastronomie* by Fernand Point, the late, great chef of La Pyramide in Vienne, France. It was not so much a recipe book as a book about a man and his commitment to a restaurant: a deep, enriching book about the life of a chef. It's a book that I still use and give to all young cooks.

In 2008, when I was fortunate enough to contribute a forward to a new edition of *Ma Gastronomie*, I asked Chef Henin what had prompted him to give me a copy all those years ago. He said that there were times when he'd watch me in the kitchen and notice how content I seemed, that regardless of whether I was having a good day or a bad day, it looked like I belonged. That sense of belonging has carried me through many chapters of my life, and I'm grateful to Chef Henin for that gift.

I could go on. My relationship with Chef Henin is deeply personal. But I am far from the only person in the culinary world who owes him a debt of gratitude. Chef Henin's influence is too vast to measure. But in the wonderful book you now hold in your hands, Susan Crowther gives us a sense of its dimension. Like me, Susan learned at Chef Henin's side. And here she offers intimate accounts of fifty others who did the same. Each chapter helps round out a portrait of the man I'm proud to call my mentor and the many hats he has worn through the years—from his tenure as an instructor at the Culinary Institute of America (where he was fondly known as the General) to his role as a coach for the American team at the 2009 Bocuse d'Or, an international culinary competition, the significance of which is hard to overstate.

The Bocuse d'Or is not about individual achievement. It is a team event, meant to elevate respect for our entire profession. Its impact is global, but it has been felt especially keenly here in the United States. I have been blessed in my career and have received many honors. But none was greater than what I enjoyed as president of this year's gold medal–winning team at the Bocuse d'Or, held in Lyon, France. At that moment, as ever, I was merely following a path blazed by my mentor. It is only fitting that proceeds from this book will go to the Ment'or Foundation supporting young culinarians and Team USA.

Forty years ago, when I was young and eager and wholly inexperienced, just getting my start at the Dunes Club, I never could have imagined the future that awaited. Chef Henin opened my eyes to the possibilities and guided me toward them. This past year in France, as I stood beside Team USA, singing the national anthem, holding the golden Bocuse aloft, my heart swelled and my mind flooded with thoughts of Chef Henin. He was with me then, just as he always was from the beginning, just as he has been for so many others.

I think I speak for all of Chef Henin's mentees when I say that I can never fully repay all that he has given me. But I've long made it my business to try to measure up by offering whatever guidance I can to others. In short: by being a mentor. It's the very least that I can do.

—Thomas Keller, Chef/Proprietor, The French Laundry

Prologue
The Salmon Run

Cooking is an accumulation of details done to perfection.

—Fernand Point

The Pacific salmon is a peculiar creature. Their entire lives are driven by one specific goal. While each species has adapted its own particular set of rules, all salmon share a common life cycle.

Salmon eggs are deposited in the river where their parents were born. Baby salmon briefly receive nourishment from the yolk sac but soon have to fend for themselves. After receiving this nourishment, young ones emerge from their birthplace, begin swimming freely, and seek food for the first time. They live here for two years, developing survival skills; navigating river currents; "schooling," or traveling in unison; instinctually hiding from danger.

Abruptly, young salmon undergo an extreme and dynamic shift: a physiological change occurs that prevents salt from being absorbed into their bloodstream. This unique adaptation enables salmon to live in salt water—actually, to be more precise, the change forces them to leave the relative safety of their homes and venture outward. Young adults begin their migration down the river and into the ocean, spreading themselves widely among the open waters. During this time, they complete their full transformations in size, physical appearance, and behavior. They will spend years in the ocean, slowly . . . steadily . . . preparing.

When adults reach full maturity, it is time: salmon make the long, arduous journey back to the rivers where they were born. Their whole lives lead to this. Most adults seek their native lands, but some never return home; instead, they travel to nearby, and sometimes far away, waters. It is important that some adults stray from their home; otherwise, new habitats would not be colonized.

The salmon run is one of nature's great, weird migrations. Life energy gained in the ocean is used for one purpose: to spawn. Salmon must fully develop in the ocean and build up reserves, for, once adults re-enter the river, they stop investing in the maintenance of their bodies. They instinctively persist, and their journey proves ultimately fatal.

There are a few theories why this is: 1) Transformation kills. Adult salmon have adapted to saltwater life, and, therefore, returning to freshwater destroys them. Their cells are unable to adjust to the change, or more accurately, unable to re-adjust. 2) Exhaustion kills. Swimming upstream—flipping their bodies in the air and hurling themselves against the downward flowing water—is no easy feat. From the perspective of natural selection, only the strongest (and, perhaps, luckiest) survive. 3) Starvation kills. Once they hit the river, salmon stop eating. Out of those that successfully return, up to 95 percent of them simply die of hunger. Whatever the reason, salmon that survive the ordeal are unable to make it back to the ocean.

Why travel out to sea if they are going to return to the river? Why leave the ocean if the journey home is what kills them? Can't they just grow up where they are born? Well, not exactly. The ocean provides things unavailable in the river, including valuable nutrients such as trace minerals. When adult salmon die and decompose, their ocean-rich remains provide nutrition for their babies, the plants, and insects. These plants and insects, in turn, provide nutrition for maturing salmon, thus preparing them for *their* journey out to sea, where they will gather more nutritional riches to bring back to their homeland. The cycle continues.

Nature has provided a cruel but successful adaptation: with no chance of survival, adults devote their resources to the quest, sacrificing themselves in the process. They take bigger risks along the way upstream. Minor injuries won't have a chance to become infected because the salmon are not going to be around long enough. The salmon's journey focuses on one goal, a race against time that ends in a singular moment.

Salmon give it their all, create life, and then die.

Introduction

How Good Could the Guy Actually Be?

Well . . . with all of this hysteria related to foods in America—some good and some bad—it was bound to finally happen. Someone in this country just wrote a fabulous book about foods and what is the most important part of the cooking process . . . *No Recipe Cookbook* or cooking without recipes. What a "novel" idea! And from Susie Crowther, a former student, on top of that . . . simply amazing!

Yes, I say "finally," because the last one in existence—as far as I know, the only one that has ever existed—was written in the 1960s by an extraordinary chef: *Ma Gastronomie*, by Fernand Point, Chef Owner of La Pyramide in Vienne, in the suburb of Lyon. La Pyramide was, in Chef Point's day, possibly one of the best restaurants in the world and where many of the "Bocuse Gang" famous chefs did their apprenticeships.

I sat stunned, reading the email from Master Chef Roland G. Henin. Chef had responded to my "book blurb request" with a 650-word essay, which immediately became the foreword for *The No Recipe Cookbook: A Beginner's Guide to the Art of Cooking*. I hadn't expected to receive a reply to my inquiry, much less an actual book blurb. Yet, here I sat, reading his response that compared my writing and culinary philosophy to Fernand Point's. It was completely overwhelming, and I exploded. Tears streamed down my face. I must have been howling for some time because my husband oddly inquired, "Are you *okay*?" In a blubbering mess, I sputtered out an explanation.

In the spring of 1983, just before entering the Culinary Institute of America (CIA), my parents invited me to accompany them on a month-long trip to Europe. My father had a conference in Paris, and in a fit of altruism, believed I ought to experience a few "two- and three-star Michelins" before entering culinary school. I was thrilled. We dined at Tour d'Argent and La Pyramide. Tour d'Argent was exquisite, but so polished and intimidating for a young American. A dozen waiters attended to our table of three. One male waiter dressed in full tails escorted me to the bathroom, waited outside the door until I finished, and escorted me back to my table. The meticulous attention to detail bordered on creepy.

Then we visited La Pyramide, and my life changed forever. Natural, comfortable, impeccable—the freshest, most flavorful and balanced tastes—simply, the most delightful meal I'd ever experienced. I had no idea such dining existed. Each bite sang in my mouth. I smiled the entire time. The amazing part was how *relaxed* we felt: so unpretentious and welcoming were the food and its people. I loved who I was in its ambience.

To be discussed in connection with the creator of La Pyramide—my greatest dining experience—was surreal. But to have this praise come from Roland Henin . . . this was the greatest moment of my life.

* * *

The last time I had spoken with Roland Henin had been thirty years prior to that email. In the week before graduation, Chef had passed me in the hall and inquired where I would be working. I remember eking out a pathetic reply: "Uh, Chef, I'm still searching for a position." He stopped, glared impatiently, and then immediately turned around, gesturing with a grunt. I followed him to his office. Chef picked up the phone and dialed a number. Within seconds, he was speaking French in a loud and gregarious voice. After a few minutes, he hung up, wrote something down on a piece of paper, and handed it to me. He finally spoke. "Take zees. You start next week." I looked down at the paper. On it he wrote: *Café du Parc, Lake Park, Florida. Pierre Latuberne.* By the time I looked up to thank him, he was gone.

Thirty years later, I find myself driving to Buffalo, New York, to meet Chef Henin at the Niagara Falls Culinary Institute (NFCI). Chef has invited me to witness two of his protégés—Executive Chefs of Delaware North Corporation (DN)—in final preparations for their Certified Master Chef (CMC) exam to be held in one month in Pasadena, California. Since his foreword contribution,

Chef Henin and I had begun collaborating on another book project. While Chef refused a biography and balked at being featured, he was open to contributing a few stories. We spoke about once a month. Trust grew. Eventually, Chef suggested interviewing mentees to offer stories about working with him to deepen the perspective. After several interviews, Chef Henin suggested the visit to Buffalo. "If you want to know me and what I do, it would be good for you to observe the practice session for the CMC exam."

The drive from Brattleboro, Vermont to Buffalo, New York is approximately four hundred miles.

* * *

As I make my way along Interstate 90 West, my mind wanders back . . . back to 1983, at the Culinary Institute of America, in Hyde Park, New York. I am at the most prestigious culinary school in the nation, at a time when "American Chef" was an oxymoron. An image of a man appears, in a place called the Fish Kitchen . . . what a silly name for a kitchen, yet this place was no joke.

Students attended Fish Kitchen just before embarking on their several-month externship. It served as a capstone of sorts—the completion of the first half of their academic journey. Fish Kitchen was also a rite of passage, run by some crazy Frenchman, the *Great Chef ROOLLAAAHHND*. Tall dude, intimidating. Apparently some big shot.

At the beginning of the unit, Chef Henin addressed his new students, announcing that if the group performed in a *particularly outstanding* manner, students could remain after class to ask him questions. Chef Henin taught the "PM" or dinner shift. Now, "after class" was around midnight, and the last thing any young alcohol-driven culinarian wants is to "have the honor" of staying after class to ask questions—questions that wouldn't even be on a future test!

Except . . .

Except that *this was Master Chef Roland Henin*. Every student understood what a rare privilege it was to speak with this great man, and that, in turn, offered bragging rights: the later we stayed, the better we looked. Culinary school was competitive, and we used any possible marker available to distinguish ourselves from our peers in order to gain the prime opportunities post-graduation. In the evenings, as classes ended their shifts and students began milling down the halls, everyone would take a moment to peek into Chef Henin's kitchen. If the lights were still on, they peered jealously at the sacred group who had performed an exemplary job and were duly awarded the opportunity of remaining in his presence to garner sage secrets of the craft.

What was it about this man? I worked with him for only one month, over thirty years ago, yet he remains as present in my mind as if it were today. Whenever someone asks, "Who was the greatest influence in your culinary career?" Henin immediately comes to mind. Honestly, if anyone asks, "Who is the greatest influence in your life, period?" The same name emerges. How can it be that, after such a brief time, this man left more of an impression in my life than any other teacher, relative, friend, or counselor?

I often wonder if I have simply romanticized our brief encounter. And now, continuing down Interstate 90, I begin doubting the sanity of making this nearly thousand-mile round trip. What did I expect? That Master Chef Roland G. Henin would present himself as some sage guru? That I would be validated in this long-held fantasy?

I mean, seriously. How good could the guy actually be?

* * *

I arrived in Niagara Falls after 9:00 p.m. and left a voice message with Chef, planning to see him in the morning. He immediately returned my call and said to come over, immediately. When I arrived, the two CMC candidates were finishing up their training for the night. I inquired about Chef. While the candidates cleaned and prepared for the following day, Chef Henin had gravitated into the adjacent kitchen where the NFCI Junior Culinary team practiced. I opened the door to the kitchen. The room appeared dim and quiet, yet active. Young students were stationed at several tables, creating pie shells. Everyone focused downward, their hands busy with the pastry.

A chef instructor greeted me with a smile and outstretched hand. I had already interviewed Scott Steiner and looked forward to meeting him. After we made our acquaintances, I asked if Chef Henin was there. He smiled more broadly, gesturing toward the back of the kitchen. I looked over to where a tall man in a long white lab coat stood with his back toward us, leaning over a workstation. Two students were on either side of him, peering in. The tall man said something to the students that made them smile and nod their heads. He patted one student gently on the back and then began slowly walking past the next table, looking at more students' work.

Chef Steiner called out to the tall man in the long white lab coat. Chef Henin slowly turned around and looked up. He walked toward me.

Roland,

There isn't a day that goes by when I don't give thanks for all you did to make my career so special. With your guidance and keen eye for details you put me on the right path on a passion I so loved. I have shared your name so many times over the years to my young cooks and upper management, to always do things right and give it your best at all times. I truly feel blessed that you gave me the chance and believed in me. I'll never forget when you called me in to your office when I was nineteen years old. You told me I had a natural gift for cooking, that I was too young to understand, but one day would. I understand now, as I have seen and taught some young culinarians who are so talented. My best to you, my friend and mentor, and have a great day.

Jerry

This letter arrived on August 8, 2015; however, it could have arrived at any time within the past fifty years. Roland Henin has received thousands of such messages, all relating the same sentiment: *You changed my life for the better, more than anyone else, and I will always remember.*

Roland Henin is a notable chef—a Certified Master Chef, in fact—one of an elite group in the United States. Since its inception in 1981, only sixty-eight chefs have earned this right. He is also a master fisherman, if one might earn such a title. Seafood purveyor Ed Brown quipped, "The man is half-fish." But what Roland Henin is most—what he is the greatest at, what matters most to him and makes him who he is—is a mentor. Chef Steve Mengel, his former CIA student, says, "Chef Henin is more of a teacher than a chef . . . his way is to instruct, inspire, transform . . . to *produce* great chefs."

Roland Henin is the *chef's chef*, the man behind the scenes. Identify a culinary rock star and inquire about his greatest influences: as an apprentice with the Balsams and Greenbrier resorts; as a student at the Culinary Institute of America; as a gold medalist in culinary competitions; or as one of the many culinarians to pass through Delaware North. Chef Henin left his mark.

This is truly remarkable, when you consider how this man was made. How is it that a man—

- whose father died when he was young
- who chose to be estranged from his stepfather
- who claims to have no mentor in his life

—became, perhaps, the greatest culinary mentor in America?

What Chef Henin leaves behind—more than any gold medal or three-star Michelin restaurant, more than any wild kitchen story or life lesson—is mentoring. His legacy is thousands of great chefs—chefs deeply rooted in the fundamentals while harshly challenged to embrace their own unique gifts. Chef Henin is the Johnny Appleseed of this industry. Every culinary venue, competition, and federation is associated with this man. Over the course of fifty years, spanning across the globe, Chef Henin has singlehandedly affected an entire contemporary culinary culture . . . one chef at a time.

Chef Thomas Keller coined it best in stating, "There was Zeus, and there was Roland, god of cooking."

* * *

Roland Henin was one in the early waves of European chefs to cross the Atlantic and bring classical cuisine to American culture. After World War II, European chefs began settling in America and opening restaurants. They brought with them their culinary secrets and cooks from their country. This culture remained insular. "American Chef" was indeed an oxymoron; it simply did not exist. American culture was caught up in fast food and frozen dinners. America was a baby—so far behind.

The first US culinary school, the Culinary Institute of America, founded in 1946 by Frances Roth, served as a vocational school for postwar veterans to learn a trade. The Greenbrier Culinary Apprenticeship Program in West Virginia opened about a decade later. In 1970, the CIA relocated to its current Hyde Park, New York location. From there, change happened swiftly. Johnson & Wales established its culinary arts program in 1973. The Culinary Apprenticeship at the Balsams Grand Resort Hotel in New Hampshire followed suit in the mid-1970s. Master Chef Ferdinand Metz took over the helm as president of the CIA in 1980, and soon after, opened the American Bounty Restaurant—one of the first in the nation devoted to American cuisine. "Bounty" was one of three student-staffed restaurants to make their debut on the Hyde Park campus in a three-year span.

The next generation of immigrant chefs longing to remain in the states, including our Chef Henin, had options. They could prove their worth not only in the restaurants, but also as culinary educators. Henin explains:

All the first American chefs were immigrants. There were French restaurants in Montreal, Quebec, New York, Chicago, and also, more ethnic cuisine—Chinese and Italian. In 1967, immigration was more lenient. Still, you had to prove you were a teacher—able to train and contribute. As a chef, I could train others to become a chef!

From the late sixties to early eighties, Old School chefs founded restaurants in major US cities, hiring only fellow Europeans, even though American cooks were now being trained by their European colleagues in US culinary schools. Mike Colameco, founder/producer of *Real Food* on PBS, recalls,

> You don't think of it, these days. It seems like such a long time ago. I don't want to say "bias," but there was a hiring practice . . . you could kind of understand it, in a very myopic way: they were trained in France; they were comfortable working with people who spoke the same language; they had the same cultural traditions and culinary reference points. If you say, *I wanna make a certain type of consommé, or I want to do a Dover sole, or a lamb this way,* everybody was on the same page.
>
> The idea of American cooks was still pretty new on the upper levels: the CIA and Johnson & Wales were producing graduates who were good cooks after they got out, or especially a few years out. Regardless, you couldn't get a job as a CIA grad if you weren't French, in those kitchens. It is hard to think back on a time when being American [laughs]—no, or being a white male in any industry—was going to work against you.

In a kind of odd "reverse cultural" discrimination, pioneering chefs like Roland Henin and Jean-Jacques Rachou became subversive radicals in this New World. Civil rights and punk rock sensibility extended beyond the college campus and into professional kitchens. These culinary visionaries didn't just embrace their new life; they forced open the doors for this first generation of young chefs, desperate to enter into their own culinary culture, and later, to establish their own cuisine. Guys like Roland Henin broke down the walls of discrimination and, quite literally, created the American Chef. Mike Colameco continues,

> The baton passed to us, from them. Now, when I look back contextually, we all stand on the shoulders of these guys. That's how it works; there's no other way to put it. We learned cooking from them. We learned the restaurant business from them. By the 1990s, Americans were chefs in their own right.

With each phone call to his colleagues and each scrap of paper he'd hand to a student, Roland Henin planted an American seed into American culinary soil. The next time you enjoy that hot new restaurant, grab a bite at a gourmet food cart, choose from an array of organic options at Whole Foods, and support artisan culinary crafts from your local farmers market, please take a moment to thank Roland Henin.

Of course, immediately after you thank him, he will most politely yet curtly remind you to thank the others—ALL the many pioneering chefs who deserve the same respect and acknowledgement: Jean-Jacques Rachou, Eugene Bernard, Fritz Sonnenschmidt, Bruno Elmer, Albert Kumin, Jacques Pépin, Gunther Heiland, Ferdinand Metz, and so many others.

This book could be about any of these great men (and a few women) who contributed as much to our American culinary terrain. Our mentor would be the first to agree; in fact, he insisted we honor them. It's simply because of my path—meeting Chef at the CIA and stepping out of the culinary world for the majority of my life—that I know only two of these pioneers, Roland Henin and Pierre Latuberne. Well, three, if you count Raimund Hofmeister, but he's a bit of a spring chicken compared to the others. . . . And through these interviews, I've come to know many others—the next generation of great chefs who stand on the shoulders of these pioneering giants.

As Master Chef Roland G. Henin says, "In good cooking . . . always."

A *note about the interviews:*

Interviews are transcribed verbatim and in the speaking style of each participant. Only minor changes have been made for the sake of clarity. Grammatical inaccuracies and informal tone are not meant to disparage the interviewee or offend the reader, but rather, to maintain the integrity of each unique voice. Also, there is some degree of expletive nature. I'm sorry, ladies, but the kitchen used to be a man's world.

As the chefs say, take it all with a grain of salt.

Navigating the River

"If you live under my roof, you do as I say."
"Well, it's pretty simple. Then I don't live under your roof."
—RGH

FOOD WAS SACRED

Roland Gilbert Henin was born on September 22 in the town of Tarare, France, a small village a few kilometers northwest of Lyon. His family eventually moved to Nancy, France, a city in the northeastern French region surrounded by rolling hills and situated on the left bank of the River Meurthe. He was the eldest son of three. Roland's father was a *chemiste* who created paints for postwar renovations (a chemistry cook, you might say), while his mother cared for the family and homestead.

* * *

RGH: My mom was born in an Italian household. Her family raised their very own rabbits, chickens, some ducks and gooses, two pigs per year, and some goats and lambs (we didn't have lawn mowers in those days) along with their very own and large garden. They did their very own wines and distillated their schnapps or different *eau de vie*, along with much canning. My mother was the Kitchen Queen—and slave—tied to the stove for three meals a day, seven days a week. My grandmother from my mother's side was the Baking Queen. On Mondays, she would bake the breads for the following week, plus all the specialty baking, such as occasion cakes and desserts. My father couldn't cook a toast to save his life. He could make coffee, but that's about it. My grandfather raised the animals and butchered them, along with making/fermenting all the alcohols: schnapps, mirabelle, cider, prunes/*quetsche* (damson plums).

Such a great growing environment . . . everyone had their assigned job. I couldn't wait to be old enough to get the job to scrape the pork and lamb casings that would be used for the sausages, *saucisson sec* and *boudin* . . . maybe eight or ten or so. All my family on both sides raised rabbits for years—rabbits, chickens, a few geese (they are great watchdogs . . . but a little messy). Once, I raised two pigs and used every possible bit of them for cooking . . . a lot of fun and a great learning experience, and the slaughtering opened my eyes! I am happy to have experienced this way of life.

I didn't have a lot of "playtime," I didn't have a bike—I was too busy helping out around the home. But in my free time, I did do one thing. I spent time on the river. I used to just go . . . no agenda, no schedule. I fished, cleaned, and gutted the fish at the public *lavanderie*, then went home and cooked it. Those were some of the best days of my life.

During the war, bombs damaged the farms and food became rare and precious. My father went through the farm country and collected rutabagas, onions, whatever he could find. We had ration stamps—each family received an amount according to their size. We would go to the baker and give him one ticket for one loaf of bread, then a ticket for milk and cheese—seldom butter. All food was rationed, and there was very little available. Food was *sacred*. You never left food on your plate. If you left it, your plate was served back to you in the evening. There was no waste, nothing thrown away. It was the philosophy of our lives: never *ever* waste food.

My father died when I was nine years old, due to inhaling the toxic fumes from the paints he created. My mom had to get a job and as the eldest of three kids, I had to take care of my siblings. She remarried when I was about fifteen, when I began my college training studying accounting. To this day, I still love the numbers. . . .

THE BIG GUY

RGH: I don't remember ever having a mentor. My first job was in pastry, as an apprentice pastry cook. The reason I was there was not because I loved pastry. I had no idea about it. I needed a room and board. I had an argument with my stepfather and left home. I slept the first two nights behind the church because it was the only place . . . I didn't want to go to the relative. I had no place to go, and I needed to do something. I bought a newspaper and I looked in the small ads, and it said, "wanted" or "needed" I don't remember, "apprentice pastry cook. Room and board." And that's what I focused on: *Room and board.* I said, "Well, I can do that." At the time, I was in my second year at the College Moderne, in Nancy. I thought I could do both. I had no idea how long it was going to be.

In France, you receive a scholarship, if you do well. I didn't need much money from my stepfather, to pay. I had about 80 percent of my tuition paid. But when you're young—sixteen or seventeen—the most important thing in your life is your gang, your buddies, your people. Not the "gang" like they have here, with the chain. Just the gang, you know, your friends. You hang out with your buddies. In France, when you get to the college level, you don't have much school class time. We have two hours in the morning, one hour in the afternoon, but you have a lot of homework. That's how they operate. I would go to school, and in the afternoon when I got back, I would hang with the guys. You don't do anything wrong, but you just hang. I would go back home at eight or nine in the evening for dinner. After dinner, I would do my homework, until one, two, three in the morning . . . and so on. I did that the first year, and I got away with it.

In the second year, in the fall, my stepfather came and said to me, "You're not going to keep doing what you did, the first year."

I said, "What do you care? I pay my tuition and everything, so what do you care about it?"

"If you live under my roof, you do as I say."

"Well, it's pretty simple. Then I don't have to live under your roof."

I didn't want to go to the relatives. I didn't want to go to the family to stay, so I left home and I had no place to go, no money, no nothing—just the clothes on my back. Looking in the paper and finding the room and board, it could have been mechanic. It could have been anything. Room and board was what I focused on.

I went to Pâtisserie Grandjean and they said they needed my parents to come and sign the paperwork. You're basically a slave, when you take your apprenticeship. You sign up, and you sign your life away. Parents sign you over to the apprenticeship, and they are in charge of you. I earned 500 francs or $10.00 per month. You could buy five packs of cigarettes for $1.00. All we apprentices lived in the same building. My room was right under the roof—right under the red tiles. Not much insulation, so very hot in summer, very cold in winter. There was no water in my room. The other apprentices had running water in their rooms, on the second floor, better rooms. The third-floor apprentice earned a bit more money and a better room.

In France, in Europe, in those days, in Pastry, they didn't have a dishwasher or pot washer. They had apprentices. They had a first-, second-, and third-year apprentice. The first-year apprentice cleaned off all the pots. Then, if you had any time left, then you could roll the croissant or the brioche, or cook the crème patisserie. You worked your ass off in order to get time to do some interesting work.

I loved working with my hands. I couldn't believe I was making those croissants, rolling some dough—flour and water!—and making croissant and brioche dough . . . it seemed like a revelation. As the first-year apprentice, you're the first one in at 4:00 a.m. to light up the big oven, and you're the last one to leave at 7:00 or 8:00 at night, and you take the shit—excuse my French—but you take the shit from everybody. And then you move on, the second year, and the third year, and then you give the shit to the last (new first-year) apprentice. That's how it works. I found it very difficult because it was my first job, basically, and it was harsh and demanding. And I lost my friend, my gang, because I had to go to bed at 8:00 in the evening in order to be up at three in the morning. That was the most difficult thing in the world.

I ate all the crap from everybody else, being the last one on the line. Sometimes I wonder, *How did I ever become a Master Chef?*

There was the Pastry Chef. He was the big guy. He walked like he walked on water, like he knew everything. If I did a good day, I was allowed to stay alone with him in the evening, when he molded the chocolate, one by one, rolling all the little candies, all the fancy work. I was authorized to clean up his table, his marble and tools, and sit up and watch him—not talking, just watching . . . watch him, watch him, watch him. If I was not a good boy during the day, I could not do that, I would have to leave.

Even the owner of the shop revered this guy. This Pastry Chef was like the king of the world, like my god. In my mind, at the time, I said, "I want to become a guy like this." The guy ran the show, called the shots. He didn't mentor me in any particular way, but I often think, *What would he do?* I always remember to him as being my god or my ideal. You can call it a mentor if you like, but to me, it was always the point of reference as where I wanted to be . . . my goal or my aims, my things to reach. This guy was the king, and at the time, I was the last piece of dirt, the piece of nothing, you know what I'm saying?

SUSAN: *That's what you did with us, in Fish Kitchen! You said that if we were exemplary in our day, we could have the privilege of staying after with you and asking questions. We couldn't believe it! It turned my way of thinking around.*

RGH: There you go. It was a privilege. If I had a good day, it was a privilege for me, and I loved it. It was very peaceful, just me watching. I couldn't talk, couldn't ask questions. I knew when to clean his tools, and I knew when and where to line them up. It was a privilege to be there, to be a servant, in a sense. That's just the way it was.

SUSAN: *Did the other superior apprentices stay, or just you?*

RGH: It was the job of the last apprentice—the first-year. In that first year of washing dishes you learn who the good cooks and who the bad cooks are. The good cooks don't burn the pots. The bad cooks burn the pots. The bad cooks have a lot of pots. The good cooks don't use that many pots. Once you do your first year, you move on to the second-year apprentice and then they get a new one. The second-year apprentice doesn't do much cleaning anymore, except their stations after they finish. They do more cooking—more brioche or whatever. They leave the small menial tasks that are a pain, like cleaning the almonds, to the first-year apprentice. Then they move up, and the third-year apprentice does more sophisticated work. They are getting close to the graduation, at the end of the three years.

I left the pastry shop about halfway through my apprenticeship and went to the kitchen. On Thursday afternoon, all the trade—butchering, baking, pastry, charcuterie, all the cooks, all those apprentices—they had the theory classes that were provided by the government. You had to attend; the law required it. You learned all those thing that are related to the profession and are the same—sanitation, nutrition, etc. We'd be at the class all day. We talked to some of the apprentices in the hotel and they said, "Look. We need an apprentice." I talked to the instructor and the chef at the hotel and I made the move.

I couldn't take the pastry any longer . . . just too hard, the hours! When I went into cooking I thought, "Ohmigod!" Like, *hhhaaaaaaaaahaah!* You know? You started at eight in the morning, you got a break in the afternoon . . . you worked all day, but had a split shift, *and* you had off on Sunday or Monday. It was more of a life, much better than the pastry. I loved the pastry, doing with my hands, but the conditions and no team, no spirit of accord . . . nothing. Just the boss and that was it.

When I left Pastry and signed on as a second-year apprentice in the kitchen at the Excelsior Hotel, I needed room and board. I had to room with one of the other guys. Somebody said, "There's room in my building." Kitchen apprentices earn a bit more money. Also, in the kitchen, you can eat! The kitchen guys were nicer, the hours were better. The environment is more social and collaborative than Pastry. Everybody helps out better. We're more like a family. You are not alone to do the work, by yourself, and everybody helps each other. The group of people, we had more team spirit.

Since I had completed one year in the classroom, I could enter as a second-year kitchen apprentice. I knew my way around a kitchen. The first year duties were not that much different—grunt work, cleaning, little prep. I had done some cooking. . . . Pastry makes gnocchi, *pâtés en croûte*, maybe some egg dishes. We prepared almonds. I would have to peel them, remove their skins, and bake them.

SUSAN: *Do you recall anybody in the kitchen there being a mentor to you?*

RGH: I've been trying to figure out what the definition of a mentor is. A mentor can be a lot of things. It could be a coach, somebody to refer to, to be your guide, or it could be a confidant. But I never had anyone really supporting me. My mother did encourage me to come back home once a month to wash my laundry. I would come, my suitcase full of clothes. She would clean it up and pack it in my suitcase, and I would leave. Other than that, I had no one who looked out for me. When I switched to the kitchen, I was able to keep up with soccer. Besides that soccer coach, I didn't have anybody who I could discuss or sit council with, or whatever it is, for my future. I was on my own unfortunately, but that's just the way it was.

Maybe I learned to become self-sufficient, which is what I've done all of my life. I never depended too much on other people. You have to look, and I'm not qualified to do that, at what made me a mentor. The lack of having one, maybe I turn around and became a mentor to other people. I do that a lot here with my chefs, in terms of certification, competitions, in terms of exploration—what's the next move they wanna make? Maybe I became almost a natural in that way possibly, because I did not have any when I was young . . . it's possible. I'm not sure.

Life was very difficult, as the apprenticeship didn't pay anything and we worked very long hours. But I made it through and passed the CAP—Certificate of Aptitudes Professional. I received my CAP Diploma, and then worked a few seasonal positions as *commis* (young prep cook). I learned discipline, responsibility, accountability, persistence, and many other skills, along with a lot of the basic foundations of cooking. I had no idea of where all this would take me. I just knew that if I always did my very best in everything, then I would eventually get somewhere.

What pushed me or guided me was the picture of that pastry chef. I wanted to be so much like him, eventually. Not because I had the ego, but because I didn't want to take any crap from anybody. I was *tired* of getting the crap from everybody else! If I became like him, I wouldn't have to take it! But you know what? I still do. [Laughs] I still do take some crap from idiots—people who are stupid or don't understand or have a misplaced ego . . . I have to learn to accept that. It's not easy, but I do. Though the pastry shop was so grueling and demanding and hard, the benefit was that it exposed me to that chef, that Big Guy. I wanted to be independent, more respected—like him. I didn't realize it at the time, but over the years, I gradually understood that. There was a reason for that, I suppose—to be exposed to that situation, even though it was so harsh. It shaped me for the future, for the rest of my life, and this, in turn, provided guidance to quite a few people in my life.

Out to Sea

What does he have that I don't have?!
—RGH

Roland Henin spends three years working as an apprentice. This consumes his time, and he eventually leaves college and loses track of his beloved gang. The irony is not lost on young Roland, who had originally left home and estranged himself from his family because he refused to sacrifice time with his friends.

After graduation, Roland makes another bold move. Without family or gang to keep him in his hometown, young Roland has an opportunity to see a new world . . . an odd landscape, devoid of culinary art. What kind of place is this—a melting pot of sorts, embracing frozen TV dinners, hot dogs, and hamburgers? Roland, a classically-trained European cook, heads to this new world . . . and, he never looks back.

A New World, a French Chef, the American Dream

RGH: I graduated from the kitchen apprenticeship, earning my CAP—Certificate of Aptitudes Professional. Afterward, graduates prepare to go out and practice their craft, where we are sent around the country for a few years. In a sense, we were not "finalized" apprentices until we earned that work experience. We were sent to a different part of the country to work for a season or to do a "stage"—working for free (often for room and board), to develop our craft. When we turned eighteen, we entered the military. After the military service, I had a few jobs in Paris, did some fill-in work. Our schedule was such that we could work until 2:30 and have a break until 5:30, then return for dinner service. During our afternoon break, we would often go to the Association. If you fooled around the night before, you'd grab a nap. Otherwise, we'd go to the club, play foosball, drink lemonade, and talk to the other guys.

An announcement board posted job opportunities—offers for cooks to fill in, like a *chef de partie* (line cook, in charge of a station). You could apply for two weeks here, two weeks there, etc. You could earn a living for a few years working as a "floater"—covering vacation times and filling in for chefs. I did that for a while. After the military, it was helpful. You could try different organizations to give you a chance to get back into the swing of things . . . a pretty good system. You still make a living, develop contacts, etc.

This is where they had this *big* poster for the 1967 World Expo, in Montreal: *Expo! Adventure! Travel! See the world! Work in the French Pavilion, representing France! Discover new horizons! Come to Montreal!* This was a big thing! At our age, you wanna have a good time, move to different places, and see new things. They speak French in Montreal. All the guys, we talked about it: *If you sign, I sign!*

Our group of twelve guys, we all went to Montreal together. The Expo ran from April to October. We worked our asses off, then played, then breakfast, then work, for those six months. We worked together, we partied together . . . I had my "gang" back. Then came the end of the Expo. Our visa lasted for six months. We were to return to France, but pushed: *You promised us "new horizons!"* We pushed and got two weeks *paid* vacation. We rented cars and took off down the Trans-Canada Highway. Expo was one of the best things I did.

Our visas were expired, we were low on money, and we didn't want to return to France. We met a recruiter looking for restaurant workers to help open a casino in the Grand Bahama at the Grand Lucayan, Beach Hotel. Our whole group signed up to work that winter at their hotel.

We kept hearing about this place called "Miami." While visiting a friend at the Fontainebleau, I met another recruiter who found me a job at a country club in Long Island. But still, no papers. But this Miami recruiter said, no problem! Come to work. Recruiters wanted us in Florida—there were no good qualified cooks for these hotels. Fifty years ago, anyone was a chef. It was a nothing job. At the yacht club, I was introduced to a family at a barbeque. The father asked what I did for work. When I told him, "I cook," he looked at me like syphilis.

* * *

Although it may be difficult to pinpoint the exact moment in time when Chef's perspective switched from apprentice to mentor, there is one man who may begin the story of Chef Henin's mentoring. If Roland is the God of Cooking, let us begin with Hercules.

Thomas Meets Zeus

When asked to describe his first encounter with Thomas Keller, Chef Henin sums it up: *He was a beach bum.*

RGH: I was sous-chef at the Everglades Club in Palm Beach, Florida, before becoming executive chef at the Dunes Club in 1976. The Dunes Club was located on the beach, in Rhode Island. We'd work a split shift—prep and work lunch, have a break, then back to work for the dinner shift. The Dunes Club closed on Mondays, so we'd pack up a cooler, make sandwiches, go to the beach, and camp out during the day. On the other days, we'd go to the beach in the afternoon for a quick swim, rest for the p.m. shift, head back around 4:30, shower, and then back to work.

During these days, we would play Frisbee, running around on the sand. I'd see this guy . . . a tall skinny guy. He'd be walking on the beach with one, or sometimes two, or sometimes even *three* gorgeous women! Every day! I see him and I keep thinking, *What does he have that I don't have?! He's tall, I'm tall. He's skinny, I'm skinny. I've got an accent . . . he doesn't!*

One Monday, we are camped at the beach, and again, I see this guy with a couple of gorgeous women on his arm. I take my Frisbee and toss it into the wind, over in his direction. I throw it right smack in the middle of them! Then, I run over: "I yahm zo zorree! Aneeybody geht heyrrt? Zo zorree . . . "

One of the women says, "Oh, you have a wonderful accent! What is your name?"

"I yahm zah chef of zaht playyce, right ovah there [points to the Dunes Club]."

The young man says, "Oh, you're the chef there?"

So, I give them a tour of the Dunes Club. I take them around and show them the kitchen. Since it is a Monday, it is all nice and clean. This guy is impressed.

He asks, "How does one get a job here? I'm a chef, too."

[Laughs] Ahh, he is a "chef!" This kid! This skinny beach bum, torn jeans, with the ladies . . . he is a "chef." He worked over at a burger joint. But hey, when you're young, you got some skills, you work on the beach, then you are beach bum and you play. It's what you do.

"If you're interested, I may have the right ticket for you. My staff cooker just quit."

"Sure!"

In those days, there was less paperwork and red tape to hiring. I said, "If you're interested, I'll see you next Tuesday at 9:00 a.m."

"Okay!"

The first day, he had on jeans. I told him, "You can't work with jeans. You see that office there? Grab some chef's pants, hanging on that door." We were about the same size.

Staff chef was a pretty pain-in-the-butt job. Fifty percent of the staff were the sons and daughters of the members. They would clean, wait tables . . . it kept them busy and legitimate with summer employment, and the parents could come visit them at the club. The kids were spoiled, always complaining about the food, being a pain in the butt. *Filet mignon, again?* Please!

When Thomas came in, I said, "Use whatever you want. The only thing is, PLEASE SHUT THEM DOWN. I don't want to hear their complaining!"

Thomas used the same products, but in just three to five days . . . SHHHHH. All the staff shut up: no moaning. No groaning. In no time at all, Thomas had turned it around. All of a sudden it became QUIET.

He took care of them, cooked properly, consciously. He did good food, didn't slop it on the plate . . . very nice. Staff were happy, Thomas continued doing well, and then around mid-August, the saucier quit. We were close to shutting down for the season, and it was late to hire someone new. I asked Thomas if he'd like to be the saucier at night, but still do the staff meal. He had no experience with sauces, so I said not to worry, I'll work with you to get you up to snuff.

He learned to make the sauces. He worked both jobs with no problem, no argument.

* * *

The interesting thing about Roland Henin and Thomas Keller is that not only was this relationship one of their defining culinary moments, but both were each other's first mentoring experience. By 1976, Roland Henin received his green card and, armed with years of culinary skill, had earned the right to secure a position of value and stature—executive chef. The Dunes Club was Chef Henin's first executive chef position. By 1976, Thomas Keller had gained enough experience to be of a mindset to receive appropriate guidance—a mentor who would expose him to the value of culinary arts. Both were in the right position and the right moment to meet each other. And besides, they both had the same pant size—a perfect match, indeed.

RGH: Being a mentor . . . it's a pretty complex kind of a situation. Who seeks who? How does it happen? How does it last? I think in terms of Thomas, I was very low-key or fortunate, in a sense. I consider myself somewhat of a gardener. I love to garden. I just started my seeds for this spring, you know? In gardening, the main thing is the soil. If you have a good soil, the rest is easy. If you have a good soil, you need to provide some sunshine. You need to provide some water. You need to pick up the weeds. That's it! The soil will do the work, if the soil is well-balanced, not too acidic or alkaline. I worked in Nova Scotia, and you couldn't grow much. The soil's just not made for growing. It's moss, or whatever it is. It just doesn't grow, no matter how much you work on it. You can put some stuff and stuff and stuff on that soil, and things are just not coming up. And then you go to California and the soil is perfect. It has the sunshine and everything, just so.

Thomas was a good soil. He didn't require very much, in terms of maintenance, because the quality of the soil was there. The rest was natural development:

provide sunshine, provide water, pick up the weed, and keep the pests away. We were able to calculate this system over the years in many ways. It just happened to work. And it worked with other people too, for different reasons and amounts of time.

Sometimes, they just need a mentor in a difficult period in their life. Sometimes they want to go too fast too soon. That's the American way: become executive chef right away, and it's too big a thing. You slow them down: *What about if you go a little sideways first for a couple of years, and get ready for that big job?* You try to help them benefit from your experience. You need to have a good soil. Like I said, I was very fortunate to have been working with Thomas. The soil was in excellent condition and the rest made it easy. It just worked, you know?

SUSAN: *I might say the same for you as a mentor. He was a plant that could thrive in your soil.*

RGH: To me, that's what it is. It doesn't require an excessive amount of work, and it was a pleasure to see those plants grow and develop. That's the real work, to see it happen. You don't do it for yourself. You do it for the satisfaction.

Recently, this young man called me and we talked a little bit. He asked, "How do I become a master chef?"

I said, "Whaaa—really? What are you doing?"

"I'm in the school at the Cordon Bleu."

"How long you been there?"

"I been there three weeks."

Aaah, bah bah bah. I'll find out stuff from *him.* I said, "Okay, how old are you?"

"Oh, I'm twenty-five."

"That's a good age. You're on the right track and everything."

We started to get into the details and he said, "I am an ex-Marine."

"That's fantastic. What else? Tell me about you?"

"Well, I got five kids."

HOOOOLEEEY COW! Five kids, twenty-five. "How long do you think that's going to take you (to be a Master Chef)?"

"Oh, I want to do that in ten years."

I said, "Waaait a minute, waaaaaait a minute, now. You're twenty-five. Even though you like cooking, you have learned little. You're starting, which is good. But you have *five* kids. You're going to have to *feed* them. You have to work and earn some money to pay for that. And they're gonna need your attention. They're gonna need your *time.* You're not going to be able to dedicate all your time to your Master Chef program. There are twenty-four hours in a day, seven days in a week, and a month is thirty days . . . for everybody. You wanna become a Master Chef in ten years. Where are you gonna find the time? How are you going to stretch the twenty-four hours? How you going to make the rent? Slow down. Develop a plan. Become a little more relaxed. It's going to take you at least fifteen years. You're a Marine and you have discipline. That's a big plus for you, but start thinking in reality."

SUSAN: *Being a Master Chef is not just in your art. It's how you live your whole life that makes you a Master Chef.*

RGH: Exactly. I refer back to my very first pastry chef that I had. Everything he was doing, he was doing that extra effort. When I saw him . . . at the time, I didn't understand much, but he was making that little stroke or those little things on top of that chocolate, or bonbon—the little *tuiles* . . . just to make it perfect. Thomas does that very well. He always tries to do one step better than last time or one step better than the other guy. He always tries to do that little thing—more, extra, better than before. Achieving mastery is not what you do the last six months before the test. It is what you do for those twenty years, learning your craft. It is a way of life.

You won't believe this, but at my age, I still don't have a TV. I never had one. There is good reason for that. I don't have the time. There are too many things to do. The second reason is I hate the crap that they feed and do to you, the subliminal messaging. They take you for an idiot through those programs. All those advertisements and everything. I can't stand it, and I *refuse* to accept it, to buy it, to listen to it. It's disgusting! It's degrading to your mind! Avoiding TV is one of the healthiest things you can do in your life. Watching TV is like a zombie, *buuuh buuuuh* . . . you are not active or thinking or feeling things.

Like the students . . . they don't think anymore. They don't figure things out. They just get brainwashed, *wuuurrrr* . . . they love the lecture and all those things. But when you say, "get up," they panic, because they don't know how to figure things out anymore. They say, *Chef, can you tell me why this or tell me why that?* I say, figure out what you think, first. Figure things out on your own and then come to verify with me if you are on the right track. You know? As opposed to, *Chef, can you spoon-feed me, because I'm too goombah to spoon-feed myself.* I refuse to do that. Some of them get upset. *Well, you get paid to tell me that.* Well, not exactly . . . I get paid to help you understand, and this is my way. Spoon-feed is just too easy. You don't learn how to think. If I was a bad instructor, then I would spoon-feed you. Anyway. That's the way it is.

SUSAN: *That's the bad soil.*

RGH: [Laughs] Yes, soil that has been mistreated, improper compost and all those things.

SUSAN: *Chef Thomas credits you with his European apprenticeship: "Chef Henin got me to France."*

RGH: In 1979, I sent him to Café du Parc. Thomas was from Florida, and it was the winter. I worked in Florida for many, many years and had a lot of contacts there. I sent him down there to work with Pierre. That was quite an awakening for him, an eye-opener. [Laughs]

Thomas kept in touch. After working with Pierre, he went back to the Catskills to work at La Rive. In those days, I was at the CIA and running long distance, to stay in shape and protect my mind. He would stop by the CIA, either on his way down to Florida or on his way up to the Catskills. Depending on my schedule—I think I was p.m. at the time, doing the Stage—he would stop in at the beginning of my lecture and sit down at the back of the class to watch what was happening. He would wait for me to finish, and then we would close and go out and have a drink or whatever it might be.

Because I was running marathons in those days (it was a great, great, great, great way for me to deal with the stress of the teaching and everything) I would go and spend the weekend in the Catskills. He was working at La Rive and I would help him—not cook, actually, although sometimes do a dish, or spend time in the kitchen or time outside, and I would run. The Catskills are great because it is hilly and good for training. So, we kept on going, there were ongoing discussions . . . he was always curious, always asking . . . and at some point the question came up that he would like to learn some more, get more in-depth.

Keep in mind that this was thirty-five years ago. In the late seventies to early eighties, we didn't have all the different talent that we have today with the American chef and everybody like this, doing good stuff. If you needed more in-depth information, most of the roots or foundation, the place to go was Europe. I was at the CIA, and we sent people—kids that wanted to learn more or expand. We would send them to Europe as a *stagiare* (or "stage," a short-term internship, to acquire new skills and be exposed to new cuisines). As a stage, you don't get paid—maybe room and board, if you are lucky.

Some did make it, some didn't. It was mostly about attitude. Some were very humble. The chefs give you a lot of crap to test you, make sure you are worthy of their kitchen. You go there to learn something from them, so you have to demonstrate that you are worthy of their teaching. Otherwise, why should they waste their time? Sure, you don't get paid or anything, and you're treated like a piece of dirt. These young American kids, they graduate from the CIA and they go there and they say, *What's the matter, you didn't hold out the red carpet? I leave from there and work for nothing? Are you crazy?* They get that attitude right away that they are the Gods of Cooking, they deserve better, and so it doesn't work. Some of them, like Thomas, shut their mouth and did their work, and they demonstrated that they were worthy of the teaching and they learned. Those guys took them under their wing. It's just how it was.

We always kept in touch, wherever he was. I would visit him—we'd have dinner or something and have discussions . . . *what's the thing, what's the next step.* Then he had some disagreement with the owners in Los Angeles and he found himself without work. They had ideas, and he had ideas, and they were different, and he lost his job. He was totally devastated, so we sat down and we talked. I said, "Look, you deserve better. It's time for you to start doing on your own." We talked about where and what and all this kind of stuff, figuring out what should be the next step. At the time, California was coming up pretty strong, especially with the wine—Sonoma and then Napa. I said clearly to him, "If I was your age and as talented as you are, this is where I would go, what I would look for and do. This is where I would open a small, classy restaurant."

Swimming Upstream

Don't get me wrong . . . it was a constant battle . . . but I could take it. I had wide shoulder and thick spine and hard head, and I didn't quit.
–RGH

The Executive Chef

SUSAN: *The years between 1967 and 1976 seem to be "the lost mentoring years." Was Thomas Keller your first "official" mentoring experience?*

RGH: I probably taught kids before Thomas, but mostly I keep quiet. During the Expo, when I was in the French Pavilion, we work and we produce. We work our station. There is no room for mentoring. You mentor when you are in a position. Until then, you work your ass off. It took me about two years to get a green card, and without the green card, you don't mentor, either. You have to keep that low profile. You don't want to draw attention to yourself.

I worked a few jobs, in Canada, Nova Scotia, Bahamas, Florida, and New England . . . summers up north, winters in the south. I loved to work in the summer in Cape Breton. There was great fishing and hunting . . . beautiful country. The cost of living was so cheap, but so were wages. I had to work winters in Florida to afford working in Cape Breton.

As an illegal, there were lots of temp jobs, working for the recruiters, working quietly, seasonally—lots of transitions. When you have no green card, you keep a low profile. It took about two years until the lawyers were paid and they finally delivered. After I received my green card, I could go out and get a legitimate job, have more of a say where I could go and what I would do. I could now secure positions like executive chef, and I could now hire staff of my own . . . tend my own garden.

Thomas Keller

Chef/Founder, Thomas Keller Restaurant Group

If he made me understand why people cook and made me want to become a chef as a profession, then he was going to be able to help me do anything I wanted to do.

THOMAS: Mentor/mentee is a difficult kind of concept for anybody to grasp, maybe especially for those in the culinary world. In the late seventies and early eighties, our chefs, whether they were the chef de cuisine or sous-chefs, expected us to actually *know* what we were supposed to do, always ahead of time. Pierre (Latuberne) threw a knife at me once, because I didn't know how to truss a chicken the way he wanted me to. Like, *How come you don't know that? What are you, a fool?*

So there's a little apprehension right away around that dynamic. When you can break through the barrier and have a true relationship, break through to where you can have a discussion with somebody . . . that's where it begins. The discussions, if they happen often enough, will lead to opinions and advice . . . and through that process, you'll start to rely on that person and their expertise.

It may begin with the mentee, because a mentor doesn't always know. You're looking at a group of people and you're not sure who wants to be mentored. It's the same thing in a classroom. At a young age, you were expected to raise your hand if you had a question. If you didn't raise your hand, the teacher assumed you understood. That's so important, *and* it's hard to do . . . to raise our hand. That's where the initial mentorship happens. It could also be from a mentor seeing somebody. I may sense apprehension or shyness, desire that is not able to be expressed openly. The mentor can then initiate the process. An organization may create a structure: when a new employee is hired, they are assigned a mentor. That could be something temporary. You can't just assign a relationship, but at least it's a way to express the idea; if it blossoms into a relationship, so much the better. If it doesn't, hopefully they'll find their way to having another mentor, or they may not need one at that time. You cannot force it; they've got to want it.

* * *

It began at the Dunes Club. Roland Henin allowed me to express my abilities through my execution of the Family Meal and help me understand the true purpose of a chef—nurturing people. Regardless of the cooking level—whether it was what he was doing for the guests at the Dunes Club or what I was doing for the staff—it was all about nourishing. I embraced the idea . . . to resonate with people in this way. That was the reason I became a chef.

Up until then, cooking was just a job. It allowed me to travel. As a young man, it was a form of freedom. You get in the car, and you end up anywhere you want to end up. You knock on somebody's door and say, "Do you need a cook?" Sooner or later, you're going to land a job.

I applied for the job, and he hired me. That period was a very short period of time—the summer—where we built a relationship beyond employer and employee, through his ability to enlighten me on nurturing through cooking. After that, because of that one learning process—that one epiphany, which changed my life—he became someone who was very important to me. All of a sudden, *he* understood. He was the person, the guiding light. If he made me understand why people cook and made me want to become a chef as a profession, then he was going to be able to help me do anything I wanted to do.

SUSAN: *There was an assumption that he would be available . . .*

THOMAS: There was never a question. I didn't ask him to be my mentor; it was an organic process. Later, as our relationship grew, I needed somebody who could help me get to France. And that was Roland. At that time, the next moment in my career was moving to France, and I was in search of somebody to help me get there. Roland was encouraging. He felt that it was extremely important to study in France during that period. Today, of course, it's not the same. There are now so many great chefs in America that I don't believe you need to go to France. But back then it was important, not just to learn the cuisine, but to learn the culture. I didn't put any parameters around how long I'd be in France; I just went. I didn't have any responsibilities here in the United States, so it was easy for me to put all my belongings in a small storage unit and move. I was there for almost two years. I had a wonderful place to live, I had friends, and I had jobs. I was very fortunate to have had that kind of structure.

Not only was I able to get into some of the greatest kitchens in Paris, but also into some modest kitchens. I saw a spectrum of what was going on—how a one-star kitchen developed its cuisine in a relatively modest way with a modest budget . . . to be able to understand, not necessarily the importance of technique, but the importance of consistency, the importance of quality ingredients, and mostly, the importance of building relationships with those purveyors: the farmers, fishermen, foragers, and gardeners.

The biggest impact was the cultural part—that, in and of itself, shaped who I became. That was truly beneficial—understanding that relationship with those people who dedicated their lives to bringing great ingredients to great restaurants and then supporting those people in a way that enhanced their lifestyle, which yielded the best ingredients. Those relationships were one of the main differences between a modest one-star restaurant and a great three-star restaurant. It was about relationship-building and realizing that you must spend the money to get the quality you want and need, in order to elevate the experience for your staff and guests.

Those were the important things that I learned. Making a veal stock, or roasting a bird, or fluting a mushroom, or things like that that were technical, yeah, those were influential, but not in comparison to understanding the relationships, understanding the teamwork, understanding the consistency, the hospitality, the general dedication and commitment that you needed to have to achieve greatness in a restaurant. It comes down to finding those exquisite ingredients. Going to a farmers market is a wonderful thing, don't get me wrong. There are great ingredients at the farmers markets, and it certainly opens a door to a group of specific gardeners who are able to deliver these great ingredients, but it has to go much further than that. It has to be much deeper . . . to those individuals who are bringing all the ingredients to your restaurant.

Take a rare or luxury ingredient, like caviar. You have to be able to work with a producer, continually evolve the quality of the product through continuous work with one another. You don't just say, "I want to pay X amount of dollars for the caviar." It's not about negotiation of money. It's about the ingredients and the quality. If you reach for the quality you want, you have to be willing to pay for it. Price should not be something that enters into a conversation with our suppliers. If we're going to have meaningful relationships with our suppliers that help benefit them, we can't have negotiations on price.

And caviar is a luxury ingredient, compared with butter, which is a common ingredient. Still, you want to have the best butter that you can possibly get. Diane St. Clair produces some of our butter, in Vermont. She makes a small amount, and we buy all of our butter for the French Laundry and Per Se—about 90 percent of her product. I don't know how much her butter costs. It's not the point, right? She's a small farmer. She has eight cows. This is her livelihood. I have to be able to support her by agreeing to pay whatever she needs to charge me, so that she can have the lifestyle that she needs. It's certainly not a luxurious lifestyle—she is a farmer, and she needs to exist. If she has to raise the price of her butter to send her son to college, then I'm not going to negotiate on that. Why would I? Negotiating on a person's life shouldn't become part of a conversation when you're trying to support someone who's bringing you the best product that you've ever tasted.

SUSAN: *Reminds me of Roland Henin's philosophy of mentoring—at what lengths he'll go to when he is "crafting the best chefs" in the industry.*

THOMAS: Roland was that model figure. He was the person I wanted to be. He was articulate, he was intelligent, and he was thoughtful. He possessed all the qualities of a person that I hoped to possess. Roland helped me, not only in my cooking, which was critical, but helped me in my path to becoming this chef and being able to accomplish specific goals. He would spend time with me, not only in the kitchen, but also just hanging out, conveying the importance of commitment and dedication to what we were doing. He helped me understand that the food that we cook, where it came from, was critical to our success. René Macary and his wife Paulette, owners of La Rive, in the Catskills, said, "Plant a garden . . . try it. You have some broccoli . . . might as well put it in the garden. Don't let the deer get it. [Laughs] But, plant a garden."

Now, Roland and I are out of that mentor-mentee relationship. He's still a prominent figure in my life. Is he helping me understand the path that I've taken? No, because he doesn't understand that path. In that generation, it wasn't something that they did—what we do today. Modern chefs, as opposed to the modern chefs of his time, were two dynamically different individuals. So he has become a very close friend, not someone who is mentoring me on what my goals are or how to achieve them.

SUSAN: *I was thinking about the shadow side of mentoring—how lessons can come in negative forms . . .*

THOMAS: Well, the best lessons come in negative forms. [We laugh]

SUSAN: *Have mentors been integral with blessing you, in this way?*

THOMAS: I'm doing a good job in failing, myself. [Laughs] I don't need other people to make me fail. Failure is a very important part—*the most* important part—of our ability to excel. You have to realize your failure and understand that you have to modify your behavior in order to be successful. If you cut your finger, you better be doing something different next time to not cut your finger—change your behavior. [Laughs] That's something pretty black-and-white. If you think about that in a bigger way, you start to understand what it is that made you fail. And it's not one thing; it's always a number of things.

SUSAN: *What are some of your values?*

THOMAS: Modesty is very important. We need to maintain that sense of humility. Trust is crucial: teaching someone something and then trusting them to do it. If you don't trust somebody, then you've lost the ability to do other things yourself—to search for your own continuous goals. Collaboration is critical: to be able to enhance an idea through conversation with others, to be able to champion that idea—not through your ego, but through theirs. *It's your idea, not mine. Give it up.* Give that success away and celebrate it with somebody else. Consistency: we need to be consistent with who we are and what we are and what we do. If you can't be consistent, then you're a one-hit wonder. Impact: to be able to impact people. To be able to give something to somebody that makes a difference.

SUSAN: *What are some delicious things that happen in the job?*

THOMAS: There are so many of them. The biggest one we need to realize is the success of the moment and being able to celebrate that success: doing a beautiful dish; collaboratively and collectively coming up with a new composition; just realizing the moment when someone does a really nice job, and you're part of the reason they do that job. Those little moments of success are probably the most gratifying: to see a young person do something that you've helped them achieve. Those moments are priceless.

SUSAN: *Are you doing what you want to be doing, in life?*

THOMAS: I'm not sure. That's a good question. Sometimes I am, sometimes I'm not. As chefs, we have a real, innate problem. We lack the backbone to say no. Or, we lack the training to say no, maybe is a better way to say it. We certainly have the ability and the backbone to instill our will, so maybe it's just the training. From the time you walk into the kitchen, at a young age, you are consistently reinforced with the idea of a "Yes." You never say no to chefs. When somebody asks you to do something, you want to give that person what they want. Sometimes it confuses us at specific levels or specific times in our profession, where opportunities abound. We can't give the world the opportunity to realize what is the most important to us . . . because we want to say yes to everyone. And then you end up having to say no to the things that are most important to you.

SUSAN: *Would you reshape something in the next ten years?*

THOMAS: I'm not sure about that, either. There is a level of seduction that infiltrates the process in choices. As chefs, we're not used to so many opportunities, such as working in television, writing books, and other high-profile branding exposure. My generation is the first to be exposed to this, so what we do is critical for the next generation. You see some of my colleagues doing things that may or may not be in the best interest or the best examples for the next generation.

The idea of good food is something that is not trendy. The Slow Food movement is here to stay. We want to eat more dynamically and have different experiences with food—more than we used to. We still find ourselves being comforted by foods that we grew up with, but at the same time, we're growing foods that we've never experienced before.

SUSAN: *What are your hobbies?*

THOMAS: I golf. And I'm learning how to fly.

SUSAN: *Fly, like, a plane? Get out. Don't you have to accrue, like, a lot of hours?*

THOMAS: Yes. It's not so much the hours, but the skills. [Laughs] They say a person's able to do something within a certain amount of hours based on the average of students in the past, but it's only an average. It's how you would determine to do anything . . . like with children on their bicycles with training wheels or swimming with floaties. They're there to protect you until you can swim or ride the bike independently. Even when you feel you're ready, your parents probably keep those floaties or training wheels on for another couple weeks, just to make sure. Right? It's kind of the same thing about flying. I'm not sure if I'm ready yet. I'm sure he'll take them off some day, even though I think I'm not ready. And he'll say, "Now you can land the plane." I can do everything else, but land. [We laugh] That's what I'm learning now.

SUSAN: *Yeah, that's cumbersome.*

THOMAS: Yes. The more you do it, the more comfortable you are with it. It doesn't seem to be a lot of things happening at once. You have more time to do the things you need to do to land the airplane than you thought you had when you first got in the airplane. The first time you watch your instructor land a plane, it's like, *How did you do all that?*

SUSAN: *Have you ever fished with Chef Henin?*

THOMAS: I have, but it's been ages. I need to get back to that. It's one of those things he continues to encourage me to do, and I continue to fail. You get consumed with other things and other people's desires of what you should be doing. That's what a chef's life is. I just need to learn how to say no. I've known that for a long time. There are a thousand wires in me that are all connected to the "yes." I don't want to be in a place where my glass is full and I can't fit anything else in it. And that's the reason we say no. I want my glass to be half-empty—doing the things I want to be doing for my career, but also for myself, which is golf and flying.

SUSAN: *So it's not that full right now . . . your glass?*

THOMAS: No. My glass is full. I'm half-empty. It's a good thing. The alternative sucks. [We laugh] There will always also be your personal and your family life, too, that infringes on your professional life—doesn't infringe, but sometimes has to . . . interface with it in a very comfortable way. The older you get, your siblings, your parents, they start to age and become sick. All of a sudden, you're faced with an idea that you never thought about before: *I have to take care of my older brother. I have to take care of my father.* That's a significant life-changing experience that might happen. And everything else goes by the wayside because you have no choice. It's not a planned process. Everything else I do is planned. Even though it is a lot, I'm still part of a plan. Someone getting sick—or yourself getting sick—is not part of the plan.

SUSAN: *Talk about the mentoring organization, Ment'or.*

THOMAS: Chef Bocuse asked us to form a collective organization supporting the US team in the Bocuse d'Or competition. He felt that America has never done as well as it could have, and part of that was because of a lack of awareness and support. He asked me to be the president of the US team and, as I pointed out earlier, you always say, "Yes." I mean, I don't think anybody has ever said no to Paul Bocuse.

Over the years, it has evolved from just supporting the US team to also establishing a foundation called *Ment'or* that basically has four initiatives: one, of course, was Team USA; the second initiative was to have a young chef competition to help identify future candidates for the Team USA; the third was our grant program. We gave close to a million dollars in the past four years; our last initiative will be our Chef's Congress. The first one will be held in November [2017].

SUSAN: *What does the Chef's Congress entail?*

THOMAS: It's a collective—a collection of chefs with significant exposure and opportunity, helping to change the path of our profession to be more cohesive and collaborative. We are very fragmented at this moment; my goal is to bring it together in the same way that the medical profession controls what they do, basically. When the Harvard Medical School publishes a paper about cancer, people listen. It's the same way with the law professors. We don't have a collective group that has the best intentions of our profession in mind, who are able to define policy and change the way people think about us.

The media seems to control our profession. If the media says that's good, it's good; if the media says they're bad, they're bad. If the media says this is the best thing, everybody jumps on it. The media claimed "Farm-to-Table," and everybody wanted it. The media claims, whatever it is, molecular gastronomy, and everybody runs to that. The media has us by the nose and it leads us around at their own whim and for their own benefit. Regulations are put on restaurants by our lawmakers, and sometimes are very unfair or not thorough or not thought out in the way that they should be. They're not fabricated for our kinds of restaurants; they're only based on the least common denominator. I don't want to say anything bad about McDonald's, but we're not all McDonald's.

SUSAN: *Could this organization help in a lobbying capacity? For instance, raw cheese comes to mind.*

THOMAS: We hope to.

SUSAN: *Is the ultimate goal of mentoring eclipsing?*

THOMAS: André Soltner, Jean-Jacques Rachou, Jacques Pic, Michel Richard, Georges Perrier . . . these are some of the great chefs of the last generation. Each one of them will admit that they cannot do what I do. I'm sitting here with these icons, these role models . . . and I can't fathom that they would say this. To me, they are extraordinary men with skills that I could only hope to aspire to when I was a young cook. To have them say that makes me feel awkward, but at the same time, it's true. They didn't have what I have. They gave me everything they had, but then, resources for me became more abundant, more refined. They didn't have food processors when they were young cooks. They didn't have immersion circulators. They didn't have the facilities that we have, the sauté pans we have.

It's like a baseball player, or football or soccer player, from three generations ago. I mean, I'm a golfer. Thirty years ago, golfers were hitting with Persimmon wood. Today, they have drivers that are made of composite metals 460 centimeters in diameter, and they're hitting a ball 380 yards. Arnold Palmer, when he started, would hit a ball 300 yards with the drivers he had. They struggle with making the fairways long enough now to accommodate these guys, with all the equipment, knowledge, and training. I was at a training center this morning and worked with a guy who was doing all this stuff with me: rotation, spinal stretching, and all kinds of things. Golfers of two generations ago didn't do any of that. They were heavy guys who smoked cigarettes and drank beer and went out and golfed. Right? So that's the point. These guys are the reason I'm here *and* they will always hold the utmost respect and admiration for me. As awkward as I feel when they say that, I have to agree with them because . . . walk into my kitchen.

SUSAN: *Right. And you want to be one of those chefs in the future, sitting there with someone you once mentored, saying the same thing . . .*

THOMAS: Yes. And I say now that the chefs in my restaurant are better than I am. They're all extraordinary, in the end. I mean, am I a great chef? Yeah. I truly believe that. I believe I have the skills, the knowledge, and the determination. I have the fortitude and commitment for everything it takes. I didn't have the training they have. I didn't have the tools they have. I didn't have the kitchens they have. I didn't have Thomas Keller giving me all the things I give them, to be able to do their jobs the way they do it. It's a generational thing.

We need to be accepting of that fact. It's a hard thing for chefs to do, because egos, in so many ways, are such a big part of a chef's life for the bigger purpose of our profession. It's not about us. If we're not positively impacting the standards of our profession, then we're not doing a good job. If it's only about me or my restaurant, then it's just irresponsible.

SUSAN: *I'm just curious, Chef, did you ever get your flying license?*

THOMAS: I did. Then I stopped flying. I realized I needed to work on it more, and I didn't have the time, so I'd much rather play golf. If I hit a bad shot, I don't hurt anybody . . . at least I have a smaller chance of hurting somebody, whereas if I'm flying an airplane and make a mistake, there are a lot of problems. [We laugh]

SUSAN: *But you did actually land a plane, by yourself?*

THOMAS: Yes, I did.

Steve Mengel

Chef Administrator, The Greenbrier

He's the encyclopedia on cooking, and I wanted to read it.

STEVE: In the winter of 1976, I was an apprentice working at the Everglades Club. My first year, I prepped and made soups with another lead chef. I didn't work with Roland directly until my second season, when I worked with him one-on-one in the evenings for dinner service. I was the garde-manger chef, and he was sous-chef. The first time I met him, I thought, *Oh my God, he is arrogant, all-mighty, and confident.* He was very difficult for a beginner. We think we know it all when we're younger, full of spunk. Roland was quite regimented. He was always in uniform at work. He expected and demanded a high standard, period.

But Roland had what I wanted to learn. He would teach you techniques and ways of doing things. You weren't just going to stand there and not figure out how to do it; he was going to make you do it *right.* He is the encyclopedia on cooking, and I wanted to read it.

SUSAN: *What did he see in you?*

STEVE: I don't know! He respected me. I think we were equal in some respects. He saw someone to have fun with, who wanted to be part of his life. It wasn't like: *I'm your boss at work and then want nothing to do with you outside of the kitchen.* Roland was not that much older than me, but he was sort of a father figure, at least when we were in the kitchen. Outside the kitchen, we were buddies. He didn't try to tell me how to live life—he wanted to share it with me. But in the kitchen, he told me what to do and I did it.

We lived in Palm Beach, so it was half work, half pleasure. It wasn't as much fun for him because he had the position and the title. Still, Chef Henin provided camaraderie. He was very car-oriented. First he had a Corvette, and then he traded it for a Jeep. I won't say he was a hot-shot, but he enjoyed living outside of the kitchen, as well: *enthusiastic* and *outgoing* are the best words that come to mind.

SUSAN: *What led to your meeting Chef Henin?*

STEVE: I wanted to learn to cook when I was sixteen, at home. My mom told me, "You want to cook? Go to school. Get out of my kitchen." I went to cooking school where my father taught, but for cooking instead of pastry. I went on to work for a country club for a few years under a French chef in New Jersey. From there I apprenticed at the Greenbrier for three years, graduating in 1976, stayed on as a cook for ten years, and then became catering chef. In 1983 I assumed a supervisor position as a sous-chef. At that time there were only three sous-chefs. Hartmut Handke then came to the Greenbrier as executive chef. After a short time, he promoted me to executive sous-chef, a title I held for over twenty-five years.

When Rich Rosendale was here a few years ago, he gave me the opportunity to buy the food for the entire hotel. I've had my forty years in the kitchen. I can do this and still be happy. I hold the Greenbrier's food quality to the highest standards. It reverts back to my earliest teachings about doing it right, and doing it right the first time. I buy the finest food, because I don't accept anything less for our guests. Since I'm buying the food, I know what they're doing with it. I don't expect the chefs to take truffle oil and pour it all over the salads and serve it for ten dollars.

Maybe Roland saw the same thing in me. Maybe he felt, *Here's an apprentice at the Greenbrier who's going to have a future*, and he wanted to latch on and help me. I don't know. At that time in life you don't realize it, but I worked with Hartmut Handke for many years, and I learned extensively from him. In that respect, Hartmut knew what I did. I was always Hartmut's right-hand man. If something needed to get done, he'd come to me. Roland found that out on his own by talking with people who I worked with, and he gained respect for me in that way.

SUSAN: *What was Roland's impact on your life?*

STEVE: Proper technique. He was the battering sergeant who would look at your tarnished star and make you re-polish it until it was shiny. He wasn't out-of-line, but he was hard on us.

During the afternoon hours, we prepped the evenings sauces—six sauces in a steam table, staying good and hot, until service that evening. We made sauce between 2:00 and 5:00 p.m. If the sauces were sitting in the steam table for two hours, he would tell you to change your *bain maries* [stainless steel containers]. We had to get clean ones from the shelf, strain the sauce, and re-coat it with butter on top. Back then we didn't use cellophane; we used clarified butter to coat the sauce, so it wouldn't form a skin. He would ask us to re-strain the sauces and put them into new vessels. I thought, *The sauces are fine. Why do we re-strain? It's ridiculous. We should do it when we're ready to serve.* But that was his way, and we had to adhere to it. We thought he was just trying to make our lives difficult, but later on I realized this was done because he upheld a standard.

Once we were peeling oranges for a large banquet of 500 people. We needed several sections for each plate—about 2,000 sections. We spent the morning at the beach and came to work already tired. We'd do a lot of fishing, then come in with sunburns and put on our chef coats. It was miserable! Two of us were trying to cut these oranges, and we weren't doing it very well, with too large a knife for cutting flatly on sides. We had a square piece of orange on the plate. Chef came over and said, "Look. This is the way it has to be done."

We thought, "God, this is ridiculous. You gotta be kidding me." But, when you see the finished product, it makes a difference. His had a nice, rounded edge.

"Fruit grows round, it doesn't grow square! Why are you cutting it square?" He came around and would completely peel the side of the orange round and said, "Do it like that."

It took more time because instead of five slices to take the edge off it took ten. The tediousness of it . . . some people tried to cut corners. He would not let you cut a corner. That's not his style.

I'd watch him turning an orange and thought, *Wow. That's great. I hope I learn to do it that way someday, too.* And now I do the same thing with my people here!

Everybody has something they could always learn. It's a different era now. More chefs experiment with chemicals and techniques. Food doesn't have to be mounted with fancy flowers or have multiple flavors so that you can't figure out what's what. That's what this industry has become . . . mustard ice cream. I put mustard on a hot dog, and I eat ice cream. I don't want mustard on or in my ice cream.

SUSAN: *Amen! Just because you can do it, doesn't mean you should.*

STEVE: Who wants it? Who says, "I gotta go have mustard ice cream today!" My tagline about that is simple: Good food, done right!

Jerry Dollar

Executive Chef, Retired, at Sea World

It was like playing basketball with Michael Jordan.
When you work with the best, you become really good.

My best friend's dad got me into the culinary field. I was working at the Hilton Hotel on Mission Bay. At that time, Chef Roland Henin was a Certified Executive Chef. When I met him and saw him at the Rancho Bernardo Inn, I was in *awe* because he was a *real* chef—not one of these people who thinks they are. He was tall, strong, young, and he sat me down in his office and asked me, "Why do you think I should hire you?" I told Chef, "I'll give you everything I got. I love to cook." He liked that and gave me a chance.

At that time, it was 1979. I was nineteen years old and so skinny you could wrap an apron around me twice. I had no idea where my career was going to be. At that time, when you worked at a hotel or nice restaurant, you worked all the stations. There were six apprentices, and I was youngest. What I liked about Chef was, he was *tough* on us, sometimes scary, but he molded us to be the best people we could be. He treated everybody fairly, but molded individually! Like clay. [Laughs] When I met him, I was making $2.95 an hour. My mindset was that I always wanted to make my boss look good. That was my job.

I did a three-year apprenticeship at the Rancho Bernardo Inn. No one wanted to apprentice there at the time. Each week when all the apprentices would meet in school, learning stocks or hollandaise sauce—whatever it was—all the other students couldn't believe how much stuff I was learning, how much knowledge I had. The way I look at it, it was like playing basketball with Michael Jordan. When you work with the best, you become really good.

He helped me in my first food competition, the Culinary Salon. I had never done anything like this. The piece he helped me on was a decorated ham. We trimmed off the ham as smooth as possible. Then we took bread crumbs and ground them up in a Buffalo chopper, and then we whipped up egg whites and folded those in to make like a smooth paste. We coated the ham with that, starting from the bottom and working our way to the top, so it was super nice and smooth. We chilled it and then coated the ham with a *chaud froid* sauce—two or three nice coats—and let it set. We made seven tomato roses and put clear aspic on them, so they were nice, firm, and shiny. We sliced radishes real thin and made a circle on this ham. We used leeks and green veggies, with all their green good color from the chlorophyll. We'd dip the leek into the aspic and put it on the showpiece. Then we put the roses on. We'd put aspic on the roses, shake them real gently, and then put them on the showpiece with a toothpick. Later on, we'd remove the toothpick when we knew the rose was attached. We put the half-radishes around the border, just beautiful. We made a papillote out of parchment paper that went on top—the same thing you'd do for a rack of lamb.

Chef asked, "Why do you think we made seven roses?"

"I know it's an odd number, but I don't know."

"In flowers, and other things in nature, you should always do things in odd numbers."

I made galantines with some different aspic decorations. In competitions, it's not about winning; it's about doing the best you can.

Chef was an excellent ice carver. He would take me back into the butcher room, back to where the freezer was. We'd pull the 300-pound ice block out and let it sit for about an hour. Chef would make a sketch and bring out his tools. He didn't have a chain saw, but he had hand saws. He never let me touch the ice block! For about three months, all I did was clean all the ice around it and into the drain. He would ask me certain questions about it. "Do you do everything on one side? Or do you go back and forth and back and forth?" With 360-degree carvings, you have to step back and look from a variety of different angles. You need to be constantly walking around, ensuring a balanced perspective. It opened my eyes and affected other things. Maybe that's another reason why he's so good at what he does; he looks at things from a 360 angle . . . instead of quick decisions, he looks at the whole picture.

The first couple months, I was just observing the ice carving. He let me touch the blocks, move the blocks around and stuff. He had a story for everything. He helped you understand why certain things happen. *What do you do when a piece breaks off? How do you freeze it back on? When something breaks, how do you work around that break?* At the end, before he left, he'd let me hold the pieces of leftover ice. You get the feel for them. I never would have been able to do this without him. He believed in me and he saw something in me—something I don't even know, that no one else did. There's no artistic talent in my family, but I became an accomplished ice carver. Over the years, I've had people ask, "How do you do this?" And I say, "I don't know. I just do."

One of the things I admire most about Roland is that he had a keen eye on all details. In the banquet: rotating everything and icing things down properly . . . he didn't miss anything! We had to order more silverware, and I tell you, Roland was pretty pissed off. He says, "Where is all this silverware going?" He goes over to the dishwasher area. He took the garbage can—and this blew me away—and he turned the can upside down and pulls all the trash apart. There were probably twenty-four pieces of silverware in there. Then he got one of those magnet things that go over a trash can, so when you empty the trash, if there's any metal, like silverware, it'd grab it. It probably saved us a couple thousand dollars. Otherwise, it's like money going right in the trash.

It's like when you're making stocks, you leave nothing to waste. He would show me how to make stocks and consommé—the clarification. When you're younger, you don't care about how something works; you just want to do it. One night I was up, sitting on milk crates, looking at our kettle, making a consommé. I was watching the raft being formed. To me, it was kind of like watching an island being formed . . . it's got the eggshells and everything in there, and all the crud is coming to the top. When we got it exactly right, we put the cheese-cloth down below it. Oh my gosh, it's so exciting to see. You make a great stock and then a great consommé, and then maybe you put in a julienne of chicken, whatever your vegetables are, and you can see at the bottom of the cup, and the flavors are just so intense.

When Roland was pissed off about something, the look he'd give you would scare the hell out of you! You're like, "YES SIR!!" There was no back talk; we were trained right. A number of people quit because they gave up. This one time, I'm making *salmon en papillote* on the table. Chef Henin's large glass office is in front of me. One of the pantry guys gets into a heated argument with him. The pantry chef goes into chef's office with a big bowl of fruit. All of a sudden, the fruit is dumped all over Chef's head and the table. Chef Henin doesn't yell. He doesn't scream. He stands up, wipes the fruit off, wipes his jacket off. Just to see how he handled that . . . to see him not kill the guy . . . was pretty interesting. It was so cool. (Chef fired that guy, of course.)

One thing that's great about Roland is, if he believes in you, he's *always* there for you. For years, he kept track of me. This was before computers . . . I don't know how he did it. I've had many health concerns. I had two kidney transplants. Roland would check on me. He sent me an email, said something like, "I wish you best, and I want you to get a kidney." That was on August 18, 2011. Two hours later, I got a call from the Kidney Foundation that they had a kidney transplant.

Once I was in a coma for eleven days and almost died—I was two hours from dying, and I made a promise that I would devote my efforts to charity. So, six other chefs and I did Meals on Wheels, and we raised over a million dollars. We did Make-a-Wish, Share Our Strength—we did many fund-raisers. Being a culinarian, you do everything to help everybody. It's not about you; it's about helping people in need and doing little things for them . . . to touch people.

In 2001, I was nominated for Western Regional Chef of the Year at an American Culinary Federation (ACF) convention. I had no idea. There were about 400 chefs gathered for the ACF Presidential Medallion, which honors the top fifty chefs of the United States. I was in the back row wearing my chef's coat and pants and my tennis sneakers. They were naming some people, and I was clapping . . . I recognized some of my friends . . . and then they called my name! I was thinking, *This can't be friggin' right!* I didn't get up, and they called my name again. I got up there, and the chef shook my hand and put this medallion around me. It was really heavy!

Whatever I'm making—a flan, a chocolate *brûlée*, or clam chowder—people will say, "Why does yours taste different?" Everything I make, I make with love. You give everything to it. I always use the best ingredients. Also, just because the recipe is in a book doesn't mean it is right. I'll make a recipe, and I'll make notes and adjust it. You have to make adjustments. Being a chef, when things happen, it's like, *how smart and quickly can you do things without panicking?* When you're focused, nothing will get in your way. Being a chef, people say, "You've been so blessed because you found a career you love." Me being Christian, I believe that this is the journey God gave me, and I believe He put Roland in my life. Roland means the world to me. I'd do anything for him. I feel like one of his kids. Roland only has one son, but he has many more.

The thing about Roland is, he's done so many things for people. He ran the Culinary Olympics. He's been in charge of teams. He's been named the best chef of the United States. He's won almost every award that you can imagine. He's just about to retire from Delaware North. He has a hundred chefs underneath him. A while back, he was always inviting me up. He'd say, "Come up! Catch some salmon! Those things are fighting like hell!" He says, "Yeah, I'm looking for a chef for the Seattle Seahawks. You interested?" I thought, "My God, if my body wasn't broken, I would do that!" But everybody's given certain things, and you just do the best with what you've got.

I sent Roland a note talking about how, as you get older, it's so great seeing people who you've trained all over the world! They're in Ireland working with Gordon Ramsay, or the Broadmoor in Colorado, Ritz Carlton, or wherever they're at. I can't even imagine how many thousands of cooks and chefs Roland's made . . . I have no idea what the number would be. The thing is, you only live once. When we're gone, people are going to look back and say, "Oh my gosh, look what Roland taught me."

The General:
Culinary Institute of America

Roland Henin spent ten years as a Culinary Arts Educator. His first year was at Johnson & Wales University, where he developed the Sauce Kitchen from scratch and created its textbook.

RGH: Johnson & Wales was one of the worst starts of any position in my life. At the Dunes Club, I had a few cooks from there, so I knew about the college. When approached to teach there, I said, "I am no teacher." The director responded, "All chefs are teachers." I was hired as a Chef Saucier. There was no Sauce Kitchen, and they hired me to develop it.

That first day, I arrive in the morning and go to the room where I will teach Sauce Kitchen. There are eighteen to twenty kids waiting in the hallway. We enter the room, and there is . . . nothing. No walk-in refrigerator. No shelves. No counters. No workstations. No equipment. No desks. No chairs. No paper. No curriculum. No food, pans, or pots. There are three steam kettles and two steam holders . . . in the middle of this empty room. That's it

I say to the kids, "Good morning. Sauce Kitchen is brand-new, as you can see. Let's see what we can do here." I sit them down, roll a chalkboard over, and begin to talk about sauce. The next day I complain, say I could do quick sauces—hollandaise, simple butter sauces—but, without pots, we had nothing. I borrow some pots and other equipment from other kitchens. By the end of the week, I have two boxes of bones—chicken and veal. I felt bad for the kids.

At the end of that first year, they came to me and asked if I would consider returning as Sauce Kitchen instructor. I said no, but proposed something else. *We are in New England. We could get support from the local fishing companies and do a Fish Kitchen.* They looked at me like I was from Mars. They said, "We'll check it out," then returned and said, "No. The director doesn't like fish."

Master Chef Ferdinand Metz became president of the Culinary Institute of America (CIA) in 1980. In 1981, a female chef colleague, Lyde Buchtenkirch (the only female CMC), and I talked. She was teaching at the CIA. She said, "Let's go and meet Metz." He was trying to rebuild a Chef-Instructor brigade.

Metz asked me, "Why didn't you go back to Johnson & Wales?"

"I did not want to continue teaching Sauce Kitchen."

"What do you want to do?"

"A Fish Kitchen."

"Why?"

I explained. It's New England and the kids cannot do fish. Fish is a big food, and it's going to get bigger.

Metz says, "Well, if you come here, I will start a Fish Kitchen with you."

In the beginning of first year of Fish Kitchen, our inventory was 400,000 frozen product and 40,000 fresh product. By the end of that year, the inventory had switched: 400,000 fresh product and 40,000 frozen.

* * *

Henin spent over five years at the Culinary Institute of America, in Hyde Park, New York. There he worked as Chef/Instructor for several units: Classical Cuisine & Banquet Service (The Stage); Classical Public Restaurant (Escoffier or "E-Room"); Seafood Kitchen ("Fish Kitchen"); and Continuing Education. He also served as student advisor/coach for national and international culinary competitions.

Henin's talent fit the Escoffier Room perfectly, except for one major detail: design malfunction. The E-Room had a "fishbowl" window, exposing the entire kitchen works to dining guests. Chef Henin's "instructional strategies" would frighten delicate diners. Apparently, throwing knifes and causing students to cry and flee the kitchen was not an "ambience promoter." (This was before the heyday of reality shows, like *Hell's Kitchen*. Who knew that Old School European Chefs were such media pioneers?) Metz had a chef of renown and ability, but E-Room was not conducive and maybe, a blessing. True to his word, Metz and Henin founded the Seafood Kitchen, in 1983. That same year, Roland Henin would take his CMC exam through the American Culinary Federation, earning the highest culinary honor attainable: Certified Master Chef.

David Burke

Author, Inventor, & Consulting Partner at ESquared Hospitality—Owner/Operator of BLT Restaurants

He threw you in the pool. At two years old. He chucks you in the pool and walks away. Even if he got an eye on you, but you don't think he does.

DAVID: I met Chef Henin in 1981. I started at the CIA in October 1980, so I didn't have him in classes until later in the second year because he taught the kitchens. I had him *twice* because someone had gotten sick and he was doing double duty. I had him in what they called the Stage, and then I had him in the E-Room. The first time I had him, he was more of a substitute for half of the block. Chef Saucy got sick or something happened. Chef Saucy was a plump, mild-mannered French chef, had his moments, blah, blah, blah . . . I was a pretty good student actually, because I had skills and confidence. I had worked in good restaurants before I came to school, and I was passionate about food. I knew more than my fellow students about French food and food in general. Also, I worked two externships, so I was probably one of the best cooks in my class, if not *the* best. I don't say that in a cocky way. That's just the way it was.

We had Henin in the second half of the Chef Saucy's block. Henin came in, and he just . . . commanded respect. And *fear*. We all feared him. He didn't play games, didn't sweet talk. He didn't care if you liked him. He was the boss . . . military-ish, the way he operated . . . he was a general in the army, man. I tell you, the CIA was a lot tougher back then, as far as discipline, and the whining, and all this other stuff: *You went to CIA; you went to work!* You went to school, but you went to work! Especially in Henin's class. He was borderline mean—people were afraid of him because you actually had to work. You had to produce.

Henin comes in, and Saucy was out. Right off the bat, he had a different way of doing French service, doing this, that. I gotta tell you something: whether his way was better or not, I don't remember. But I got to see another way. He didn't care about the other guy's way. That was the other guy's kitchen, and that's not how you do it. He just came in and turned that class upside down. I don't know if it made sense, if it was harder or easier, but the final product was better.

SUSAN: *Can you riff on that, a bit?*

DAVID: Let's talk about poaching quenelles or timbales—fish mousse in cups. He wouldn't let us cook them ahead of time and let sit. They had to be cooked and then served. There was no paranoia, it wasn't *Hurry up, and get it ready, and then we'll wait to plate.* He took more chances, but he also didn't hold your hand. He told you what you had to do, and you would do it. He threw you in the pool. At two years old. He chucks you in the pool and walks away. Even if he got an eye on you, but you don't think he does. He creates nervous energy.

So we get through that class, and then we had the Sheraton dining room with a great chef named Elliott Sharron who liked me—I got a 99 in his class. We saw eye-to-eye. I was one of the leaders in the classroom. He came to me and said, "Burke, you got great hands. I like your style. Your classmates respect you. You've got instincts. You're a natural. If you need a job in New York City, you let me know." I appreciated that. I was the team leader or whatever you called it. We put out nice food with Elliott. I was boning out salmon, did butchery for the class. I cut a salmon in a certain way, and it came out fine. I'm not saying it was great, but I could get it off the bone.

Next block! I get Henin in the E-Room. We weren't supposed to have Henin. He switched from days to nights, and now I wind up getting him. By mistake. *Twice.* Since we had Henin once before, he knew our class a little bit. He might have failed people in our class already. I did okay with him in Saucy's class—I don't think he paid much attention to me. E-Room is our last class before graduation, and we're getting excited. We're popping the cork a bit early . . . but now we got Henin, and everyone was scared, including myself.

The *first* day of his class, my car breaks down on the mid-Hudson bridge. I used to have a green Gremlin. I had to park it on the top of a huge hill—walk about a mile and a half to get to it from my house I rented. I'd push it down the hill and pop the clutch to get it started. And it worked, it worked. So this is about April. The thing worked all winter through the snow. I mean, I've had this beast since *high school.* And all of a sudden, today . . . it doesn't fucking start. I get on the bridge, and my car breaks down. I got a hairnet on, I have the yellow necktie—we were the last block of the yellow neckties and the white pants. I break down, and *I see Henin's face in my head.* I don't see the truck behind me. I don't see the blinker, the motor, the radio . . . all I see is his face. I shout, "Oh, no. Oh, *no!!*" I'm like, "Holy shit!" I *leave* my car there. I just left it! No note, nothing. I jump down on Route 9 and start hitchhiking. I am *not* gonna be late.

And anyway, I'm late. I gotta walk into Henin's class *late*—and I'm late by forty-five minutes—half an hour, at least. I got my knife roll and my hairnet, I'm huffing and puffing. And I get in there, and he starts in . . . and I'm like, *whoaaaah . . .*

He says, "Do you think you can walk into my class late?" He was like Jack Nicholson in . . . what's that movie? When he says, "YOU CAN'T HANDLE THE TRUTH!!!"

SUSAN: A Few Good Men.

DAVID: *A Few Good Men!* That's what it was like! I'm not arguing with him, but he goes on and on for like, three minutes. Finally he says, "What's your excuse?"

I'm like, "My car broke down on the bridge."

"THAT'S THE *BEST* YOU CAN DO!?!!"

"No, I could make up a great story! But that's what happened! What do you wanna hear? You wanna hear that—"

He screams, "That's ENOUGH! SIT DOWN!!"

He's pacing around. He says, "I got to tell you something." (I can't do his accent.) "I asked the whole class about you. They said you're a good guy, and this and that, and blah blah blah. . . . So, I'm gonna let it slide. Everybody—the class you've been with for two years—they all basically stood up for you. They said it's unlike you. You should be proud of that." He said that! He says, "But, I'm not fucking proud of you."

Anyway, so we put that aside. I kind of had a backhanded warm feeling about it. I was also scared shit. He goes, "I got my eye on you . . . you get one more mistake, and that's it."

The next couple days go by, and things are fine. Elliott Sharron is in the kitchen right next door. Elliott treated me like I was his little brother. So day one, day two . . . then, Henin demos a salmon. "When you cut a salmon, you got a big, slicing knife." He did it in one fell swoop . . . impressive. He says, "That's how I want the salmon butchered." He takes another salmon, and in one fell swoop—like a samurai warrior would take his head off someone, like an archer would put an arrow five hundred feet into a bull's-eye—that's how he did it. It wasn't even an effort. It was like he was buttering toast. It was the best fileting I have ever seen. He goes, "This is the way you do it. This is the way I want it done. Am I clear?" I like, "Yeah, okay, I can do that." I'm picking my jaw up off the floor.

I looked at it, and okay, that's one way of doing it. I think to myself, *It's not the way I do it, but okay.* I start butchering the salmon. I'm going to cut it the way I am comfortable. I know I can't do it the way he did it because I don't have the confidence to do it that way. If I think about doing it his way, I'm going to mess it up. So I'm slowly doing it the way anybody would, by going down the back and fileting it with a smaller knife, and pulling it. I'm gently easing the knife in as a first-timer would gently ease anything in . . . I'm being more careful not to make a mistake. I'm on the low diving board, not the high one.

Henin sees one of the filets. I'd say it was pretty good . . . I'd give it a four. He gives it a zero. He comes over, and he just starts bashing me. I gotta tell you something . . . I can still hear it. He's *tall*—about a good foot above me—yelling with the accent. And let's face it, he's not the softest looking guy. He doesn't look like . . . what do I wanna say . . . he doesn't look like Michael J. Fox. I'm looking up and he's beating down on me, and he's screaming and F-bombing and *Fuck you* and *bap bap bah*, and *what the fuck are you thinking*, and *get the hell out of my class!* I'm like, "Holy guacamole! What the fuck?" It's a fucking disaster.

The whole class stops because he's borderline . . . what would be harassment these days. Elliott Sharron hears him from in the next classroom down the hall and comes in to my defense. He goes toe-to-toe with Henin, like an umpire and a coach of a baseball team. Elliott's no joke, either. He is a highly respected instructor, got more tenure there, and is more of the All-American-likeable guy, although strict. Anyway, he comes in and he goes right up to Henin. I'm standing at the cutting board, and he says, "What the hell is your problem? Leave him alone. He's a great kid and *bap bap bap* . . ." Henin's defending his class. It's *his* class, and Henin throws Elliott out of it. They go into the hall and they're going at it, they start having an argument. It was like a husband and wife that just needed a catalyst to fight about something else. I think there were other things they wanted to get out in the open, and I just happened to be the excuse. I don't know what to make of it. They're out in the hallway, and this goes on for a couple minutes. Henin comes back. He showed me another salmon, and he showed me slowly. I did the third one his way.

SUSAN: *How'd it come out?*

DAVID: It was okay. The way he did it, he must have done thousands of fish, no exaggeration, that good. I don't do it that way today because I don't cut a lot of fish. If I was a butcher, I would do it that way. It's a technique you have to master. But you know what? I got to see it.

Boy, he embarrassed me. He was actually disappointed in me more than anything else. That's what upset him . . . because he knew I could have done it. At the moment it was happening, I didn't know he was disappointed in me. I was just thinking, *This guy's a fucking mad dog.* As I have gone through my career, I realize he would have never yelled at me that much if he didn't know I was gonna be great because he wouldn't have wasted his time. He would have walked away and said, "There goes another schmuck."

Anyway, we calm down, we get the service done, yada yada, anyway, fast forward. I did well in his class after that. We had some jovial moments, especially toward the end. Later I found out, he's just a puppy, a nice guy! He had a human side, but didn't want anyone to know that. He was the kinda guy that would laugh without smiling—you know what I mean? You'd have to get to know him a little. He'd look at you without opening his mouth. He'd be laughing, but you didn't know it.

I have to choose my words carefully. . . . After the class, I'm still intimidated about him. When I left Elliott Sharron's class, he patted me on the ass, roughed me up on the shoulder, and said, "Good luck, kid. You got a great future ahead of you. You got good hands, good instincts. Call me anytime, with any questions. I'll help you get a job in New York. Keep in touch." To the rest of the group he said something like, "Good-bye, good luck," or whatever. Or, "I'll see you guys in the unemployment line."

Just before graduation, there's a job fair. I'm walking around and get approached by a few guys. This one guy comes up to me named Jean LaFont, a big-time recruiter hiring for a hotel group down in Texas. He says, "May I speak to you, Mr. Burke?"

"Yeah, of course."

"Are you interested in moving to Texas and joining our team?"

"Well, I was in Dallas for my externship . . ."

"We've got some big developments there, a hotel group. I'd like to offer you a job."

I said, "Why?"

"Roland Henin says you were the best student he's seen in a long time."

"What? You mean *Elliott Sharron* said that."

"No. Chef Henin. Sharron said it, also."

I was like, *"Reeeeallly?"* I got this warm feeling. Henin must've pointed him to me.

I looked across the room, and Henin was there. I saw him out of the corner of my eye. I kinda gave him this look, like, *you son-of-a-gun.* He just looked at me and smiled, nodded his head, and walked away. It was one of those things. I'll never forget that moment. I was beaming with pride. He didn't say a word, and it meant a million words. He said to me, without saying anything: *I'm proud of you. You're a good kid, and you're gonna do well.*

That recommendation from him meant so much more than anybody else's . . . without him even saying anything to me. He was thirty yards away, with a grin and a nod of his head, as if he was saying thumbs-up, and he had his hands in his pockets and he just kept on walking. It was all I needed. It was the seal of approval from the strictest and one of the most talented chefs in the school. Chef Henin was the School of Hard Knocks, and not everybody gets a trophy. I had goose bumps. I was like, "Cool."

In past interviews, people always ask, *Who do you remember?* I always included him. That was the moment in my career that gave me confidence. That was what I needed the most. I was always a confident guy, but he gave me a confidence that was the punch in the arm I needed to take the job I did take. I didn't take that Texas job, but I found a job going to Norway to be a chef in a private residence for a wealthy family. Without that nod of confidence from him, I wouldn't have had the balls to go to Europe by myself.

SUSAN: *What is your mentoring style?*

DAVID: I was the same at the beginning. When I took over the River Café, I was a no-bullshit guy, *My way or the highway*, demanding. There was an old joke: *If he yells at you, he likes you. If he really yells at you, he really likes you. If he ignores you, you're in trouble.* Maybe I should've been more complimentary, but people don't respond to that. I give a guy a compliment, and he calls in sick the next day. Been out celebrating. I did take the good guys in my crew out to eat and drink. Then, times changed. I'm in the process of interviewing people right now, and as I'm older, I talk about what I'm looking for in somebody from the ground up. Not just like recruiting soldiers. I used to recruit soldiers like a Marine: *I'd make a great man-chef out of you.* Teach you and berate you, and *Do it my way.* That works for a lot of people. These days, it's a little different. I like to have fun, so I'm a little bit of a wisecracker, and I do it in a way that creates an ambiance of fun, with team spirit, like Little League. There's always going to be someone you pick on a little, always someone that leaves the pack.

SUSAN: *What are you doing these days?*

DAVID: I do everything. This morning I'm in the kitchen, believe it or not. I just made a filet mignon hot dog. No one ever knows what to do with the scraps . . . you can grind them, do this and that. I've finally come up with a way that saves the scraps in long strips, 'cause they're strips, right! I wrap them in plastic like a hot dog, *sous vide* them, then brown it off and put it in a hot dog roll—best filet mignon hot dog ever. I like taking scraps and making something great.

I'm in Maryland working with crab cake. I'm going to do a "Cake and Coffee": crab cake made with onion crumbs, simple—no breading. I'm going to use my dried onions crumbs as a coating, and we're going to bake it, so there are no carbs in the cake at all. But still, it'll have a little crunch, a little texture. If you're in DC and you want to put crab cake on the menu, you've got to keep it as pure as possible. "Bi-crusted this" . . . I'm sure everybody's done everything. The creativity is, "Let's go back to the basics."

We'll serve the cake with a Maryland crab cappuccino next to it. The espresso is made out of crab stock, and the foam is topped with Old Bay and lemon zest. These days, when you buy crabmeat, where is the shell? The real essence, the flavor in the crab is not in the meat, but in the shell. We're going to make a reduced crab broth from the whole hard shell that nobody gets because they just buy picked crab meat. I get hard crabs year-round, so it becomes one of our signature dishes. Then I've got crab stock for minestrone, soup-of-the-day, and all that. We'll make an intense amber stock, and that will be the "coffee." We'll put a little foamed milk on there, garnish, and we're off to the races. Cake and Coffee, like grandma! I get to charge eight bucks more.

SUSAN: *What life lessons have you learned from Chef Henin?*

DAVID: What I've learned from Henin at a distance—and something I need to learn—is how to enjoy nature and life a little more. It seems like he's having a helluva time in his fishing and his life, based on the note he sent me and his invitation to go fishing. I admire that. One thing I hate about him is I'm never gonna be able to be better at him at fileting a fish. I'd love to see him do it again. I do want to get together with him, but unfortunately I can't go down in October because I'm opening three places.

Life is short, and you cross paths with some unique people. They don't have to be your neighbor or best friend. These certain people leave a mark on you, and that's what he's done for me. I'm glad that we can express what he's done on paper because he's the kind of guy who doesn't look for the spotlight and notoriety.

Henin did a lot more in those few weeks in school than he could imagine. When you're young and you look up to guys like him, you don't realize how much of an impact you have on people. They're looking at you like you're the Gods of Cuisine. The little things you do and say are taken with such magnified glances that you sometimes don't realize the importance of your words or your actions.

Mike Colameco

Host / Producer Mike Colameco's
Real Food TV and *Food Talk*

This was the first guy that had ever, on purpose, sabotaged a recipe.

MIKE: I was in my early twenties, toward the end of my studies at the CIA. Back then, your last two units were the Sheraton Room and the Escoffier Room (E-Room). Both prepare you for the real world. The Sheraton Room was set up in Roth Hall. Half the term was working the front of the house, Russian Service—serving food off of your left arm from big trays, serving diners the best you could by using the back of a spoon and a fork [laughs] . . . picking up tourney potatoes and cuts of meat and putting them on a plate. Your customers were CIA students. The other half of the term was in the kitchen. The E-Room had the same rotation, but the clientele were the general public.

I graduated in January 1982, so would have been in the E-Room in December 1981. Roland was the Sheraton instructor. I was a slightly older student, having worked in kitchens for nine years before I went to the CIA. I started young, at thirteen, in Philly. By the time I got to school, I already had good solid industry experience, in terms of what you could do in those days. Because I had worked in kitchens, I recognized different things in the instructors.

Henin liked me, luckily, because if you got on his bad side early, it would be a long ten days. He was a quick study. You walked in and you were sized up. He was an imposing kind of figure, French, with a dry sense of humor. Big hands and a big schnozz (I have one too, so it's one big nose to another). He was a big shot. There was no bullshit about him. You could tell that this was *not* going to be an easy ten days, in any way. If he didn't like you, *good luck*.

Cooking schools are a concept, right? You learn the cooking trade in the field, so "cooking school" is kind of an oxymoron. You're better served doing a long apprenticeship in kitchens. To that end, what Roland would do, and he was kind of famous for this, is, he'd mess with you. You're working on your recipe and have to get it ready for lunch or dinner—whichever a.m. or p.m. shift you were on. You'd have your roast leg of lamb in the oven at 375, come back an hour and a half later, open the oven . . . and he had shut it off. [Laughs]

His pranks were on a daily basis. It was great because he gave you a sense of working in the real world! If you've got several things going at the same time, you better check on them every fifteen minutes [laughs], just in case. Did someone turn the oven off, or is the pilot light on? All those things happen in the trade. He'd sabotage stuff in the kitchen and explain to whomever was his victim that *this is what happens*. If you're working on something, and you leave your *mise en place*, you're playing around and you walk away and do something else and come back twenty minutes later, maybe it's not going to be there. Maybe the pot washer took it. It was, basically, a reality cooking class in a school where there was no reality; it was all kind of a setup. This was the first guy that had ever, on purpose, sabotaged a recipe. He'd teach them a lesson that, *Hey, when you're out there in the real world, big boys and girls, this kind of thing can happen. When you get out there in a month, get ready.* I had a lot of respect for him.

SUSAN: *Too bad students had to wait until the E-Room to receive that valuable lesson, instead of all chefs doing that throughout the program.*

MIKE: Yeah, well . . . it's not the way culinary schools work. I am a graduate of the CIA, and I learned a lot when I was there. When people ask me about cooking schools, I tell them it's not a *bad* idea, but a costly one. When I was a student, culinary schools weren't that expensive; now they charge upwards of $50,000 for a degree. It's crazy. I would say, find a good kitchen in the town where you live and even work for free for a couple of years. You'd be better served. Henin was great that way! He brought the real kitchen to the students. He was this salty French guy who clearly had a lot of industry experience and was trying to pass that on to the students. In terms of the CIA, it was more of a "hard knocks" fashion.

If you visit the CIA now, it looks different from the Culinary Institute when I was there. It looks like an Ivy League campus, with these beautiful brick and wood buildings, media centers and gymnasiums, and dormitories that could pass for million-dollar condos. When I was there, it was Roth Hall. Students lived upstairs, the library was on the second floor, and working classrooms were below. You either lived in Roth Hall or in one of the cinder block three-story East German dorms that were a little walk away from Roth Hall, down by the river. That was it; that was the whole campus. It was much more blue-collar looking than it is today.

The instructors then were almost exclusively retired, European-trained chefs—French, Swiss, German, Belgian, or northern Italian, plus a couple Asian chefs. They were all great at what they did, and you could get vastly different experiences depending on the instructor. Growing up in Philadelphia, other than Georges Perrier at Le Bec-Fin, there wasn't much of a restaurant scene. At the CIA, suddenly it was like being in a treasure trove of knowledge. We were able to tap the brains of these guys who had an entire career in the industry, who started in their early teens and were now bringing thirty to forty years' experience aboard. We had some world-class pastry chefs in the school at that time. There was this one Swiss guy, Chef Albert Kumin, who was still kicking a decade ago, making chocolates with his daughter. He was just amazing. This guy . . . we were doing eight-inch cake trays . . . he had those great big hands, reaching in and taking out these trays in a 375 oven. I'm thinking, *Are you kidding me?* He pulled sugar all the time and had these ginormous callouses. We had some of the best culinary talent in the country at the time, no debate.

I was obsessed with trying to get my money's worth out of the CIA. If I felt there was a better instructor during a block, I would switch my a.m. and p.m. blocks, or I would take both a.m. and p.m. shifts. This was a long time ago, but yeah, they'd let you do that. It was different then.

After graduation, I got busy in my career. I was a chef at the Ritz-Carlton in 1987 and my girlfriend/now wife was the pastry chef at the Pierre. We were going to open a restaurant in New York City and had backers . . . then the stock market tanked—October 19, 1987, Black Monday—the stock market fell 22 percent in a single day. It was the single biggest loss of money in history. There was no "off" switch when the selling started . . . that meant our investors said *no money.* For weeks, all the chefs were like, *Oh my God; every phone call is a cancellation.* The market wiped it all out. Thomas Keller's Rakel was less than a year old . . . everyone was struggling. Officially, the New York recession happened a few years later, but for restaurants, it happened that day.

We dusted ourselves off. Instead of building in New York, we'd build somewhere else. We traveled around and noticed that there were great restaurants outside of the city. I would not advise [laughs] anybody to do this. We ended up in Cape May, New Jersey, with a seasonal place. For six years, we ran it in the summer and came back to New York to work with friends in the winter. Then we sold the restaurant and had a few dollars because we owned the real estate. I did some food importing and odds and ends. Finally, the cooking show came about in 1999. Since then, I've been doing a mostly local PBS cooking show in New York City. I still do some radio for WOR. I went from being a chef to being in food media, once that became an actual viable thing to do. When we were in cooking school, media wasn't on anyone's list of things you were going to do at any point in your career because it didn't exist.

SUSAN: *After graduation, did your relationship continue with Chef?*

MIKE: I wish it had, but no, it didn't. Once I got out of the CIA, I packed up whatever it was that I had—my cookbook collection, my knife kit—into my Ford Pinto, and I drove down to Manhattan. When you think about graduating in January, in retrospect, it's not the best time to try to enter the New York job market. It's one of the deadest times of the year. I put my shoulder to the task of navigating the world of Manhattan restaurants and building my résumé. I wanted to see if I could get into some of the best kitchens that were available in New York City. It wasn't just all French or three-stars. I wanted to do volume, so ended up at Tavern on the Green for a few years as the night chef because you never know where you're going to be in five years.

The old European guys were tough to work for, with the breaking down of barriers. I was lucky to have the guys who I had, coming up, who were generous with their experience. Jean-Jacques Rachou was a super-important guy in New York because he was *the* first French chef. He had three-star restaurants—La Côte Basque was one of the greatest in that era of the late seventies–early eighties, like Lutèce, like Le Carrousel . . . all of those. Jacques was like a Horatio Alger–type of story: Rachou was the first French chef to hire American line cooks full-time. All the other kitchens only had French staff front and back of house: Lutèce, La Grenouille, La Caravelle etc.

Rachou was an orphan, which, back then, was second-class citizenship. He lived like a slave with no schooling. When he first arrived in America, he could neither read nor write, in English *or* French. Rachou was completely uneducated; literally, he was illiterate. Despite this, he found his way into kitchens in France, worked his way up, and ended up at the top of his game in New York City. He was the first French chef in Manhattan, with a restaurant of note, who would hire American cooks, full-time. No one else would hire them. Charlie Palmer, Rick Moonen, and Frank Crispo—these were the guys graduating from the CIA around that time. If you came to New York in the late seventies and tried to get a job with André Soltner at Lutèce or any of the other restaurants, the answer was no. There wasn't even a question. They would say it: *We don't hire Americans. You could come in and when our poissonier is away on vacation, you could work his fish station. When he comes back, you leave.* There was a bias among that generation of French chefs. Jacques was the first guy who felt that these guys were as good as anybody else. *I'm gonna give them a chance.* They threw him out of the Vatel Club briefly because he was hiring Americans. It was kind of scandalous.

You don't think of it these days. It seems like such a long time ago. There was . . . I don't want to say "bias," but there was a hiring practice . . . you could understand it, in a myopic way: these guys were trained in France; they were comfortable working with people who spoke the same language; they had the same cultural traditions and culinary reference points. If you say, *I wanna make a Consommé Royale,* or *I want to do a Dover sole or a lamb this way,* everybody was on the same page. The idea of American cooks was still pretty new on the upper levels—that the CIA and Johnson & Wales were producing graduates who were good cooks after they got out, or especially a few years out. It was hard to think back on a time when being *American* [laughs]—no, or being a white male, in *any* industry—was going to work against you. You couldn't get a job as a CIA grad if you weren't French, in those kitchens. Jacques was so important; if I were to list for you all the cooks that came through his kitchens in that era—the late seventies and early eighties—it's a *Who's Who* of what would become the first generation of American Chefs: Charlie Palmer, Rick Moonen, Henry Meer, Frank Crispo, Ali Barker, Waldy Malouf, Todd English, Stefan Kopf, Neil Murphy, and on and on and on.

The baton was being passed to us, from them. Now when I look back contextually, I think back . . . yeah, Thomas Keller . . . we all stand on the shoulders of these guys. That's how it works; there's no other way to put it. We learned cooking from them. We learned the restaurant business from them. By the 1990s, Americans were chefs in their own right. Then, by the aughts . . . David Bouley was probably the most famous guy for a long time, and I think Thomas Keller is probably one of the great—if not the greatest—spokesmen for what would become the Great American Classical Kitchen.

When filming out at the French Laundry in 2000, my cameraman pulled me aside after a day of filming and said, "So, what do you think?" I had eaten in most three-star restaurants in Europe.

"This is the first three-star Michelin restaurant I've ever seen in America. That's what I think. He's killing it. It's perfect. He's nailed it."

Thomas and that generation of Americans were the first generation of Americans to take over kitchens and move the ball forward, but very much standing on the shoulders of mostly French chefs. As kids coming up, there was still that sense of rigor, discipline, integrity, and technique.

SUSAN: *It's interesting that he was a product of apprenticeship and classical European foundations. He's perhaps also a spokesperson for learning in that traditional manner, compared to the culinary school path. I've seen that a lot, in people's stories: the benefit to apprenticing. It seems to be a road less taken, nowadays . . . a lost or dying art.*

MIKE: Yeah, it's a shame and it shouldn't be. I have a call-in culinary radio show, so I tend to answer the same types of questions: *Why is my cheesecake cracking? Where do I go for dinner in the theater district?* My rote answer about cooking is: If you're interested in cooking, culinary school is an option, but a much better one would be to find the best restaurant you can talk your way into, work for free or minimum wage if you have to, and just keep your mouth shut . . . and learn, learn. The European models of starting young and not going to school, but doing apprenticeships, were more formalized. That's the best way to learn this business, not spending a crapload.

When I was a chef in New York in the late eighties and nineties, kids were coming out of the CIA with their thermometers in their pockets and their neckerchiefs tied perfectly, expecting to be hired as sous-chefs. They had no résumés to speak of, and it was hard to explain to them. We had a lot of Dominican and Puerto Rican immigrants before them who were amazing line cooks, who came to this country knowing nothing . . . people who'd work in restaurants and said, *teach me.* They are the Spanish contingents, now including Peruvians, Ecuadorians, Salvadorians, and now, Mexicans: the backbone of New York kitchens. They are phenomenally good cooks: disciplined, reliable, and hate to say it, but, dollars to doughnuts, they are ten times better than most of the CIA graduates, easily—humble and less entitled. For them, it's a job. If you show them how to work fast and clean, they are great at producing a recipe consistently.

People who come out of cooking school have a false sense of their abilities. They think they're worth something that they're not. It's just an illusion. Part of that comes from the culinary school. They give you that. They're not gonna take your fifty grand and tell you the *whole* truth [laughs]. When we went to culinary school, there were just two: CIA and Johnson & Wales. Now, every city has its own cooking school. There are satellite programs, multiple campuses . . . it's become a huge growth industry, and they can only sustain that by selling the myth that a) Cooking is fun to do for a career, and b) Come to my school. You'll be good, when you graduate. Both of those things may be true, but it's still a business.

SUSAN: *Chef Henin is a French chef who persisted in the United States . . . spent his life mentoring American students. It's complex. He speaks so highly about how quickly the US changes, and the creativity it allows. Changes that took a couple of years here would take two hundred years in France.*

MIKE: That's completely true. It's our greatest asset as a country. Back in the eighties, we'd have a couple weeks off in the summer. We'd buy the cheapest plane tickets we could and go to Paris. We'd book tables to eat at these three-star restaurants because that was the Gold Standard. What you were seeing in those kitchens, you were not seeing in America. There were a few reasons for it, not the least of which was ingredients! In New York City, in the mid-eighties, we were basically buying everything off Sysco trucks. Right? There were no farmers markets, no Farm-to-Table movement. There was no good bread. Butter was crap. We accepted that level of ingredients. In retrospect, it was junk.

To Roland's point, once cooking became cool—once restaurants and going out to eat became the talk of the town, once it became fashionable—we ran with that ball. By the late nineties and the aughts, I would go to Paris and be bored silly. They hadn't done *anything new*—nothing new since nouvelle cuisine. I'd think, *Christ, I could eat better than this in New York any day of the week.* And now look at the ingredients we have: the bread that's available; the butter; the American-made cheese; the artisan ingredients. Yeah. Once we decide we're in as a culture, we're in. We just move at Grand Prix pace. It's crazy. It's the absolute truth.

SUSAN: *And your legacy? The PBS show?*

MIKE: One of the things these younger writers find useful with me is that sense of historical context—how it got to be this way. It's easy to be smart and young in New York, just move to Brooklyn and think it's always been like this. If you go back to the first generation of American chefs, the kitchen was such a small community. The restaurant scene in New York in the eighties was so tiny, compared to what it is today. I teach people . . . I add to the conversation.

SUSAN: *Some of your favorite restaurants these days?*

MIKE: They're all over the place! The ingredients these kids have to play with and the dedication these kids have . . . I am a huge fan. A lot of guys in my generation, you'll hear them bemoaning, *back in the old days* . . . I tell them, dude, you're crazy. We were doing the best we could with what we had. If you picked any of those *New York Times* four-star restaurants in the era that I was in New York, if you could pick any of them, go back in time, and eat dinner there, you'd be lucky if that chef would get one or two stars today. That was all we had! It was the same menu, the Dover sole, the lamb chops, and some kind of beef done a certain way. Now people are just playing with superior ingredients.

My job is to go out and eat at restaurants in New York and then curate which restaurants are going to make my show. The kids at Battersby in Brooklyn are doing amazing stuff. Two restaurants that opened up in the lower East side: Fung Tu, run by Jonathan Wu, a Chinese-American guy who worked for Thomas Keller at Per Se, is reinventing a Chinese-American cuisine. It's this little hole in the wall. On Orchard Street, by Canal, there are two chefs called Contra and Wildair on the Lower East Side, doing downtown casual. There are so many great spots these days, it's crazy.

There is a whole generation of chefs who are just absolutely killing it. The ingredients are the best. The wines coming to America are from around the world. My friends come in from France, and we'll go out to dinner. They're in the business, and they're like: *How did this wine end up here? I can't buy this wine in France, and I live in Paris.* There is so much interest in good wine and so many good importers . . . producers with small allocations who want to be in New York City, and San Francisco, and Chicago . . .

The wine scene, the food scene—the whole thing just keeps getting better. There's never been a better time. Back to men like Roland Henin and Jean-Jacques Rachou: we stand on those guys' shoulders. That's the legacy. This is the history of how we got here. Let's not forget it.

Edward Brown

Chef Innovator, Restaurant Associates for NYC

Even being a young kid, I recognized that these people were just wasting energy on complaining, instead of absorbing the lesson being taught.

EDWARD: Roland is one of the most important mentors in my life. Although we've stayed in touch all these years, I only spent, literally, three weeks of my life with him. He was my instructor back in 1982 or '83, toward the end of our time at the CIA, followed by a final blast in the American Bounty. He had a big reputation for being a real hard-ass. It was a difficult class, famous for making people want to quit, cry, or any combination of these, but having said that, everyone thought he was the best chef in the school.

When our class arrived, I went in with the attitude: *I want to make this the best experience I can.* He was aggressive, direct, and firm. Prior to going into the kitchen, we would have our class meeting. Henin would rattle off the prep and work assignments and expect you to get it. If you had intelligent questions, you could ask them and he'd respond. Once we'd left that classroom, he'd expect that we all got it. When you get down there, you better be on the money or you're going to hear about it. And hear about it you did—I mean, he's not afraid to scream and yell, not afraid to give people a hard time. I thought it was okay, because first of all, I didn't get too much of it, so that was good. It wasn't that he was attacking anyone personally. It was about the job. He would put them under pressure for real-life situations to make them feel like, *Listen. You're about to go out in the real world, and you need to know what it's going to feel like.* I felt like I was working in a high-end, high-pressure restaurant. We were responsible for serving great food, to a lot of guests, in a short period of time, under pressure.

I still have my notes from his class, including the sweeping schedule of when it was most efficient to sweep the kitchen and sweeping at the end of service. He drew a diagram that included instruction: start here; follow the arrows, etc. Sweeping is as important as any other task. Those are the kind of details that I got from Chef: how you start the fish; how you clean the fish; the sauce you make for the fish. Every element is as important as the other, and it all comes back to being disciplined, organized, and prepared.

I was in charge of the fish station, which it happened, remained throughout my entire career. He demanded that if you are in charge of the station, then you

owned it. This was not an experiment; this was the real deal. You need to do
your research the night before, to know as much as possible about the product
in your station that you're cooking. You're part of a team, and you contribute to
making this service happen. A restaurant doesn't live on just one station. It lives
on several stations, and you contribute to the whole picture.

One night, there was a guy who was serving butter sauce with one of the
dishes, and he ran out. Chef calls out for the sauce, and the student says, "I'm
out."

Henin says, "You're out. So, what? You're out. What do you want me to do?
Go out to the dining room and tell the guests, 'We're out?' How could you be
out and not have a plan?"

Chef jumps behind the stove and makes the sauce. It was a sauce that required a longer process, but he made a shorter version of it on the fly, which was
real-world experience. I will never forget him doing that. It made me think that
there are ways to do things, and there are ways to do things when *you have to*. It's
about serving our guests and never having to say no to them.

Within the first fifteen minutes of our class meeting him, he informed us:
*Most of you will get the absolute minimum grade to pass this class—69.5. Quite a few of
you will not be here on the last day. You will fail.* That's how it went. That was the
starting point. I like to call that Henin's welcome speech.

SUSAN: *So, that was how he started the class? Wow! What was your response?*

EDWARD: I loved it. It made me so excited, because in my mind I'm saying, *I'm
not gonna be the guy who fails, and I'm not gonna be the one who gets 69.5. This thing
is gonna be about who does the best work. It's not about who studies more, or who writes
a good paper . . . it's gonna be about the guy who acts the most like a chef.* I picked up
on that right away. You were in for something different than anything else that
you had already done. It was gonna go one of two ways: sideways or great. Everybody, from that first welcome speech, had the same chance. I saw an opportunity, a time to step up. I was absolutely inspired. I'm proud to tell you that I got
a 90. There was another student, Lou Piuggi, who also received a 90 or even a
94. [When we asked Chef Lou, he said, "I wish I could say that I remember the
numeric grade, but I'd love a 94, if you're handing them out!"]

Henin was a controversial chef at that school. A lot of people were unhappy
about how he treated students and how he conducted himself. Even from my
vantage point as a student, and being a young kid, I recognized that these people
were just wasting energy on complaining, instead of absorbing the lesson being
taught. One of my absolute best moments at the CIA was that class. I took a lot

of what I learned there and what I had prior to coming there, and I thought, *Shit, I might actually be able to become a real chef!*

SUSAN: *Did you want a career in fish at the time?*

EDWARD: To some degree. Having grown up at the Jersey shore, being at the ocean, fishing had been a big part of my life. I worked at seafood restaurants before going to the CIA, and I realized then, there was so much more in the way of finesse and technique with fish. Remember, we're going way back to the early eighties. There was little opportunity for someone to say, "Fish is my thing." Two-and-a-half extra minutes on the grill with a steak, and it's still pretty good. But two-and-a-half extra minutes on a piece of turbot, and it's burnt. I also realized that, in those days, everything on a meat plate was basically brown, yet on a fish plate, there could be five different colors on one dish. I saw the opportunity to be a craftsman as well as somebody who delivers "edible art," if you will.

SUSAN: *Did he know any of this, when you were in the E-Room?*

EDWARD: No. We have become good friends, but I pride myself on the fact that I was not his friend at the time. We didn't have any kind of relationship, outside of the hours spent in the class. It was, "Yes, Chef." Otherwise, I had my head down, working.

In my time at the CIA, Fish Kitchen hadn't been developed yet. I feel like I missed out. I would have loved to have been in the Fish Kitchen with him. But, I had a micro-version of that, being the "Fish Guy" in the Escoffier Room. In those times, the early eighties, you graduated with a great job. You could have gone anywhere in the country. The market was so hungry for American cooks. Chef placed me in my job, after graduation. He was consulting for a restaurant— a wealthy couple in Nashville, Tennessee, of all places. They traveled the world and spent a lot of time in New York. Basically, they wanted to recreate Lutèce, in Nashville. That was their model, and they bought a free-standing house in the middle of the city. They traveled to France, found a European chef, and got this restaurant going. The only problem was, their chef would take a certain period of time off every year. They would be stuck, because Nashville did not have people who could do what he was doing. The owners thought, *Where are we going to find the best of the best?* They got in touch with the CIA and Chef Henin. He may have even gone down there to cover for that chef. When I graduated, he said, "This is a great opportunity. I'd like to send you down there. It's a small

French restaurant, Julian's, a super boutique French restaurant, in a small house in Nashville."

I worked with the great Dijon-born chef, Sylvain Le Coguic. We came in early, baked bread, did the *mise en place*, all the sauces and preparations, took a break and returned to do the dinner service, with a maximum of seventy covers. Everything was scratch cooking, done the right way. You work hard, but it would be like learning in a few different restaurants in one location. He said, "It doesn't matter where on the planet you work; this is the right place for you." So, that's where I went.

I stayed there for about one and a half years. At that time, Lou Piuggi was working at Maurice, in the Hotel Parker Meridien, in NYC. They were looking for a fish cook and wondered if I would consider returning to New York. It was time to keep moving, and this was a huge opportunity. In the early eighties, New York was the mecca of French dining. This was the right moment for me to be working with one of the stars of the moment, Christian Delouvrier, Executive Chef. Alain Senderens was the consulting chef from Paris (Lucas Carton Restaurant). It was an opportunity to move up the ladder, so I did it.

When I went to Nashville, Chef and I stayed in touch, with occasional calls and a letter . . . obviously, we weren't emailing at that time. It's so different now. Today, if you have a mentor, you could be sending him an email once a week to check in. Back then, you had to call or write a letter. The interesting part is, the communication channels were so much less than they are now, but I feel like I never disconnected from him. There are few people in my life that are like that, and he's one.

We stayed in touch over the years. When Chef Keller received some huge honor and invited Roland to be there, he invited me into town and we had breakfast. Again, we went right into talking about what I was doing, does it make me happy, is it important for me . . . no bullshit, no *how's the weather* kind of thing. Listen, I'm a successful guy, I'm not afraid to say, but we immediately fall into our roles. He's the teacher, and I'm the student. I don't mind that, and I don't give that up for a lot of people. We all need teachers and we never stop learning. He has my respect in that I'm not beyond listening to anything he's got to tell me, even today.

I saw him at a job fair at the CIA. Our company was there, and he was there representing Delaware North. It was an unexpected pleasure for us both. He immediately called me by the nickname he gave me—Rattlesnake. In letters I've sent to him, I would sign, "Sincerely, Rattlesnake." If I spoke to him on the phone, I'd say, "Hello, Chef, this is Rattlesnake." I don't even know why he called me this! You could picture him saying this: *"Aah, Raahtlaahsnaayke!"*

SUSAN: *Better than Shoemaker.*

EDWARD: Better than Shoemaker. He called plenty of people Shoemaker. Clearly, we have a good relationship, so it was a good connotation, but . . . I thought it was funny. It was from the E-Room. For some reason, one day, he says to me, "AAAAh, *zeez eez ze Rattlesnake.*" And that was it. From then on, it was Rattlesnake. That's who I was. It was clear that most of the others were called *Shoemaker*, preceded by *Fucking.*

There are many people out there who thought Henin was the worst experience of their career. Those people probably haven't done much with their careers. Honestly, he never did it because he was a nasty dirtball. He had a mission, and that was his style of getting you to your endgame as a winner. He believed in it. He does what he believes in, period. I would say that this philosophy has helped me, as well. I also live by that. If I don't feel right about doing something, I won't do it. At times, it's been difficult, but mostly, it has worked out.

SUSAN: *How has Chef impacted your life?*

EDWARD: We've had a nice relationship over all these many years, but the whole thing is based off of spending not even three weeks together. I would still call him out as one of the top three mentors in my life, just because that formation was so important to me: it was a combination of the things that he taught me and the awakening of my own self, finding my own way. I made it through the CIA and did well, but, you're with a group of people, and everyone's caught up in, *Who got an A? Who got a B?* When we got to his class, it was a level playing field where he basically said, *You're all going to come close to failing or just make it. You're all on the same playing field, and the strong will survive. Stand up and be strong. Show me who you are.* I got to stand out in that moment, and I've never looked back. It awakened that in me. I was never passive or lazy, but it was like the bell was ringing. His voice was that bell and now was the time. Sometimes it takes that spark to awaken that thing inside you. I was always ambitious and very motivated. I always wanted to work, but we're talking about a whole other level.

You went there the same time as me. We were in the generation of respected American cooks, hoping to be chefs. The generation or two prior to us were still blue-collar cooks. I mean, look what we've seen, just in our time. Then we have this opportunity . . . and what's happened from then until now is crazy!

It annoys the crap out of Henin to see these TV-level rock star chefs. It annoys him to no end, but he is as much a rock star in his own right. Yet, he also realizes that they serve a purpose. If you are a chef on television, you are furthering the public awareness about cooking and what we do, which helps garner more respect for all chefs. Some of us use it in the right way, and some of us don't. And, by the way . . . I don't mind being forward in saying all this love fest is for Roland Henin. He is not the most humble guy in the world. He likes the attention.

He came to visit me while I was in Nashville. When the chef was away, Chef Henin and I would work together. What a small kitchen it was . . . just two other guys in the heat of service. I'm looking over and here I am, standing next to my instructor, chef, and mentor who, just several weeks ago, was the guy giving me terrifying looks. Now here I am standing next to him, cooking. It was great.

Anyway, I brought my girlfriend to meet him—this guy who was my mentor, my chef at school, how I got here . . . the whole thing. Chef reaches out to take her hand. You know how someone takes a woman's hand, to plant a kiss? He grabs her hand, pulls it toward him, kisses his *own* hand, and says, "It's a pleasure for you to meet me." I mean, is that him, or what?

SUSAN: *[Laughs] No one has told me that one before!*

EDWARD: That's why I am the Rattlesnake. We both absolutely share a passion for the opposite sex. I would say, he's a tamed lion at this point.

SUSAN: *What is your mentoring style?*

EDWARD: It's the same. I help expose my chefs to what their direction is—not by preaching, but by sharing my experiences and leading by example. When they tell me what they want to do, I ask questions nobody else has asked them: *You want to be the chef of this hotel. Why? What's so great or different about that hotel?* Make them spell it out. *Tell me what intrigues you about it.* Maybe it's not such a great choice, and I'm not afraid to expose that. I want to be the devil's advocate. That's a good mentor.

The other good part about being a mentor is expanding that person's network to be in places where they might not be exposed. I'll introduce them to people who might be able to help them in the direction that they are heading. When a guy is doing a great job, with great attitude, going as far as he can go on his own, I want to help get him even further. I wish everyone I talk to had that attitude and talent, but the truth is, they don't. A chef came to see me last week. I had blocked off forty-five minutes, and we stayed there for two and a half hours. The conversation was so rich that I would have stayed there all day. If he or she wants it, and we have a connection, I have all the time in the world.

SUSAN: *My, you sound an awful lot like somebody we know . . .*

EDWARD: That may well be the best compliment that I get.

Author's note, *in response to Chef Ed Brown's "Rattlesnake" story: My nickname was "Slash," earned on the first day of Skills Development. I slashed open a fellow student's hand while we both reached for a bowl (with my French knife still in my hand). Poor guy was out of school for months (sorry, Martin). Also, referring to Rattlesnake's "69.5" story, I am proud to tell you that I received an 81 in Chef Henin's Fish Kitchen. Slash ain't no Shoemaker.*

Lou Piuggi

SRVP Culinary-Executive Chef, Patina Restaurant Group

I owe him everything, because he saw me.

LOU: I first met Chef Roland as a student at the CIA. I graduated in August 1983 and had him in Escoffier Room. For his class, I chose to work the *saucier* station. He wasn't a Master Chef yet, but he had the reputation for being severe—throwing knives in the garbage if not sharp, etc. There was a lot of trepidation among the student body before entering his class. The Escoffier Room unit was defined as a "real" restaurant experience, a place where you would be treated like a serious cook. A lot of my classmates shifted to the a.m. group, thinking it would be easier to get a better grade in a less demanding environment. So, we entered the kitchen with only seven students—just enough to cover each station.

It was the best experience of my student career. On our first day, we filed into the lecture room. He took attendance. He'd call your name and size you up with an intent look. In that moment, I could see all of his intelligence, his intent as a teacher. In the classroom, he clearly communicated his expectations. You knew what was expected of you and what your role was to the team. He listened to us and challenged our ideas. We refined the dishes we were developing. He happily shared his work and knowledge with us. I knew the past two years of my culinary studies were going to be tested and his leadership helped make sense of it all.

He wrote a manual—a saucier guide he made when he was a teacher at Johnson & Wales. He mimeographed sheets of paper and gave copies to students. It was so detailed! In it, not only were there all the basic recipes of the mother sauces, but also ratios, stocks, and consommés. The book also explained that the recipes are not static; all recipes can be manipulated, varied, and improved upon. The things he stressed were selection of ingredients, reverence for technique, practice, and patience. He included little drawings. There was a hand-drawn diagram of a saucepot over the fire, to insure the proper cleaning of the impurities.

In the kitchen, he empowered us to take chances, test our abilities, and be in control of our stations. He forced us out of our comfort zones and prepared us for any situation. He seemed to know what our individual limits were and pushed us to perform well beyond them. He walked around the kitchen, watching, correcting, tasting a sauce here, testing a knife edge there. Was the walk-in swept and mopped? *Sanitour!* Each position was important, from *saucier* to *sanitour*. The kitchen was spotless, our stations organized. We truly learned what *mise en place* was and that it takes the entire team to have a successful kitchen.

As a student, you begin to realize what it means to open your peripheral vision. He was everywhere, saw everything, and demonstrated what it meant to be a chef. Chef was confident, indefatigable, passionate, knowledgeable, encouraging, empathetic, observant, organized, foresighted, and humble—a true mentor!

The Culinary Olympic team was practicing at the CIA and booked a dinner in the E-Room on our last night of class. What an opportunity to be able to express all that we had learned. Our assignment: develop the menu, simple as that! Each station chef—garde-manger, *saucier*, *poissonier*—came to class with ideas for dishes to serve. Chef vetted them, adding sophistication. He ensured they retained their original essence and made sense as a multi-coursed menu. He never made this about him; this was about us, the students. This was our experience.

That last night was amazing . . . one I will always remember. In just seven days, Chef helped me realize that my dreams were attainable. Through hard work, I had the ability to accomplish and conquer any obstacle. I saw the potential he saw in me and that was powerful! After we finished cleaning the kitchen, put all the pots away, took out the garbage, and sanitized the cutting boards, we ended our night and class sharing a cold beer with Chef . . . a "real life" restaurant experience!

SUSAN: *What do you think he saw in you?*

LOU: I hope he saw a bit of himself. I imagine he recognized my cooking ability, my passion and focus. I was respectful, hardworking, curious, and indefatigable, and wanted to learn everything I could. He chose to recommend me for a job that set me on a path for success. It was my first job in New York City, with Christian Delouvrier at the Maurice Restaurant in the Parker Meridien Hotel. "Roland has told me that if I didn't hire you, it would be a big mistake. When can you start?" I've always felt that, whatever position I held, I never wanted to let him down. Wherever I'm working, I always imagine he is in the dining room and I'm cooking for him.

SUSAN: *What advice do you have for up-and-coming chefs?*

LOU: Show up to the job on time and prepared. Have a great attitude. Be patient, passionate, and willing to work hard. Also, focus on a few people who are of a generation ahead of you. See what they've accomplished. Stay focused on them and what you admire about them. Don't get caught up in what your peers are doing (this is a distraction that keeps you from accomplishing your own goals).

SUSAN: *What is your legacy?*

LOU: That's hard to think about. I hope that if I am remembered, it will be because I have left the same mark upon many young cooks and chefs that Chef Henin has made on me and my career. I hope I am able to encourage their curiosity, explore their passions, and help them to become complete chefs.

What I find ironic is that Delaware North just purchased our company. Chef Henin brought a certified program to DN, which brings the focus to chefs. This continues his legacy as a teacher and lets them be something more than they imagine. I haven't yet had opportunity to meet with Chef. It seems to have come full circle for me. When I do speak to him, I don't know if he'll remember me. When I think of the people who have pushed me forward and challenged me, he was my first serious person. I owe him everything, because he saw me.

Pamela Williams

Hospitality Instructor, Miami Dade College

No job is smaller or less important; everyone is equal in the kitchen.

PAMELA: I started at the CIA in the fall of 1983. During one of my first classes, Safety and Sanitation, I noticed some chefs sitting in the back of the lecture hall. One day this booming voice asked a question to the instructor. I have no idea what the question was, but the voice and the accent were hypnotizing! I turned around and saw Chef Henin for the first time. He was a tall man who spoke French. He had long legs. I timidly spoke a little high school French to him during one of the breaks, and he was gracious, as you might expect. That was the start of our friendship.

Unbeknownst to me at the time, these chefs were in the midst of preparing for their Master Chef exam. Chef Henin was "bucking up" on Sanitation and Garde-Manger. Several days later, their buffet catering platters were set up in the main hallway. I had no idea what I was looking at, exactly, but I will never forget the garnish of hard-boiled eggs Chef Henin had decorated to look like little fish. There were tiny carrot pieces cut like dorsal and tailfins, maybe a piece of truffle for the eyes. The whimsy of it all made me smile.

SUSAN: *What qualities attracted you to each other?*

PAMELA: I could understand him—his good work and good heart. He was alert, enthusiastic, and prepared. He stressed the *basics*, the foundations. He'd say, "Do those well, everything else will fall into place." I understood French and, therefore, his temper, and was able to come to his aid. I think he was grateful that I took the effort to speak with him in his native tongue. *"Bon jour, mademoiselle."* He was gracious and humble. When I realized he was a professor at the institute, I looked forward to working with him. Chef Henin ran the Fish Kitchen. He was "not so great" with my classmates—kept losing his temper. He had a great French temper! Half the class didn't know what was going on! We received our grades before externship. Chef Henin took me aside and said candidly, "Mademoiselle, you have a heart of gold—but switch groups." I was kind of shy, so he made a point to show me. He had a gentle manner and a charming way . . . the girls all had a crush on him. He spoke in a pleasant way, never condescending.

He's a regular guy, but he's not. In a word: un-pretentious! He's so gracious and humble. When you speak to him on the phone, it's as if he's in the room. As busy as he is, it's as if you're the only person that matters. Wherever I have worked, Chef Henin would come and eat dinner. He would not tell you he was there, and then later, send a note. He is no fame-seeker, his work is never about the glory. He is all about the outdoors—fishing, hiking, nature. He'll retire somewhere with no phone or TV.

SUSAN: *What are moments you recall from his mentoring?*

PAMELA: Several years after I graduated culinary school, Chef was trying out for the Olympics and invited me to be one of his *commis* during the actual competition. I flew to Chicago. When I arrived, the kitchen was a beehive. The work at this point was all about the glazing. Glazing food in aspic is a specific skill set, one that I learned over the course of that weekend. Each item that goes onto the competitors' platters and plates must be coated, at least three times, in an aspic solution. The method of application is different for each item: meats and pâtés are laid out in numbered slices and dipped in the gelatin with a fork; similar small items, such as peas or beans, are individually skewered on picks and lined up neatly on a Styrofoam block. This way, you can dunk a dozen or more beans at one time. The aspic has to be at a certain temperature, so there is a window of time you can work before you have to stop and re-temper your aspic.

This aspic is sticky stuff. There are to be no fingerprints or drips; that counts against you. Here we are, a small group of *commis*, working nonstop in the cold walk-in, working against the clock as we dip beans, baby carrots, and little vegetables. It is a rhythm: one tray in the walk-in, another one out; one team dipping, while another team irons off the gelatin drips. Through it all is Chef Henin, guiding our work. Peas! On toothpicks! I was so chilled, but you didn't sit down, and you didn't complain. Sleep was not an option; we stayed up for over twenty-four hours together. He was going for the gold, and you *wanted* to be part of that.

When the time came, we brought his *mise en place* upstairs to the competition hall. We watched in awe as Chef put his table together—the way he laid the food on the platters and placed the sauces on the plate. It was poetry, the ballet, and what a Master Chef is.

SUSAN: *What did Chef teach you about life?*

PAMELA: Care for my tools. Keep knives sharp. I'll always remember him throwing students' knife bags in the trash. If they didn't care for their tools, they didn't deserve to keep them. I learned to properly set up my station. I'll always remember the *tourney* demo. The lesson was a sauté Trout Doria. These kids were not doing a good job. Chef comes in, snatches the cucumber with his big hands and lays it out so clearly. He broke it down, step-by-step—the *mechanics*. We were so mesmerized. He would *tourney* six potatoes in thirty seconds. To this day, I love teaching *tourney* and I'm good at teaching it, because of him. Finally, he taught me to be a gracious loser.

We did fish together once . . . went out on the river together on a beautiful fishing boat . . . it was fun, and I just let him fish. He might have cast the reel for me a couple times. It was a leisurely kind of day. *Let me just take the girl out.* He caught a few big salmon. Roland has a fond expression: If it's not wiggling, it's not fishing.

SUSAN: *What is your mentoring style?*

PAMELA: I've spent the past twenty years as a professional educator at the Art Institute of Fort Lauderdale and just recently switched to Miami Dade Hospitality. I give back to young culinarians. Attitude reflects leadership! I am the first to arrive and last to leave. I walk the walk and lead by example. I'm the head chef. I do my demos and *they* produce tastings. Students respect me, because I'm in the trenches. I'm on the line. I show them how to do things individually. I make a point to do multiple demos and to correct their technique. At the end of the night, I'm the first one out with broom. I make it fun! I love having new students, value my friends and time with loved ones. I like to set an example for today's culinary field.

Everybody is so excited to be at culinary school! They arrive early. Some students are more challenged, so they make an effort and shine! For instance, some young women raise children and have a job, all while attending school. They know what they have to do to better their lives. They love their children, have such heart, and are so excited to have an opportunity. I will connect with them and learn their names . . . connect individually and in groups, develop groups and teams. I remember his un-pretentiousness . . . everyone has a part to play, a job to do. No job is smaller or less important; everyone is equal in the kitchen.

The Coach: Team USA, Culinary Olympics

O ne of Chef Henin's first assignments for me in training for the 1988 Culinary Olympics was to create a Styrofoam display of eight hors d'oeuvres. This entailed making an exact visual replica of real edible hors d'oeuvres—their exact size, shape, dimension, and color. When I accepted Henin's apprenticeship, the amount of time and commitment it entailed was beyond my comprehension. At the time, I was a newly promoted executive chef of my first hotel chain and I was a new father to my first child. When Chef Henin came to review the work I had done, I had only six of the eight completed. He turned and looked at me with a piercing, deep-to-the-core, angry gaze. He said to me, "So, I've done my homework. I'm going to go out and play now, while you finish yours. I'll be back in a few hours." The mood in the room, the pitch in his voice, and Chef Henin's character translated those words to mean that, if the assignment was not done in the next two hours, I was forgotten and it would be as if I never existed to him. This would become the Chef Roland Henin that I would train under: All in, or not in at all.

—Brad Toles, Chef/Owner, Savoury's Catering

RGH: I was always involved in the American Culinary Federation. I competed, but in an old-fashioned way. My real exposure to competition came when I was at the CIA, where the Olympic team practiced once a month. I wanted to watch, clean pots, take it all in and be part . . . this was where my teams started.

The lessons learned in competition, or perhaps their magnitude, can never be replicated in a teaching kitchen or restaurant. You can never put the pressure on, like in competition. Even in a dinner service or catering, the pressure is different. Competitions are about you and your team. You have to care as much about you and your team as you do your hundreds of guests. Self-motivation can be more difficult. It is easier to do something for someone else, and this is where our motivation grows. Say what you like about culinary competitions or the American Culinary Federation, but at the end of the day, they still provide a vehicle for the serious chef to be challenged and recognized.

I was on the competition circuit for many, many years. Competitions definitely improve the breed, whether they are cats, dogs, horses, chefs, or anyone else. I did impact a lot of people, mostly young and upcoming. They were totally "brainless" and had no idea what the hell they were getting themselves into . . . or they would have never done it. But at the end, after all the aggravations and tribulations and "black" nights spent dealing with monster *gelatine* and no sleep for over forty hours . . . after some rest and upon reflection . . . they definitely found themselves much better cooks and certainly better human beings.

These were certainly some of the best years of my life. Most of these kids ended up with gold medals in national and international competitions and wound up getting somewhere in their professional lives.

Larry Banares

Chef, Sharp Grossmont Hospital, CBS/LA

Chef Henin has an interesting style of teaching.
He makes you learn by answering your own questions.

LARRY: My dad joined the US Navy in the Philippines. Many Philippine immigrants came through the Navy as stewards and cooks. My dad parlayed his experience in the Navy to a culinary career when he got out and worked his way up to executive chef. He was at the La Jolla Beach and Tennis Club when I began working with him in summers. After he figured out that I could do it and wanted it, he arranged an informal apprenticeship for me. I spent about three years working with different chefs who were his friends in the area and then wound up taking supplemental courses at a community college. I've been blessed, but this was an entirely different story, one of those love/hate relationships. As a dad and my boss, he expected me to know everything by genetics or osmosis. I wasn't successful at the beginning. I couldn't cut a club sandwich straight. Many times I was dragged physically into the storeroom and told I better do it, *or else.* That was back in the old days.

At this time, I was the executive sous-chef at the Disneyland Hotel in Anaheim. There would be kind of a circuit of shows or competitions, "culinary salons." If you wanted to get outside of your comfort zone, you'd go to the local shows and compete. I was a young executive sous-chef of a large hotel property, and around that time, we had an ACF Regional Conference that put Master Chef Raimund Hofmeister in our hotel for a number of days. He saw me in action, running the operation, and told me, "You would do well at competitions. Consider going out for one of the teams." That inspired me.

I first met Chef Henin at the early formation stages of the 1988 ACF Western Regional Culinary Team. We were put together as a team to compete in the Culinary Olympics in Frankfurt, Germany, in 1988. It was a unique team because, at the time, it was the first team to be sanctioned by the ACF, other than the official national team. This was Raimund Hofmeister's idea, formulated to create a regional presence on what was, at the time, a national US culinary team heavily represented from the East Coast. We'd represent the Western region in the national competition and also create a template for future regional teams. He, Chef Henin, Walter Leible, and another CMC began to look for talent. I worked hard competing and winning local competitions. They wanted me to try out for the new team—the new ACF 1988 Western Regional Culinary Team.

When you're in competition, up for forty-eight, seventy-two hours without sleep or food and trying to get it just right, to be put on display, critiqued and picked apart by three normal ACF judges is nerve-racking, but knowing that you're being considered for a culinary team to represent your region and the United States in an international arena, and to have three Master Chefs critique you . . . that's a tense situation. Chef Henin critiques you directly. He addresses the mistake—the issue on the plate—but he'll also offer a bit of comic relief. If your food is too big on the platter, he'd say "That's a beautiful platter for eight people, if you're serving sixteen." Little things would put you at ease: *This guy is hard, but I can work with him.* They were picking team members who would be working with them over the next two and a half years, for competition in Germany. It was an honor to be the first person named. Collectively, they thought I had what it took to be on the first team. They traveled around to all the local competitions and finally put a team together.

The most interesting thing with the Master Chefs was their confidence—not a confidence to show you what they know, but confidence in their manner and how they teach you. Chef Henin is one who will tell you something, maybe in a meeting or a coaching session, and you may have forgotten about it. Later in the kitchen, he'll call you over and say, "*Monsieur* . . ." He'd always say, "*Monsieur, monsieur,* come here," and then he'd execute it. He remembered, with all the stuff he was doing, to teach me that lesson—bring you over and show you what he meant.

Raimund Hofmeister was team manager, Roland Henin the team captain, and Walter Leible team co-captain, but they were also competing themselves, putting their own work on display. They didn't want too big of a disparity between some of the younger guys on the team; it was a learning environment. When I take inventory of that, having the opportunity to work two and a half years with three Certified Master Chefs . . . not many people would get that opportunity, that intimate training. The most interesting part of that experience was hearing them speak! A casual conversation about Wiener schnitzel or making spaetzle would turn into a master class. In those days, we had "on demand live programming" whenever we walked into the kitchen and went to meetings. We worked hard in the kitchen and would finish the evening in the hotel lobby for a nightcap. I'm not a big drinker, but I always enjoyed a nightcap before turning in. If we threw out a term like *Royal glaçage,* we would sit there for hours, usually with Chef Henin winning out on the technical side of it. *Royal glaçage* was hollandaise-based sauce that you glaze, as with *coquilles St.-Jacques*. So the big conversation was, "What is a *glaçage?* Is it a mousseline or a sauce on its own?" The chefs would give us these passionate reasons why it's called this and take us through a culinary history. If you needed a final *final* answer—if you needed a lifeline on classical cuisine—you'd call Roland Henin. He'd always get the last word, or it would be shelved until breakfast, and they'd bring up the *royal glaçage* again.

Chef Henin has an interesting style of teaching. He makes you learn by answering your own questions. If you came to him with something easy and he felt you didn't put enough effort into the answer or the solution—like rolling the galantine the right way or if your aspic was cloudy—he wouldn't tell you how to correct it. He would take you through the steps of how you made it and then you're like, "Oh, I didn't cool my galantine in its own protein liquid, and *that's* why it broke up and the texture wasn't as smooth as it should have been." He changed you from someone who just expected an answer to someone who would look a little bit deeper into the process and figure out why it didn't come out the way it should have.

All those Master Chefs reminded me of my dad. In those days it was a different set of rules, a different mentality—tough love. I got that my dad was doing it for my benefit—dressing me down in the kitchen or taking me apart in the storeroom about something I messed up. You would have the end result—that *aha* moment—yup, I should have thought of that. That's what drew me to Chef Henin. He was a disciplinarian—even in a team environment, even if we were up against a time limit to get our displays, even moving things into a van to take them over for a practice. He never hesitated to call us together. *We're working as a guest in this hotel's kitchen. Before we leave, we're going to organize the walk-in.* If that walk-in isn't clean and organized when they come back, how can they possibly set up to work and feel good? It was those things that made you better—not just a guy who makes a beautiful platter and wins gold medals, but as a chef who stops and takes care of those things . . . not necessarily at the most convenient times, but I think at the most *important* times. You are a reflection of your work, both on a platter and in your workstation.

The chefs put together a number of "tune-up" competitions, whether it was the National Restaurant show (NRA) in Chicago, the springboard to Frankfurt, or more exciting for us, Expogast in Singapore. We'd have to prepare some things in our own kitchen and bring them in the coolers—a galantine, a terrine, different garnishes, etc. Some of the guys came up with an idea to pour aspic in the gelatin; that way, when the air freight guys were throwing luggage around and stuff, all our stuff inside would be protected, surrounded by the gelatin. Then we could re-melt it, clarify it, and use it for aspic on our platters.

We drilled down and got to work, making mock platters out of Styrofoam or cardboard to simulate our exact platters. We practiced our layouts with these cutouts. We used Polaroids of the previous platters. I've never seen anyone in competition as organized or meticulous as Chef Henin. Whether it was the diagrams, the addendums to the diagrams, the numbers coordinated with the diagrams, the individual Post-it notes that were taped to each individual sheet pan or tray . . . down to a science. These were just as important as cleaning that walk-in.

He would stake out an area in the kitchen. It was kind of a joke. While checking in and getting room assignments, Chef Henin would always be suspiciously missing. He wasn't so concerned about "Did this cooler get there?" or what room he was staying in. He was already staking out his area. He would go back into the kitchen and bring our coolers in, and you'd already see his station set up, his cutting board and tools already there. Typically, it was the nearest station to the cooler. He'd already have some cases and speed racks lined up. He'd put a tag on 'em—*RGH*. After all these years, I don't know what his middle name is, but he marked *RGH*, *RGH* on all his stuff.

He was all about getting down to business. Sometimes we'd wanna go relax, take our shoes off, change into our uniforms and stuff. We'd come back and Chef Henin would have all of his diagrams, prep lists, and stuff for the next day, everything all organized already on the station. We knew the reason; he had to compete and set himself up for success, because he and Chef Hofmeister also had to worry about our table. They had to put together our centerpiece and deal with logistics. It was just a running joke, when arriving: "What is the kitchen like?" However the kitchen was, rest assured that Chef Henin claimed the best spot.

Chef is wired to do it correctly. I've never seen anyone quite like him, who wants to make sure that everything is done absolutely right. We were at the Westin Stamford in Singapore, in a competition called Expogast, a tune-up for Frankfurt. Chef Henin had to deal with logistics: organize our table, find a florist, get tablecloths, etc. We knew he was taking care of team business and had already organized the cooler, so we didn't have any concerns. We started early that morning and asked Chef Leible, "Chef, when's lunch?"

He says, "I haven't heard from Chef Henin." We would eat meals together as a team; that was kind of a rule. "But you guys have been in all day. Okay, as team captain, I'm gonna say let's go eat."

We came back in the kitchen, feeling good about having some nourishment, and went back to work. Chef Henin came in with a couple of bags, decorations from a local market, and a centerpiece for our table. He spent the entire day outside the kitchen, not being able to work on his stuff, and he was hungry, too. He said, "Let's go have dinner."

Chef Walter walked up to him and said, "The guys have eaten already."

I think maybe he was a little bit irked that we didn't wait for him. He said, "Okay, fine."

There was an open space in the kitchen. Chef Henin rolled a table in—a standard size banquet table. He rolls it in and sets it up. We're looking at him: *Maybe we're going to display there or plan our centerpiece? We're going to mock it out and see where the food's going to go, and maybe do the setup?* He sets up a sixty-inch round table, gets a tablecloth, and places it on the table. He comes back with a chair and puts the chair next to the table. Then he—I don't know where he found it—finds a bud vase, and a flower, and puts them in the center of the table. We're like, *Is he inviting someone for dinner? It's only set for one person. Did he invite the general manager? Are we going to cook something for our host—reciprocate his taking care of us?*

Henin heads into the walk-in and comes out of the cooler holding some eggs and a bunch of herbs. He minces these herbs meticulously, and I mean, minces the herbs *down*—if you were to lay them out under a microscope, they'd all be about the same size. He places the minced herbs on the table, cracks the eggs into a stainless steel bowl, and whisks them gently with salt and pepper, then gets an omelet pan hanging above the range. He makes this perfect thin herb omelet—the most beautiful omelet I've ever seen. By this time, we've all stopped to watch him. He barks out, "What are you guys looking at? Go back to work!" He slides the omelet onto a plate and gets a glass of water. He sits down at that table and enjoys his dinner.

To this day, I don't know if it was an example for us or a pushback that we didn't wait for him to have dinner. Either way, it showed that when this guy does something, even fix himself a meal, he does it with that degree of detail and precision. (I would not be surprised if that's the way he fixes his meals at home.) He finished his omelet, broke down the table, and started working on his competition stuff. It was amazing. Most of us would pull up a milk crate and head off to the corner, and that would have been good enough. He followed through: his omelet needed to be served on a draped table. I watched him fluff his eggs, how he whisked them together in the bowl. It was about watching him, learning from him, seeing his moves, not necessarily saying a word sometimes, just observing the technique. We looked at each other in disbelief that he would go to that extreme making himself an omelet, but to him, his food commanded that type of service. *Make the best food, even for your own self.* That message stuck with me.

Chefs are great people. We have a good work ethic, but we also have a mischievous side. Once, we were in the Bismarck Hotel in Chicago getting ready for the NRA show. We were able to recommend our own apprentices from either a local culinary school or even in our workplace. If you got a confirmation from another chef, they would be considered for the team. I brought this kid named Robert, an apprentice who was assigned at a previous competition. Chef Henin said, "I'll take Robert anytime. He's good, he's quiet. He's fast. He gets the work done." I put that as a feather in my cap.

Some apprentices had a sense of entitlement, however. They had worked with Master Chefs and were full of themselves. One of those apprentices, Jeffrey Mora, was assigned to work with Chef Henin. This apprentice thought he knew a little bit more than he probably did, but he soon found out that Chef Henin doesn't play. You got to contribute with actions and production, not just with words. Jeffrey would come out and blow off steam, complaining about having to work with Chef.

Another chef on the team, Mial Parker, looks over at me. "Man, Jeffrey's an A-hole. Bigmouth needs to be put in his place."

Chef Mial came up with this plan. "You know how Chef Henin has all of his stuff organized on the speed rack?"

"Yes, to a high degree." Chef labeled all garnishes, emulsions, and everything on his trays, so if he needed to build a duck platter at any point, it would be easy. Even the shelves on the speed racks had Post-it notes saying what category each was: tray one, category A, item number one; tray one, category A, item number two, and so on.

Mial goes into the walk-in cooler and comes out a couple minutes later. "I'm counting down. Henin is going to explode, going to blow a gasket."

"What did you do?"

"I switched Post-its on a couple of platters on his speed rack."

We go back in the kitchen and it's getting kind of hot and heavy. Chef Henin is barking at Jeffrey: *Hey, bring me this, bring me this! Bring me this!!* Jeffrey goes into the walk-in and brings Chef Henin the wrong item for the platter. He brings out the seafood garnish for the meat platter. Chef is screaming, "No, no, no, no, no, get me the *right* garnish!!!" Jeffrey goes into the cooler and comes back with the *same* platter. Needless to say, Jeffrey couldn't find the right garnish, and Chef tore him apart. Mial got a big laugh out of it. I got a chuckle out of it, too. Henin didn't appreciate it at all, because he was the one losing time. The apprentice was humbled in the process; that was the good part. The bad part was that Chef Henin kicked him out of the kitchen. "I don't want you here! You're messing me up! Go!!"

I looked over at Chef Mial and mouthed, "How you going to fix this?"

He says, "Watch this." He went over, took Chef's platter into the cooler, put everything back, and fixed everything. It was wild.

The thing was, it was like a silent movie. The kitchen was part of a butcher shop. Chef Henin appropriated the entire place. We were on the outside of the shop, looking through an enclosed glass window. You could see him in there, from the waist up. We were looking through the window. Henin was just taking him apart . . . just seeing that apprentice's head nod . . .

SUSAN: _Did you ever come clean and tell Chef?_

LARRY: I don't think that we ever did, and Mial passed away a couple years ago. He was the only one, other than me, who knew about it. I know what Chef Henin would tell me, though. He'd probably call _me_ an A-hole!

I look back on my career as a chef. I got involved in media in San Diego—having my own radio talk show and cooking show—with a local affiliate ABC chef, for ten years. Henin loved it and would ask me, "How's the TV going? Are you a star?" He would always know what was going on with me, but he'd ask to hear it again because he was proud.

I'd done the culinary team and worked at the Disneyland Hotel. They had management rights to a place called the _Queen Mary_, the big ship docked at Long Beach, California. I went there as part of a Task Team. Disney wanted to turn it into an aquatic theme park. I went there on a task force and wound up staying about five years. Long Beach didn't want to give them as much control as Orlando had given them to build Disneyworld, so Disney pulled out. As a result, I had an option to go back to the Disneyland Hotel or go east to the Epcot Center Contemporary Resort, in Orlando. I chose neither, getting a job instead, in San Diego.

A number of years later, I get a call from Chef Henin. "Monsieur, how are you? How's your family? How are your kids? I have a project for you. I'd like you to come up and have dinner with us. We're taking over a property that you may be familiar with—the _Queen Mary_. Come out. We want to use you as a consultant. You were there with Disney. You know the place better than any of us. Come up and offer your knowledge. Walk the property."

My ninety-day consulting agreement turned into two years. My family continued to live in San Diego, but I wanted to rejoin Chef as a professional in a work environment rather than in competition—in a company who has Chef Henin on their webpage as their authority on food. Once I started, I would go too long before reaching out to him, so I'd get emails like, _Monsieur, are you still alive? I am. Give me a call._ He wasn't being mean or facetious; he wanted to know how

I was doing. I'm humbled to have been taken under his wing in such a personal way. Even to the point of telling me, "You may need sometimes to take a step down to move up." To this day, I always look at it as a learning experience. Having worked with him, I have a stronger respect for my fellow chef, as a craftsman and as an artist. I owe that to Chef Henin.

Jeffrey Mora

Chef/Owner of Food Fleet

That ostrich saved my ass.

JEFFREY: I worked at the Century Plaza Chef with Raimund Hofmeister when the Tower opened in December 1984. My first exposure to Roland was in 1987, as an apprentice on the 1988 Western Regional Culinary team. I joined them at the springboard to Frankfurt competition in Chicago in 1987. From there, I competed on the Culinary Olympic team from around 1990 to 1996.

I met him at the ACF Regional Convention in Anaheim, California, for our very first regional team meeting. Roland Henin and Franz Popperl were leading us and Hofmeister was the team manager. This was a springboard to competing in Frankfurt, Germany. All the chefs on the team were gathering at the Anaheim Hilton. I had to pick up a bunch of 'em at the airport. There was a team meeting that lasted till 11:00 at night. We began walking to our rooms, all set to go to bed. Roland looks at Franz and goes, "We're getting ready to go to work, aren't we?" We looked at each other and Roland says, again, "We're going to go down and get started, right? Right now, no?" There's no saying no, so instead of getting a good night's sleep, we spend the whole night and all through to the next day working on a display. I believe that was a thirty-six-hour stint, being awake. It was me, and Franz, and Roland. Roland was constantly harping on Franz. Remember, it was an Austrian and a Frenchman—not exactly a good combo. [Laughs] Franz is probably one of the most talented guys I ever met . . . way, way, *way* ahead of his time. Franz was the first guy to do the whole concept of Nose-to-Tail.

SUSAN: *Nose-to-Tail?*

JEFFREY: He utilized everything. Franz did that on his first display, with rabbit: a terrine with the head, a dish with the shoulder, a dish with the rack, a dish with the loin, and a dish with the leg. When he did his salmon platter, he smoked and cured the belly. He utilized every piece of the fish or animal, according to what it should be. That was back in 1987, and people weren't necessarily doing that back then. Franz definitely was an innovator on that. How much Roland influenced him on that, I don't know. That would be a question to go back and ask Franz. It would be an interesting one to find out.

In order to compete in Frankfurt, the team had to first compete in Chicago. Hofmeister wasn't going, so I asked him if I could go work with Henin. Hofmeister said sure, so I took my vacation time and bought myself a ticket to Portland. Franz picked me up. I spent the night with Franz, and then Roland picked me up to take me up to Salem. Roland told me to bring a sleeping bag because he didn't have an extra bed. I'm thinking to myself, *What the hell do I need a sleeping bag for? I can probably just crash on the guy's couch.* From Salem, we'd go straight to Chicago, and I wasn't about to drag a sleeping bag all around the country.

Henin picks me up. We go to McDonald's. He absolutely loved McDonald's breakfast. He explained it in terms of the quality, the price, and the consistency. We get to his house, and yep, he doesn't have an extra bed . . . or a couch or a TV. He had a kitchen table. He had a dining room table that he had bought without legs, because he was taking that to the show in Chicago . . . a *whole* dining room table, six-plus foot. I ended up sleeping on the floor in one of the spare bedrooms. Underneath his sink, he had giant buckets of vinegar with the fermenting mother. He made us some sort of dinner with giant peeled asparagus—the care he took in perfectly peeling it. The larger ones, he peeled with a peeler.

We get to Chicago and we're working at the Bismarck Hotel, which was an absolute shithole. In fact, Walter Leible had to re-glaze his platter, because a rat ran over the aspic! We spent five days making food for the food show. Each day we'd go to the kitchen, and he'd shove me against the wall, making *fleurons*. For *five* days. I wasn't allowed to turn my head and see what he was doing. Never. There were few people who were as much of a perfectionist as he was, in a good way. But you're twenty years old and you're like, *What the fuck am I doing?* You know? [Laughs] It was, "Yes, Chef!" no matter what, back then.

SUSAN: *What attracted you to each other?*

JEFFREY: One of the reasons I was brought on the team is that I'm resourceful, can scrounge, and know how to get around things. He was the cheapest son-of-a-bitch I ever met. Roland told Franz he was only allowed to bring one bag, instead of four; Roland needed the extra suitcase. He told me the same thing. Franz was displaying a full program, just like Roland. He was telling Franz he couldn't bring what he needed, but Roland could. I'll never forget that.

Roland is panicking, because he knows he's going to have to spend money at the airport to check his bags. He had, like, twelve bags. This is before electronic ticketing and self-check-in.

I'm like, "I got it."

"What are you going to do? What are you going to do?"

"I got it taken care of. Don't worry; it's not going to cost a penny. I got this covered."

I'd worked in airports, so I knew. I said, "Pull the van around, grab a skycap."

So we pull the van around, and I give the guy at skycap four bags and a tip. I say, "Drive around again."

I rip the tags off the airline jacket ticket and check four more bags into another skycap. We did this thing four more times and got all the bags checked in . . . free.

"Wow, wow, wow, that's amazing. That's amazing!" He was impressed.

Roland was one of those guys, without a doubt, by-the-book, very straightforward. To call him easygoing would be quite the opposite. [Laughs] He was not an easygoing guy: very rigid, scheduled, and disciplined. I was quite the opposite. I grew up more with common sense and those things. I was always the scrounger on the team. *Go figure it out. Go find it. I need this.* That was me. Even on the '92 and '96 teams, I was the guy who got things done. Whatever was needed, I got 'em.

I went through this brutality in Chicago—the *fleuron* making, facing the wall—all of it. After we left, I didn't bother to go to the airport with him. He got stuck with a pretty huge bill having to pay for those bags to come home. [Laughs] Still, even after getting screwed with the bill, I did get an apology letter from him, like two months later. I was shocked. A handwritten note! I still have it. I believe I may be only person who has received an apology letter from Roland Henin.

SUSAN: *How did Chef Henin affect you?*

JEFFREY: He was an asshole! [Laughs] There's a photo of him with Raimund Hofmeister. Somebody's holding a French flag in Roland's crotch. Roland is out cold, on the table.

I love the guy. There are few guys with his knowledge in the world. He's a technician, a perfectionist. That's what it takes. Could you get away with the stuff they did thirty years ago? No. But, it wasn't just him; it was the culture. One chef hung one of the catering managers on the meat hook in the walk-in, overnight. I used to put in a hundred hours a week on my apprenticeship. He wrote me up once, for not coming in on my day off, to clean the walk-in.

Without a doubt, in terms of knowledge of cuisine, knowledge of the profession, and keeping the profession a profession, there are few guys in this world like Roland. You wish you were able to do some of those same things today and carry them forward. Forget about the abuse and treatment; the discipline is hard to find, in this day and age—to continue to expect those higher standards. He's never let his guard down, and he's never compromised his standards or his efforts. *Never.* Love him or hate him, there was no one who didn't respect the guy. It was impossible not to respect him.

He was always willing to learn, which was amazing, too. He was constantly looking to see what was going on and to keep getting better. Anything different, any type of technique, he was the first guy. He'd say, "What's that, what's that? What are you doing? How are you doing that? Show me. Show me." Not that he would always show you! [Laughs]

SUSAN: *What great crazy stories stand out?*

JEFFREY: Orlando. The first team practice. We all made the Olympic team, and they flew all the regional teams down to Orlando to practice. Everyone had to do a display of cold food. We took a break for dinner, and at this first team meeting, Henin stands up and tells the story about how they fired a guy *that day* at Epcot for eating a roll. It was just a little disconcerting, the strictness and the way he was laying it down. We remembered thinking, *If they fire a guy for eating a roll, what'll happen to us!*

As the judges critiqued the displays, they always got more and more angry. I was almost the last one to be judged. They got down to the last team, and I was like, *Aw, shit. What's gonna happen? This isn't good.* There was this one guy, Chef Mike di Maria, who made a Hawaiian plate. He created a chicken breast with sweet potatoes, pea pods, and broccoli. Right? Roland is judging the plate.

"Now look at zees plate. Eez vary nice, vary clean . . . I can tell zees is Hawaiian theme . . . I see the pea pods . . . zas vary nice . . ."

Henin is laying into him, nicely. Chef Mike is getting a little bigger, he's smiling now.

Roland goes, "But, then I see zees . . . zis *broccoli*. Where the *fuck* do they grow broccoli in *Hawaii*? I see zis, and I think you're jerking me off."

Then he just rips into the guy. Roland sets him up to rip him to shreds. I swear, all of us, to this day, still say, "He's *zhherking* me off!" It's a Roland Henin term.

I'm supposed to be judged after the next guy . . . after Roland's all revved up: "They don' grow fucking broccoli in Hawaii! I see zees, it tells me you're trying to *zhheerk* me off!"

I'm sweating my ass off, going, *Holy shit. I'm coming up.*

The next guy had an ostrich plate. *Ostrich.* No one was doing it, at the time. The chefs are laughing so fucking hard by the time they got to me, they were all saying, *Fuck it. Fix this, this, and this, and then let's go. Let's go home.* I lucked out so much. I thought I was gonna be bleeding after that one. I was waiting to be ripped to shreds in front of fifty guys. It didn't quite happen. It happened plenty of times after that, but not then.

That ostrich saved my ass.

SUSAN: *There are probably whole cults of people out there who have been touched by Chef Henin . . .*

JEFFREY: Oh yeah. That's a whole other line of questioning. . . . What happens in the kitchen stays in the kitchen. I'm not getting in the middle of that one!

After these practice sessions, he would cook food in the back and take it home on the plane—braised rabbit legs, or whatever it was—back to Oregon with him, to eat. When we were in Anaheim, we had time to kill, so I took him to a mall. He found this turkey platter, but it was about fifty bucks and God forbid he buys it, right? He was doing a platter for Germany and was working at it. This mall was an hour and a half from my house, easily. When he gets home to Oregon, he called me up, he goes, "Jeffrey, Jeffrey. Go get me that plahttah. I need that plahttah. I need that plahttah. You gotta buy me that plattah. Go get me that plattah."

I drove an hour and a half, each way, bought the platter, and sent it to him. "No no no, this isn't it. This is no good. Send it back." [Laughs] It was one of those . . . he could have bought it right then and there, but he didn't want to pull the money out of his wallet.

When Roland and Keith Keogh were writing *The Art and Science of Culinary Preparation*, Keith had a photographer there. They gave me the recipe to make the veal stock. I'd been making veal stock at that point for quite some time. I was already on the '92 team, and the way I was taught was: roast the bones for the first couple of hours; add the *mirepoix*, then add tomato paste; get it nice and caramelized; add the wine to deglaze it, and then it goes in a pot.

He's watching me, and after I got through that part he goes, "What's *zees*? What's *zees*?"

I go, "What do you mean?"

"Tomato paste! Tomato paste! Why you put that in there?"

"What are you talking about? There's tomato paste in veal stock, in a brown veal stock."

"No no no, Look at the rahsipee! Look at the *rahsipee!!* It's right here, right here! It says Optional! *Optional!*"

"Yeah, *I opted to put it in!*" [Laughs] And I walked away.

Blood was boiling.

SUSAN: *So he doesn't put tomato paste in the brown veal stock, eh?*

JEFFREY: He may have not on that one, because obviously that was the recipe he wrote. If you look at the '92 Olympic book, there are a few pictures of me making the stock.

Author's note: *Chef Henin responded to this: Veal "fond blanc" does not require a tomato product (NON-optional). Veal "fond BRUN," meaning roasted bones, does require a tomato product (NON OPTIONAL).*

SUSAN: *You and David Burke should do a comedy routine at a Henin roast. I'm going to back up. You talked about . . .*

JEFFREY: French flag sticking out of Henin's crotch? That was after Frankfurt, 1988. We were waiting for our critique, and he had passed out on the table. I don't know who it was, it might have been Mial Parker or Larry Banares, but somebody stuck a flag in his crotch. I don't know if there was ever a photo taken, but it's a vivid memory. I can tell you that.

SUSAN: *What is your mentoring style?*

JEFFREY: I took everything that Henin and Hofmeister told me and did the opposite! He's not humble. Just not in his nature! Our background was all yelling and adversarial. We all thought that was normal. My first job outside of the Century Plaza was as sous-chef at the North Ranch Country Club. At the club, the front of house and the back of the house had all been traveling together, working together, and were like a family. There was no yelling and screaming, no beating the crap out of each other. It was everyone together—one big team.

You can't do what we did anymore. Although, I think the work ethic today is a lot less than it used to be. Few people are willing to put in the time and the energy to do it right. There aren't many great chefs out there anymore, and a big part of that may be the culinary schools. The schools today aren't the same as they were thirty years ago. Now it's about how much money you can make. Back then, they would have kicked somebody out or failed them. But today, they're not going to give up the money.

SUSAN: *What do you think about culinary competitions?*

JEFFREY: I think they're great. Competition teaches you things about adversity, being able to get through things. You can't trade for that information. Roland was a tyrant in a good way, driving home the seriousness of it. We'd be in Orlando working until midnight or 1:00 a.m., having to be up and ready by 6:00 a.m. If you were twenty seconds late, he'd be tapping his watch, pissed off. Banging pots, *let's go, let's go,* driving it. It wasn't easy, but I wouldn't trade it for anything. You don't realize what you end up with, until long after: how to get yourself out of the weeds quickly; how to adapt when you don't have a kitchen or when you don't have a stove; how do you get the stuff done.

He always worked backward! It was always last minute. You'd fly to a city, in a different country, with no resources, and you gotta pull it all together. In Frankfurt, we got knocked out of our kitchen. We ended up having to go cook at a military base, in Nestlé, thirty miles out of town. We had to adapt to get the whole thing done.

SUSAN: *After that, you can do anything.*

JEFFREY: Chefs like Henin would turn off ovens. Unplug a fridge. Force you to cook on Sterno. Bring in live eels. Everything that could go wrong always did. So you couldn't get pissed off. You had to keep going, because the clock was ticking, regardless. *Always feel like you're behind. Never think you got more time. Rather be an hour early than an hour late.*

Culinary schools are not teaching this to kids. How much can you learn in three weeks? You never got the real experience. Externship helped, but three weeks per unit? Come on. Only 30 percent of the graduates remain in the industry. Plus, schools put students so far in debt. It's not what it used to be. When we went to a culinary school, you had to have a culinary background, and there was a two-year waiting list. Nowadays, *your wallet is full, I'm happy to help you.*

SUSAN: *How has your relationship changed?*

JEFFREY: It's less mentor-mentee, more like colleagues. We're peers now, because of the respect we've had. The whole point is to eclipse your mentor. That's the one thing about Henin and Hofmeister . . . they would never tell you that, but, they always wanted you to be better than them. They didn't want it to be *right then and there,* but eventually. If I can't train the people to be better than me, then I didn't do my job. That's what I learned from them. Keller is the epitome of it. But guys like that are few and far between. I'd ask Roland, "Chef, how'd you make this?" He'd say, "If I tell you, you take my job." He'd joke about that, but he always gave secrets of the craft—all of it—away.

Franz Popperl

Chef Instructor, Arts Institute of Seattle, Culinary Olympics, Retired

When you have Chef Henin coaching you,
and he thinks that you could win it, you will.

FRANZ: I'll start off with a little story, first. I was one of four judges up in Seattle for the state competition—the Northwest Regional Team. Roland Henin was there but not as an official judge. We started the first competition and judged the first competitor. We gave him a high score, and so we're thinking that maybe we are already starting out with a gold medalist? We gave our critique and then Roland gave the last critique. There was something wrong with the way the competitor put down his finishing touches, and Roland noticed this. We enter another kitchen, and Henin starts saying the same thing. There is this big, burly, angry elderly guy growling, "Who is this A-hole French Guy?"

I said, "That would be Roland Henin, Master Chef. He was my team colleague. I spent four years on the national teams and had to share a room with him when we were traveling. He is an amazing guy!"

The chef argued, "*If* he would do more listening and less talking, this whole thing would already be over by now!"

The funny part is how the people he rips apart the most are the ones he gives the highest score! You always think he's crushing you, like you're zero, and you have no idea.

SUSAN: *There are two kinds of people: those who respond to his way, and those who . . . don't.*

FRANZ: You have to know his history. Growing up, Henin apprenticed in France. I had the same experience. We went through the same kind of treatment: stabbed and burned; banished and punished. If we burnt something, we had to pay for it out of our wages. It was harsh, especially for Roland, since he was older; conditions were even harsher for him than when I went through it. In six years, I barely ever heard anything good when I worked, but if I did something bad . . . oh, boy!

To understand Roland Henin, you have to be able to visualize him when he's fifteen years old, in a French kitchen. The times, the history about the whole thing . . . you have to visualize it. If you can see the chefs around him, mentoring him, then you will understand Roland Henin. Otherwise, you walk away with your mouth hanging open, going, "*What?* Who is *that?*" You will not understand where he's coming from. There was hardly any refrigeration. Stoves were heated with coal and logs; apprentices had to make a fire in the morning. There were dishwashers as big as a gorilla, lifting and washing copper pots so big you could take a bath in them. Technology? No way. You were not allowed to use cookbooks, not allowed to read a recipe! If you wanted to look something up when you were working, they would just scream at you, "You should know this before you come in here!" You must show the chef respect.

When I was working my kitchen as an apprentice, it was always a pot that was holding the fat in the deep fryer. Just a special pot we have in there, and a basket that goes into the fat. When we wanted to find out if the hot fat was hot enough, we always spit in it. *Pop!* It's always bubbling up, so you have a bubble bath. *Oh, it's hot enough!* If we wanted to see if the oven was the right temperature for baking, we put our hands in it. *Aaah! It's the right temperature.* We had to turn the sponge cake with our hands when we were taking it out, because if you forgot it was rising higher on one side, it would not come out level. The chef charged me for the part that wasn't level. One hundred dollars a month was my pay, back in the day.

SUSAN: *Chef Pierre (at Café du Parc) made me remove foods from the boiling oil with my fingers. [Laughs] I got good and calloused, fast! Was it different in Austria compared to France?*

FRANZ: Well, I don't know who were the bigger A-holes. I think the French were pretty strict, because in Austria we cooked all our French/Classical cuisine all day long. We had butcher days; half cows and pigs came in and the apprentices would break them down. The hotel I was working in basically made their money off having apprentices running the kitchen. We had one chef and one sous-chef and that was it. They hired five apprentices per year. We worked 8:00 a.m. to 2:00 pm and then 5:00 p.m. to 8:00 p.m. If you did something wrong, you had to work through the afternoon break, peeling potatoes. We were only allowed to use the mixer for making mayonnaise and meringue. That's it. Everything else had to be made by hand.

The second-year apprentices cleaned pheasant. We were in the basement and in came this one woman. She takes the pheasant out of the apprentice's hand

and hits him left and right over his face with it. The guts came out all over behind his neck. One of the owners of the hotel had a daughter who was a little bit younger and always came down in the kitchen to flirt with us. This apprentice was stupid. There was a cinema next to the hotel and it was free for us to go, when we asked permission. Well, he was caught smooching with this daughter, in the cinema. Oh boy, oh boy. He got fired.

SUSAN: *You and Chef Henin must go way back.*

FRANZ: I've known Roland since 1987. He joined an ACF chapter, and he had this idea to start a regional team. Competitions were never a big part of my work, but he reminded me of why we do them. I was teaching for the Culinary Institute in Portland. I always thought teachers should compete! It helps educate the students. It shows the craft and gives a good name to the school. I asked the school for a plane ticket for support, but also had to fund-raise for competitions.

Roland inspired me to rise up to the whole thing, and I did pretty well. The first time we competed together on the regional team, in 1988, in Frankfurt, Germany, was a disaster. Our task was to bring not too many suitcases, to lower the costs. I had everything down to one package. I had one apprentice with me. Roland Henin came to the airport, looked at my luggage, and said, "You are not my friend anymore! You could have offered to take some of my luggage!"

I said, "You never asked! You never called me!"

"You should have called, as a courtesy."

He went off on me, to the point where I am standing there, and I say to him, "You know what, Roland? Just shut up! And, go F yourself!"

Whenever we would compete, it always came to this point where I had to tell him to go "F" himself. It was amazing. He just flew off the handle like a real, good old European chef. He demanded from you, loyalty. He demanded from you, respect. We had our ups and downs, but it was okay. Roland said it was good to travel to the competition location, before you compete on teams. If you're flying to another town, it's a different experience. I already experienced that in Los Angeles and other places and had one experience behind me, so I knew how to pack, etc.

Roland's last competition was in 1988, in Chicago. The display was beautiful! He had a whole table set up with his Thanksgiving theme. The table was made by carpenter and it was heavy as hell. We had another guy who filled up a container. You couldn't send it by plane, so we had to pick it up by freight. He had a big toolbox—like the kind people have on their pickup trucks? He put all his food in there, and then he put in his aspic. The whole thing weighed about four hundred pounds.

In Germany, we got to the hotel, and they didn't have a kitchen for us; we had to prepare in a corridor. There were two guys on the loading dock prepping. I had to work near the elevator. It was pretty bad. Everything went so smoothly getting to Germany, I thought, *Something's got to go wrong.* We enter the exhibit hall and there are no tables for us! Chef Raimund put the application in three days before it was due. The person who was supposed to submit the application for him didn't, so we are now scrambling. Chef Raimund was having a slight heart attack over the situation. He was so mad that he jumped up on the tables! It was quite a scene. Roland Henin kept his cool, with a toothpick in his mouth. He said, "It's not my problem." He always walks around with a toothpick in his mouth. It helps him to think.

My stuff was critiqued by Ferdinand Metz. I came up with the cold display, with an exhibit of rabbit. I don't know if you ever heard, but I got this nickname in the United States as "Rabbit Man." My work pleased him; he criticized me the least of all.

Roland Henin will always be my mentor, my barking little Quasimodo. Lots of people have a hard time with criticism and start to crumble. There's absolutely no backbone on lots of people I meet. You try to get them to compete and they say, "Why should I do it? It's too hard. What I get for it? Nothing." It's pretty bad. The craftsmanship is absolutely misunderstood.

There are too many kitchen shows. Everybody thinks they'll become the TV version of Master Chef or food critic. They have absolutely no idea what we're talking about. It's more about entertainment than the ritual of eating . . . molecular gastronomy and all that—not for nourishing, not for necessity. Twenty-four courses? You need more chefs in the kitchen than customers.

SUSAN: *What pisses off Chef Henin?*

FRANZ: When someone tries to question him! [Laughs] You can see him like getting *red* in his face and he just gives it to you. He usually starts out, "You know what? You are coming here, wasting my time!" He sees that they haven't done the research.

Once in a competition, he came out of the kitchen with a blown-up food handler's glove pulled over his head. [Laughs] He had his five fingers right on the top, like a chicken. He'll lighten the mood when people are too tense, but he's a serious guy. Roland Henin coached the German Master Chef, a *big guy,* Hartmut Handke, for the Bocuse d'Or competition. When you have Chef Henin coaching you, and he thinks that you could win it, you will. I mean, Henin is down to every little step, every little move in the kitchen. He will question you, and he will be in your face: *Why are you doing it this way?* Every detail. *Why are you turning left, you should turn right!* That's what he is; that's the brilliance of the guy. He sees everything: every wrong stupid movement that you make because you're nervous, or you're off, or not well prepared, or whatever.

Recently, I had a nightmare. I was in this perfect, nice chef's outfit. I'm walking through the kitchen, and I said to myself, "Oh, man, there's no food here. I don't have any food." There was no time to prepare anything, and here comes Roland Henin. He says, "Where is the *food?*" I just walked out. I had to say to myself, "Wake up! Bad dream!" You can't blame Henin for your nightmares, when you're unprepared or lazy. Oy yoy yoy.

Keith Keogh

Owner/President, Total Food Network, Orlando

Me just dogging him and persisting and not letting him say no.

KEITH: I met Chef Henin in April 1988. We were competing at the Culinary Show in Chicago on the main floor. I competed with the Disney team, and he competed as an individual. We didn't know each other and got into a conversation behind the table about how he executed his platter. What stood out in that conversation was his ability to teach and his focus on detail: why things were cut and presented in a certain way and his philosophy about it.

For instance, on his plates, he executed a loin of rabbit. He described the slicing technique: if you slice a loin straight up and down versus at an angle on a plate, it changes dramatically. Presentation is completely different on a bias and diagonal slant. We compared ours to his, and you could see a difference. Imagine if I take a stereo and put on any kind of music and turn up the treble all the way, and then I take it all the way to the bass. It's the same exact music, but the sound would be completely different. We had tremendous debates about these fine tweaks.

We spent the first four years of our relationship debating the nuances of cooking—ingredients of a stock, or roasting vs. baking. People would be astonished how much time we spent on this . . . from how to use a knife to how to stand! Of all the people that came to compete, no one else would debate me but him. In preparing for the 1992 Culinary Olympics, Roland was one of the first people I called for his thought process, going through plates, platters . . . his ability to bring everything back to the fundamentals. He would never ever let something go by, which was, actually, a big part of the team success.

How do you make a chicken stock flavorful, in a four-hour period, in this particular kitchen? We ended up grinding the bones by running them through a Hobbs food grinder, making the raft, and then cooking the bones and raft all at once. *How much do we have to add? Do we add gelatin? What do we have to do to get the texture in the stocks in that short period of time?* A lot of that was Roland. What do we have to do to make sure that the *bâtonnet* are correct every time? This is what they judge in Europe; that's the norm. In America, we're just a little bit more "creative," giving things classical names, but not executing them the same way. When you get to an international competition and don't execute in precisely the way they are asking, you don't succeed. We were fortunate in the World Cup and several other first-place finishes, and a lot of it was attributed to Henin stressing the fundamentals. In the end, that's what separates the teams: Everybody is working under the same time limits, right? So, who executes it right?

In Europe, they have a grinder where you can take the chickens and run them coarsely through it. It would grind the bones, chop them through and squeeze them. So, when we made our stock, it would extract everything at once, and we got that great flavor. We ended up putting a little touch of gelatin in it, because we didn't get the texture in that short period of time, but we did get the flavor, while other teams were bringing (soup) base. The judges come around looking at your stuff, and they're impressed when you execute fundamentals like that.

SUSAN: *They used chicken base?*

KEITH: Yeah. They weren't successful. Different people approached that time constraint differently. We approached it and executed it from the fundamentals, and I think that's why we were successful. Again, it's the details. He executed a loin of rabbit and we spent a lot of time talking about it. Take the slicing . . . the bias fits in a little better and each slice locks in, together. It's the nuance of the same protein, same idea, but thinking through that dish to its last possible degree. Once you bring it to center where everything is balanced, once you get it right, it's perfect. That's where Roland helped us, in between that treble and bass. You're messing with your radio, it sounds a little better, and you mess a little more until it comes in, perfectly.

Roland's got a sense of humor, once you learn to recognize it. Once we were at a practice session with the '92 team. Each team presented their platters in the middle of a large amphitheater-like room. Everyone got to hear the feedback; it was a learning process. One kid who tried . . . he just didn't have his platters together. Roland looked at the plate and then he put his finger down his throat, like he was gonna throw up. The whole audience was quiet at first, but then exploded in laughter, including the kid. It released a lot of tension.

In 1991, when I took over as president of ACF, I asked him to take over the certification process because of his attention to detail and precision. When Chef Henin was chairman of the search committee, he'd redline grammatical mistakes in a chef's application and ask for them to be corrected. The ACF had never experienced that before, but he wouldn't allow misspellings on an application. It was hard for people to handle, and he took a lot of heat. Henin would never back down. He had a standard in his mind, and he stuck to his guns.

Despite all their complaining, these same ones who got their certification considered it a banner of knowledge and approval.

Henin brought the ACF standards out. In the eighties, chefs weren't a big
deal. Sure, there were people like Paul Prudhomme, but the schools and everything didn't come along until later. Henin upheld ideals and integrity. He
demanded the cooking or practicum, in certification. Until then, certification
only required you to fill out paperwork and send in the application. There was a
written exam with two hundred questions: *describe how to peel a carrot*, but there
was no *show me a hollandaise*.

At Delaware North, he brought in certification, doing internal classes and
educational seminars. They had their summit events and internal competitions
from different regions. I judged them a couple times in Buffalo. The way he
handled those people . . . they worshipped him. You don't see a brigade of chefs
look up to a corporate chef. Usually, it's *here comes the corporate chef, telling me
what to do*. He had a whole different level of respect than most corporate chefs
I've worked with. It was amazing.

SUSAN: *What attracted him to you?*

KEITH: Me just dogging him and persisting and not letting him say no. I was
on him until he said yes about the certification and until he said yes about the
team, and let me tell you, it wasn't the first time I asked him. In any case, he did
it. I think he just dealt with me to get me off his back, most of the time. [Laughs]

When we competed in Europe, somebody needed to get ingredients for the
hot food competition. Roland and a couple of our apprentices would go, driving all night to Belgium to get stuff, because we wanted it fresh off the market.
There was such a level of trust. Think of twenty people, representing five teams,
who had worked four years to be in Europe—Luxembourg or Germany. All these
teams get to represent their country and had to trust somebody to get the food
that they were going to put on their platters and in somebody's mouth: that was
Roland. If the market didn't have something, he'd figure out how to get it. He'd
go to a charcuterie shop or somewhere to get the right meat, if they didn't have it
at the open market. We knew that when he came back, we'd have everything we
needed. Sometimes he didn't always have great friends with purveyors at the market, because he demanded such a high level. He wouldn't just take what they'd
give him; he'd send it back. *We're not going to take that. This is the way I want it.* But,
those clashes are what made him so effective and helped the team out so much.

A lot of people don't remember that during those four years, we won two
competitions and we lost two competitions. We won the two competitions by

less than .15 of a point. I'm talking all-around championships—the World Cup and the Escoffier Cup in England. Then we lost them the same way in Basel, Switzerland. When you're dealing with that kind of detailed measurement of success, an overcooked rabbit or fish with just a little bit of an off flavor or a potato that's too soft translates to .15 of a point, overall—the difference between winning and losing.

Roland would leave Luxembourg around ten at night and be back by five or six in the morning. The market would open at 3:00 a.m., and he'd be there, ready with their list. If something got misused or didn't come out right during practice and needed to be done again in the afternoon, Roland would get in the car and find us something in Luxembourg or Germany, in Berlin or Frankfurt. He'd find a charcuterie shop and get us a shank. Instead of our concentrating on how we were going to replace it, it was, *Okay, they're going to take care of us. Move on to the next thing and we'll finish it up when they get back.*

Competition took incredible stamina, and that's why I retired. It's a young man's game. My feet told me after '96, no more. You get two hours sleep. We had a coach who said, "If you can't sleep for more than four hours, you've got to sleep for less than two." If you slept three or four hours, you felt worse. There were nights when everybody got two hours of sleep or less. Everybody was totally committed.

I will tell you one more story and if it doesn't make the book, I want you to make sure he gets it. When I was president, we had a Northwest Regional Conference in Salem, Oregon. Roland always talks about fishing. I used to fish competitively way back in the eighties here in Orlando for bass, right? It's a different kind of fishing. Roland got himself a new boat and wanted to take me out, so sure enough, we went. Roland rowed and instructed. "This is the way we fish. You sit in the boat. You cast this spinner way downstream, and just let it float downstream." That is totally opposite of what bass fishing is, where you just drop little artificial bait off rocks or drop them off weeds. After about an hour, we didn't catch anything. I said, "I'm not going to do it that way. Here, let me just hit along the shore as we go down." I caught a thirteen pounder, one ounce Steelhead trout . . . got it in the newspaper, there! He told me he would never take me fishing again! [Laughs]

SUSAN: *And have you?*

KEITH: No, I've never been fishing with him again. [Laughs] First and last time! We brought that salmon back and cooked it. I was working at Disney at the time where we had team meetings. I brought everybody in who knew Roland, and I showed them. It was a thirteen-pounder, so we fileted it, did a little brine on it, and then stuck it in the oven, Florida-style—lemon, just a touch of horseradish, salt and pepper—and baked it. We cut it up and ate it. It was so good . . . there were about eight of us and we each got a little bit. Roland always told us how to fish and always had stories, and we harassed him about that, forever.

I'm so glad you're doing this. He's a handful, but he's a great person.

SUSAN: *He sounds like a four-year-old boy you're dropping off at daycare.* [We laugh]

Kevin L. Ryan

CEO/Executive Director, International Corporate Chefs Association

He would take all of his toiletry items.
They'd be set up on the bathroom counter from shortest to tallest.

KEVIN: I first met Roland through the US Culinary Olympic team. I got to see him as a leader helping younger team members with all the different techniques that he knew, and people he knew. They all looked up to him. The wealth of knowledge he had . . . especially in traditional cuisines! When you compete in an international arena, you have to know a lot of everything around the globe when it comes to cuisine. That's the one thing Roland had—that kind of knowledge. He had competed on the stage as well, so he knew exactly what to do: what judges would be looking for; how you couldn't cut corners; how to have everything down to perfection.

Speaking of perfection . . . here's one, about the NRA show in Chicago in 1992. We always had to share rooms because it conserves money. Everyone roomed around with different people and decided who they liked and who they wanted to room with—basically, who they could tolerate. After everyone bounced around a few times, *nobody* wanted to room with Roland. He's so eccentric. He would take all of his toiletry items, any tubes, etc. They would have certain heights, and they'd be set up on the bathroom counter from shortest to tallest. Any tubes and things that were laid down, the same thing: shortest to tallest. It had to be *exactly* to perfection. I don't have an issue with that, because I call myself a recovering perfectionist. It was no big deal for me, and we got along well. We had hit the road now for a few years, and we traveled all over. We went to China together, on the road, for twelve straight days and come back to Hong Kong. Guys are running into McDonald's to eat and he and I are going out to a fine dining restaurant to eat sushi.

Fast-forward to the next year . . . the American Culinary Classic is happening in Chicago. Media was my job—they had to go through me. This particular time, I needed to be up at 3:00 a.m. because the NBC morning show was filming (or one of the top network shows). I get back to the room around midnight, get to sleep, and the next thing I know, the lights are flying on. Roland cracks open a Heineken and sits there, relaxing. *I'm only gonna get two hours of sleep.* I'm kind of mad . . . but no big deal. I come back after filming, and Henin's out working with the team. I took all of his stuff and messed it up: all the bottles, the tubes, moved everything around. I even rearranged his clothes in the closet. He came after me: "You asshole!" It was hilarious, but that's the kind of stuff we would do.

The team manager was Keith Keogh, corporate executive chef of Epcot. Keith is a Florida boy and fancies himself as a fisherman. Roland is an *excellent* fisherman, and they would constantly go at each other as to who was better. They had "sparring fishing bouts," if you will. Keith would go up to Washington State and fish with Roland and when Roland was down here for the US Culinary Team, we would fish. The first time, we went out on Bay Lake in Walt Disney World—a manmade lake right in front of the Magic Kingdom, where they have the paddleboats. You can't go on it to fish. Nobody knows this, but really, you can. There were two pontoon boats available for mostly key Disney staff members at Fort Wilderness that you could take out and go fishing. Of course, Keith knew that. We get out on the lake, and the day before, Roland pulls me aside. We're gonna go bass fishing, and he doesn't know a lot about that. I said, "Here's the trick. I know Keith. He's going to use artificial bait. If you want to get some big fish, you need to use live bait." Roland says, "You got to get it for me."

We were leaving at 5:00 a.m. I had to go to this bad part of Orlando to find a bait store that was open, just to get shiners . . . I mean, a place where you really didn't want to be at five in the morning! These shiners . . . they were the size of my hand! Huge! I've never seen shiners that big, in my life! [Laughs] I said, "I definitely want some of those." When we got out there, we caught these monster fish! Then we went to one of the Epcot restaurants, back into the kitchen, cooked them up, and ate them. This is where the fight came up between those two. It was so funny, because Roland, of course, is giving him a hard time. *Why would you use artificial?* He's going off on him, how it's wrong, it's plastic, you put plastic in the water, why . . . that's the kind of guy Roland was—such a naturalist!

Oh my God, one time we were in New York City in 1995 for the ACF National-al Convention. We had serious judges, and Roland was always one. Some were European and some were not, so it was a good balance. Another Roland was Roland Schaeffer, a German chef. The two Rolands were the key judges in this competition. At different times of the day, they were judging different things. Roland Schaeffer was another extremely good judge, always nitpicking things down to the dime. We had been going at this for three days, videotaping the entire time. It gets to the point where there are just so many dishes, even for the judges.

The theme of the convention was like a Letterman show. We were doing like *Stupid Chef Tricks.* So we go to McDonald's. I swear to God. We're in Times

Square, at the Marriott Marquis, and we go to McDonald's and buy a Happy Meal. Roland Henin takes the Happy Meal and displays it on a plate . . . I mean, to the point where he even put the toy on, as a garnish. It was done in such a way that it looked *really good*. The food runners would come in for the food. The plate was completely covered and the runner opens it up for the judges. I'll never forget Roland Schaeffer. He's looking at it and sees the toy. He's like, "Hmmm . . . this is interesting . . ." Oh my God, it was one of the funniest things I had ever seen. We were in tears; crying . . . it was so funny. The judges were laughing, when they finally figured it out.

We videotaped it, because nobody saw it live but us. We showed it at the General Session, in front of 1,800 members, the next day. The whole place—it was just a *roar*. It was that short hesitation . . . taking it seriously . . . that made it so funny. If we had just put the Happy Meal on the plate it in its original paper, it wouldn't have been as funny. But the hesitation of taking it halfway seriously . . . made it. And it was Roland Henin who pulled that off.

Another classic was the trick he learned from me. When we arrived at a hotel, I would hang my clothes up in the bathroom, turn the hot water on, and steam the wrinkles out of them. He was trying out the technique. This is another Chicago event—I think the team tryouts for the 1996 team. I'm up early, in the hall . . . there's nobody up this time of night, of course—just the competitors. All I can hear is Roland coming down this long hallway, and I mean, *nobody's* around now, not even the union workers. It's just us back in the competition area, and I hear, "YOU ASSHOLE!!!"

I'm like, "Whoa, whoa . . . what's the matter? I didn't *do* anything. What are you *talking* about?"

"Because of you, my clothes are *ruined*!"

"Whaddayou mean?"

I would always hang my clothes up on the shower curtain. The way he did it, he pulled a little white string across and then hung his clothes on *that*, on hangers. Of course, as the clothes got more moisture in them from the steam, they got a little heavier . . . and so they drooped down . . . they landed in the tub, and then everything was soaking wet, all of his clothes. He had to take everything down to the lobby, and it all had to be dry-cleaned. He was so pissed at me.

SUSAN: *What attracted you to each other, other than perfectionism?*

KEVIN: It was mutual respect between the two of us. We enjoyed our conversations. We both love to travel, we love food and wines. One of my favorite lines that Roland said . . . we were doing Mystery Baskets way before the Food

Network ever thought of doing them. The Culinary Olympic teams were doing them forever. You don't know what you're going to get. There's just product, and you have to make whatever you're given. Some of the team members were complaining about Mystery Baskets, and his line was, "I don't know why you think Mystery Basket is so, so, so . . . big of a problem! My mother, she did that every day. She come home! She open the fridge! She make what she have." It's *true*, when you think about it, especially with Europeans. My grandmother was like that, too. She used whatever was around! They raised rabbits, so we ate rabbits! They raised chickens, so we had chickens. You had what you had, and you made the best of it. You go into market, and you find the best ingredients you can find, and that's what you ate.

Roland came to my house a couple of times. My sister was dating a guy who was a big hunter, so he would bring over wild game. That was fun to get into the kitchen with Roland, because some of that stuff is pretty tricky to cook properly. Little things reversed my way of thinking. I was steeped in Northern Italian cuisine. We raised all the animals we ate and all that. Roland taught me some things, even about *salad dressings*, which was totally reversed from what my grandmother did. She would always put the olive oil on the lettuce first and then put the vinegar in afterward, saying that the oil coats the lettuce, and the vinegar will stick to the oil, which, if you think about it, doesn't make sense *at all*—like oil and water! If you're going to emulsify it, okay, maybe. Roland said that if you're just going to make a quick salad, you put the vinegar on first. That coats the lettuce, and then the oil goes in. That's how I've made my salad ever since, plus you use a hell of a lot less oil. He showed me that salad technique like, twenty-five years ago, and it changed me, from then on. Once he said it, I was like, *duh*. That makes all the sense in the world. We'd do little stuff like that and marinating meats, venison, etc. We worked with a lot of game. I grew up eating rabbit. Marinating the venison, you'd use shallots and red wine. He was so good at the balance between sweet and acidic and adding richness to dishes. He'd marinate something and then make a sauce with the marinade afterward . . . he utilized everything.

SUSAN: *Did he influence your own mentoring style?*

KEVIN: Yes, there's no doubt. There are people who know a lot but want to keep the knowledge to themselves, as a kind of advantage. He truly wants to share his knowledge to help people get better. A lot of people stay competitive; he was *collaborative*. The culinary field lends itself to an apprenticeship and mentoring type of industry. It's an industry of passion and you share that passion with the people around you. Roland has one of the biggest hearts in the industry. He is so good at helping the younger generation, instilling the values of what makes this industry great.

With the Chef's Associations I run, we reach out to these young up-and-coming rising star chefs and get them involved in the events that we do in their cities. Chris Gould is one of them! He's definitely someone you're going to read about five to ten years from now, as one of the generation leaders. One of the things I love about these events is hearing people say, "The first time I saw that chef was with you, Kevin, at your ICC summit." I'm always looking for these gems out there who are going to be something.

Kevin Doherty

Executive Chef, TD Garden, Delaware North

He must see something in me,
because he put a lot of time and energy into trying not to kill me.

KEVIN: My first impression of Chef Henin was about fifteen years ago: *Uh oh. Angry French chef.* Didn't know what to expect and had never worked for a Certified Master Chef. The question that runs through your brain: *Are they that good?* Sitting here after the fact—yes, they are. You think you know a lot until you stand next to someone like Chef. He forgets more in one day than I know.

Chef as a mentor . . . this is an interesting concept. Chef will never spoon-feed you anything. We'll have a conversation and if your ears are on the right way, he'll help you get to the answer through a roundabout conversation. He'll tell you about growing up in France or working for this particular restaurant or hotel or club or doing the Olympics . . . If you're listening, you get the story as well as an idea of next steps. If you're giving your 50 percent, he'll give his 50 percent, but if you're only giving 10 percent, he's going to get angry and not further the conversation or the commitment that was started.

His method of teaching is unlike anything I've ever seen. A good example would be boning out a pig trotter. I sent Chef some examples of pictures.

"Oh!" he says, "I used to carve ice."

I'm thinking, *What does ice have to do with a pig trotter? I'm going to bone out a pig trotter and he's going to tell me about ice carving.*

He says, "When you're carving the ice you have those nice chisels and some of them are rounded."

There was the story. My ears were open.

"You know, those chisels are quite handy for different things."

It was his way of getting me to understand the bone structure of what that trotter is. I didn't use a chisel. I brought it in to see what it would do, but eventually I got to do it with my boning knife. I sent Chef the finished picture later and he goes, "You see, it's not that difficult." Yet, he never showed me . . . directly.

The first real experience with this was getting ready for Germany. The team of chefs were like, "Put up a garde-manger platter." I was like, "Oh my God, I've never done this. I have no idea. I have basic skills." Practicing for Germany, one of the garnishes for my platter was asparagus. *I can peel asparagus.* No, I can't. I had been peeling asparagus for probably three hours and chef was getting frustrated. "Chef Kevin, you need to think about what you are doing. Why would you peel asparagus with a peeler?"

"I don't know. I'm stupid, Chef."

"Maybe you need to go wash a pot."

My ears are open, but I was frustrated, and now I'm going to go wash my dishes! And then . . . Wow. A green scrubby is an amazing thing. The green scrubby takes off that ultra-thin layer of that vegetable, removing the fiber. It's a life lesson. God! I'll talk with other chefs, Chef Percy or Chef Scott Green. They'll ask, "Do you think there's a solution to every single thing?" My answer is yes. I just think we have not been exposed to perfection around us, our entire life. We were brought into the game late. I wish I had met Chef Henin thirty-five years ago. He probably would have killed me, but I think about how far along I would have been. He probably would have killed me, without any doubt. The mentorship blows your mind to think about it.

Taking the ProChef Certification through the CIA, I would update Chef on my progress. At the end, I said, "Chef, I scored 97 percent on one of the disciplines."

"Why didn't you get the 100?"

"I couldn't peel the pineapple correctly."

"That's five bucks and I'll show you. You peel one and I'll peel one, next time we're together."

Knowing how to peel the pineapple correctly cost me three points on this exam. I had never known.

SUSAN: *How does he peel a pineapple?*

KEVIN: You take the top of it off and you take the bottom of it off, so it's flat. When you look at the pattern there, it tells you how to peel it. So gently—and I believe Chef uses a serrated knife—you take off the smallest amount of skin you possibly can. You're still going to leave the "eyes," if you will. Then you lay it on its side and you look at the pattern of the eyes. They make a corkscrew pattern, so if you take your paring knife and you make a "V" channel, you V and you spin it and you V it back in this tiny little canal, you remove all the eyes. His waste is 50 percent less than mine, *and* his pineapple is already garnished by the time he gets to that stage of the competition.

We did a GM conference in Florida ten years ago. He said, "Chef Kevin, I'd like you to clean the fish for me."

Oh man, I'm in trouble. I'm not a hack; I can clean fish, but before my knife even touches the skin, he stops me and says, "You're from Boston and you can't clean fish?"

"Yes, Chef. I must be stupid, Chef. I'm sorry."

So there was a demo for all of the chefs on the right way to handle that creature. Do justice to the animal that was caught, killed, and now used for food. It's the right thing to do. A lot of people take it for granted—whether vegetables or fish or whatever the product is, it needs to be given the utmost respect. I mean, we're a wasteful society. I think that's one of Chef's messages, indirectly.

Chef Ambarish Lulay was in Germany with us. We've had multiple conversations about how Chef knows how to clean all these fish. He's a fisherman, but I believe he was a fish in his last life. Seriously, he talks to them. He *speaks* fish.

There was a group of us back in the day that did some competitions—Scott Green, Ambarish Lulay, two folks who are no longer at Delaware North, and me. There was talk with Buffalo that Chef wanted to take a team of chefs to Germany to compete, because our competitors do it. We did the whole project in eighteen months. Just think if we had done what the national team does; they're three and a half years into training! We practiced once a month, for eighteen months, and then hopped on a plane and went to Germany, not knowing what to expect. We were young, dumb, and stupid.

The first day of the competition, we're waiting outside at around four in the morning in the rain. There's a group of chefs there with us.

"Oh, Chef Henin! Nice to see you. We haven't seen you in twenty years. What are you doing in Germany?"

"I brought my team to compete."

Here's the five of us from the United States, and we were like clowns.

"What?"

"Well, this is my team from America."

You talk to these other chefs. We had no idea, the company we were in, during the Olympics.

They were polite. Instead of saying, "Aren't these guys out of their league?" It was, "Wow. What are they doing here?" [Laughs]

We did all right. Held our own. You spend eighteen months training, twice a month. We spent three solid weeks together, in Germany. We're a lot more than just colleagues who work for the same company, now. These are friends, but also kind of brothers. And, here's Chef Henin, steering us along.

"All right, we need to do this."

"Why do we need to do that, Chef?"

"We need to know where the place is, right?"

"Well, yes."

"We need to know what the drive is going to be like at three in the morning, when we have your platter and all the ingredients to build the platter. Do we know the way? Will we get lost? Is there a detour? Is there going to be traffic?"

Wow, that's brilliant. Not get up the morning of and find out the road's closed due to construction. Nothing is left without a plan. I go back to that. It's too valuable that we were all there, competing, and nothing was left to chance.

SUSAN: *What did Chef Henin see in you?*

KEVIN: He must see something, because he put a lot of time and energy into trying not to kill me. Whether it is commitment or integrity, I don't know. I like to think I have integrity. It's trying to do the right thing, whether or not I know what the right thing is all the time—maybe that's the piece. He forces you to understand: you need to be able to stand there and look in the mirror and say, *How do I rate myself?* You know the devil and the angel on each shoulder? Will you listen to that voice that's been pounded into your head for ten, fifteen years? The shortcut is unacceptable. You know the right thing to do, and that's the hardest piece. Most everybody wants to take that shortcut—that's the easiest way, but not always the right way. Chances are it's the wrong way.

What else can I explain? The other pieces where I think we are alike? I won't give you the answer. I'll give you what I remember of Chef's story: the late nights, the early nights, the early mornings, where everything possible that can go wrong to a dish did. You make your own mistakes and you learn from them. Some of those apprentices or even chefs who worked as my assistant got the benefit of seeing the results: *Wow. That works great for him, the second time.* Well, they didn't see the twelve times before that didn't work. They have that quick insight, which almost doesn't seem fair—learning to do something without the pain and agony.

That's my 50 percent of the bargain: write these menus and practice the Mystery Basket, so when I show up to cook and demonstrate my skills in front of Chef, who has flown three thousand miles and has lost four hours of sleep due to the time change and has missed out on two fishing trips, I don't go backward. So long as you're making progress, you're going in the right direction. But sometimes we weren't moving in the direction fast enough. That's the same with my staff. We talked about how you should do that project and yet, they chose to do the opposite. "Well, we were short staffed," or "Well, I didn't have the right product," or, as Chef says, "Save zee excuses for the judges."

SUSAN: *What is Chef passionate about?*

KEVIN: Everybody's going to say food. I truly believe it's every person or thing that he can touch. He's passionate about a clean chef coat. He shines his fishing lures with a silver or copper polish, before he goes fishing. That's why he catches the big fish! He's passionate about his integrity. All a person has is their integrity . . . nothing more, nothing less. Without integrity, we're nothing. And of course, Chef is passionate about food. Chef was strictly food—not payroll, not HR, not the babysitter, not the shrink. He was the chef. At the end of the day, he was the chef. He was responsible for food going to the guest. There was somebody who did the schedule and somebody to do the payroll. His job was to manage that kitchen and cook.

You try to tell Chef, "Hey, I have a meeting to go to."

"That's bullshit! That's bullshit! That's somebody else's job! You need to cook. This is a food business, not working on a laptop!"

"Yes, Chef."

I know he gets it, but he doesn't want to get it, doesn't care. There was one goal.

When you look at the meetings, the scheduling, the PR, all that crap as he says, you don't need it. A lot of the kids today get all locked up into that. They forget why they're putting on that white coat. It's not to go to the meeting, and it's not to, *Oh, I gotta do my hair.* They don't even wear kitchen shoes. They wear dress shoes! They walk around in their Monday-through-Friday and somebody does something and, *oh Chef, I need you to take a picture here now.* God forbid if they get in somewhere and need to cook. They need a person who cooks for them, now. I guess that's the difference between "Then" and "Now." I would have liked to have seen "Then." I think "Then" was a good place, but it was probably twice as hard; everything you wanted to research, you truly had to research: go to a library; reach out to somebody; go work someplace for a few months, to learn about a menu item or a technique.

SUSAN: *How does Chef differ as a CMC coach, versus as a boss?*

KEVIN: He was never my boss, per se. He was a reference, somebody to keep you in check—that humble pie, so you didn't get too big for your britches. We did parties all around the country: Lake Placid, Florida, and Buffalo. He can smell what you're made of, and he pushes hard. Some people he will acknowledge and be cordial and professional, but he can tell they're not in it for the long haul and are just looking for the better position or promotion. There's a group of us who see that, because wow, he doesn't bust anybody else's chops. Or somebody will say, "Wow, he busts your chops hard!" Well, yeah. I'm worth it. Plus, I

Young Roland Henin

The French Pavilion, 1967
World Expo, Montreal, Canada

Ma Gastronomie, by Fernand Point,
Published by FLAMMARION,
Paris (1969)

Thomas Keller

Jerry Dollar

Steve Mengel

David Burke

The author, "Slash" (Fagelson) Crowther, CIA, 1983

Ed "The Rattlesnake" Brown   Mike Colameco

WELCOME TO SAN FRANCISCO!
THE 1988 AMERICAN CULINARY FEDERATION WESTERN REGIONAL CULINARY TEAM

The 1988 ACF
Western Regional
Culinary Team

Karl Peters, Jeffrey Mora,
and Master Chef
Raimund Hofmeister

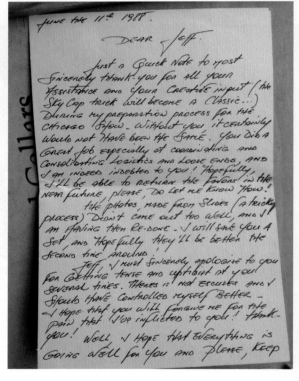

"The only apology letter Roland Henin
ever wrote," to Jeffrey Mora

Lou Piuggi helps
out his Patina Group event

Roland Henin, William Bennett,
and "Bunny Ears" Colin Moody

AMERICAN CULINARY FEDERATION
IS HONORED TO CERTIFY THAT

ASHLEY K. MILLER

HAS MET THE NATIONAL
KNOWLEDGE AND SKILL STANDARDS FOR

CERTIFIED EXECUTIVE CHEF

Ashley Miller
receives his CEC

Keith Keogh

Cowgirl, Jill Bosich

Dan Thiessen

Susan Ettesvold

HOME PLATE

FROM HOT DOGS TO HAUTE CUISINE

Home Plate" Cookbook Project,
Delaware North Corporation, with Beth Brown

Is it good enough? Think again!"

One of many training seminars
at the CIA Greystone Campus, Napa

Colin Moody creates
an ice carving

Ambarish Lulay
and Roland Henin

Scott Green
and Roland Henin

Randy Torres is hugged by team members
as the Professional Culinary Institute wins
the California State Culinary Championship!

The "Travel Hospitality Group:" Adolfo Calles,
Roland Henin, Dawn Hedges, Nick Catlett,
Juan Carlos Velez

Larry Johnson

Rich Rosendale focusing
at the Bocuse d'Or
Competition, 2013

Roland Henin
and Ron DeSantis,
Cancer Nutrition Consortium

Master Chef Dan Hugelier does his stuff

Roland Henin
and Percy Whatley train
for the 2014 CMC Exam

Ambarish Lulay receives
critique from Roland Henin

The 2008 Culinary
Olympic Team

Roland Henin and Kevin
Doherty train for the 2014
CMC Exam

"Three Little Pigs"
Competition Platter,
by Kevin Doherty

"The General and his Soldiers" head to the Whitehouse

A lighter moment
with Roland Henin
at the Ahwahnee
Vintner's Dinner

Roland Henin
gives his graduation speech,
Greystone Campus, 2009

Delaware North Chef Summit, 2012

Brian Williams, Roland
Henin, and Jeff Wong

Current titleholder,
"Best Boat B-tch,"
Kevin Doherty

"Behind every great woman..." Wife Joni Badley
"out-catches" Roland Henin

2017 Bocuse d'Or Competition.
Team USA brings home the Gold,
for the first time in the competition's
thirty-year history. Shown in the photo
is Bocuse d'Or President Thomas Keller.

2009 Bocuse d'Or Competition,
Team USA, Left to Right:
Adina Guest, Timothy Hollingsworth,
Coach Roland Henin.
Team USA placed sixth that year.

A man and his mentor—Thomas Keller and Roland G. Henin

The late great Fernand Point,
owner of La Pyramide,
once considered the best
restaurant in France
when Chef Point was alive.

Master Chef,
Roland Gilbert Henin

A Master Chef finds Balance—newlyweds
Joni Badley and Roland Henin

got thick skin, I'm not going to curl up into a ball and roll away in the fetal position. I'm a big boy. I can take it.

We were meeting in my office here in Boston, and he looked at me and started raising his voice. "You should go back to Johnson & Wales and ask for your F'in money back! You got shortchanged! Stupid!"

"Yes, Chef! I'll write a letter today."

"They taught you nothing!"

That's the beauty of it. There's no punches and nothing held back. He's not going to sugarcoat it. "Why, why would you do this?"

"I don't know, Chef. I don't know. I don't have an answer."

"Well, that's bullshit!"

And there you go. You can hear him say this, correct?

I got him in a good mood, in a meeting . . . everybody's in a great mood. An article came out in the CIA about lobster bisque. I said to a couple of chefs, "I'm going to get Chef angry."

"Why are you going to do that? Why? Why?"

"Chef, look at this article. I don't think this is right."

He puts his glasses on and he's reading it and he slams his fists on the thing. "They are stupid! I'm going to write to the dean! I'm going to write to CIA!"

The article thickened lobster bisque with roux, and he got so mad! He looks at me afterward and goes, "Why would you do that to me?"

"I don't know, Chef. I thought it was payback."

He goes, "Ohh!"

SUSAN: *Describe your own mentoring style.*

KEVIN: I hate to say it. I'm the same way. Spending over ten years with somebody, I used to say that I was the product of the last chef I worked for, because I worked for so long with him, but I can honestly say now that the style has changed almost to mimic everything Chef Henin does. Like the patience level. *You gotta do your part. I'm not going to just give you the answer . . . back to the thought process.* Any mentoring differences are based upon how the world is today. Everything is go, go, go and technology-driven. Yes, it's easy for me to pick up my iPhone and Google it. Technology has helped, but it's also kind of hindered.

SUSAN: *I don't mean to sound like an old codger, but it's an entitled generation. They expect a lot of praise and everything spoon-fed. Google solves all their problems, so they don't learn how to solve on their own.*

KEVIN: Yep. You have a conversation with somebody about something that either is incorrect or non-usable, and they get all upset. *What do you mean? I showed up for work. You need to praise me. You need to give me more money. You need to give me a raise.* I don't need to praise you. You need to give me 100 percent. That's what Chef has given me. One hundred percent.

Andrew Friedman

Food Writer, Author of *Knives at Dawn: America's Quest for Culinary Glory at the Bocuse d'Or, the World's Most Prestigious Cooking Competition* (Free Press, Simon & Schuster, 2009)

Don't let your sensibilities be offended.

ANDREW: I first met Roland Henin when preparing to write *Knives at Dawn*, about the Bocuse d'Or Competition. Roland was coaching the US team. He had previously coached his colleague, Hartmut Handke, in 2003. Two thousand eight was the first year the USA effort was under the auspices of Daniel Boulud, Thomas Keller, and Jerome Bocuse.

I went into the project with *no* prior experience of cooking competitions— none at all! I went to the team tryouts in Orlando before I sold my book project, gathering material for a book proposal. During tryouts, there were four competition kitchens set up, a facsimile of the real Bocuse competition in Lyon, France. Tryouts lasted two days. Teams were going through these long—five-plus hours— cooking routines.

I met Roland the night before tryouts. At several points during the next day, Roland took my arm and walked me along these kitchens, pointing out things the judges should be noticing. This was invaluable, because a lot of the people involved in the US team—including Thomas Keller and Daniel Boulud—didn't know much about cooking competitions. There were not a lot of people who could impart this information to me. We'd walk through the kitchens and he'd say: *See how organized this person is, whereas this person is more chaotic, doing it on the fly. See how this person has a "Punch list" or schedule of their preparations on the wall, and this other one doesn't. This person keeps cleaning as they go. See how these two people have this down to a routine, and these two people don't.* The first time he did this, I audiotaped him, taking it all in. With the legend of Thomas Keller, Roland is a figure that looms pretty large. Thomas will tell you that Roland was a catalyst in his transformation from an anonymous American cook in Rhode Island to one of the most important chefs we've ever had in the United States.

Roland is huge [laughs]—I mean, he's a very tall guy with exaggerated features—huge hands, and this deep throaty French voice. All that could have been intimidating, but he was this incredibly nurturing guy with somebody he'd never met before. During those two days, I would go over to him and say, "Feel like washing the windows?" He'd go, "Well, you got five dollars?" A few times, he had Hartmut Handke join us. I believe the two of them are fishing buddies. Hartmut is basically what I describe as a "Competition Junkie." I went to his house to interview him, and he literally had a trophy like a cup, filled with medals from dozens of competitions. Roland got Hartmut involved, and the two of them became my guardian angels for those two days in Florida.

The French Laundry team won the Bocuse trials: Timothy Hollingsworth and his *commis*, Adina Guest. I traveled to Yountville four times, between October 2008 and January 2009, to observe training at what they call the Bocuse House, dedicated as a training home for the team. The regional notion was that the chef representing the US would take a three- to four-month sabbatical—leave their job to train. That ended up not being the reality; Chef Tim continued working throughout training. Roland made no secret of the fact that he was displeased: you could not be working full-time and preparing for this competition.

Tim had figured out what he wanted to cook and put out his meat platter for the first time. Roland flew in for this demonstration, and the smile on his face was just . . . impressed and proud. The team ended up coming in sixth place. Henin believes that if the candidate had been training full-time, he would have come away with a medal. The food was good enough and his skills strong enough, but there just wasn't enough time to deliver it. It bothered him, in terms of unrealized potential.

I accompanied the team to France about ten days before the competition to get over jet lag and do practice runs. The funny thing between me and Roland is when we went to France. I didn't know this when we all went over there, but it was his strong opinion that having a writer present in France was a distraction for the team. They didn't need "mental interference," seeing a person with a tape recorder and notebook out of the corner of their eye.

At some point in the trip, it was like he turned off a switch. The team met each morning in the little breakfast room. There was a stretch of mornings where he wouldn't acknowledge me at the table. Sometimes I would be the first down and he would be the second. He would just [laughs] get his food and sit at a different position at the table. Sometimes everyone would get their food and they'd sit down and say, "Good morning," and he wouldn't. If I contributed to the conversation, he would never pick up on it. It was as if I, literally, ceased to exist to him.

"Chef, is there something I've done? Are you upset with me?"

"Don't let your sensibilities be offended."

He explained that the team should now be in a bubble. My point of view was that the Bocuse d'Or committee was in charge—not me or him. I had a book to write and there was no way around it. He understood that, but our priorities were different. Nothing else mattered to him but the mission, as the day grew closer.

SUSAN: *You could feel the tension in the book, without it being stated explicitly.*

ANDREW: Roland trained at a time when kitchens were boot camps: sink or swim. European apprenticeships were like medical school, normal to work six days a week, lunch and dinner, with a nap on the banquette in between meals. Things are different now, with a slightly more human view of the kitchen. For instance, there was a point in the book where, just before the Bocuse event, Chef Timothy decides to take a surfing vacation instead of having another round of training. I don't know that it *wasn't* the most useful thing for Tim to go surfing, yet he might have broken if he didn't. Maybe he needed that break . . . I don't know. I see both sides. But Roland was insistent.

After the competition, all the team equipment had to be packed into a van to be stored at Daniel Boulud's parents' farm. Henin was so upset, I assume, by the results, that he did a lot of the loading by himself. I don't know how old Roland was at the time, but he had to be well into his sixties. He got there before the team, and in like a fit, was loading the van—I mean, carrying *big* boxes out of the catering hall, into the van, and almost throwing them in there. Nobody was going near him. It was something to see! Also, he had a bit of a hip or knee injury from running. It was a very impressive physical and emotional display of raw emotion. No words or anything . . . the body language spoke for itself.

The team went for a final dinner. It was probably stress about working on my project, plus being the night after the competition, but I got sick and couldn't go and say my good-byes. I sent Roland an email from my hotel room thanking him for everything, for putting up with me, and saying that I'd see him again soon. Of course, now with the competition over, I got the loveliest email back, clearly from a different man than the one I had experienced in the last few days.

Roland gave me time in person. He was being honored at the CIA-Greystone campus and he invited me. He gave this great speech about this cooking instructor and these four students who go out and party the night before a big test and come in and lie about having had a flat tire. The cooking instructor, in his wisdom, asks them the one question that proves the lie. First of all, it's a great story about smart-ass kids being taught a lesson. It's a distinct story about the kitchen and what you can (and cannot) get away with—a very Roland story.

Here is a guy, way too big to be described as the Yoda of the Culinary World, but who is definitely one of the Mystical Elders.

Funny thing is, he's not known that way. Roland had been an instructor at the CIA during a very important time in the United States. People talk about his relationship with Thomas, but Roland had been an instructor in the late seventies and early eighties. A lot of now-famous people went through there at that time, chefs who remember him vividly! Not just Thomas Keller! There are a ton of people who are now in their mid-fifties to late sixties who went through the CIA when it was, by a mile, *the* place where aspiring young American cooks went if they could afford to go to cooking school. There are a handful of classic instructors that get talked about by people who went there—Sonnenschmidt was one of them, Eugene Bernard . . . and Roland Henin!

A lot of people will tell you he was *incredibly* demanding, but they learned a lot. I interviewed a guy named Mike Colameco who has a show called *Real Food* on PBS. He told me that Henin would do things like: you'd be cooking something, and you'd go and get something, and he would turn your oven off. Why would he do that? To teach you to be ready for the unexpected. That's the kind of thing some guy might do to you in a professional kitchen at that time, just out of competition. Henin knew that, and he'd do it to prepare you. Roland is one of these people who may not win the *Who's Who Award* at the James Beard Competition and is not enshrined anywhere, but is one of those people from that time who had a profound influence through his being a CIA instructor. That is an underappreciated role. Everyone talks about the chefs they worked for in restaurants, early in their career. It was an incredibly important time in the Culinary Institute of America's history, challenging the cliché of the French chef having no regard for America as a place where people knew how to cook or even having raw talent. Roland loves the United States, how open it is! In terms of culinary evolution, what has happened in this country in thirty years would take two hundred years in France.

Paul Bocuse's original utopian idea about the Bocuse d'Or was that representatives of different countries would come and cook food in the style of their country. Most people think that doesn't work, unless you're from Europe. If you come from Mexico, how are judges able to evaluate your food if they are not from Mexico? Roland is enthusiastic about food products perceived as "American" and believes they should be represented in the American platter. He always would bring up maple syrup; it was this great American ingredient. He knows more than I do, so I say this with all due respect, but my feeling is that would be something too sweet for a lot of the palates on the judging panel in France. There are people involved who would disagree with Roland on that point, but I thought it was interesting that, here was a guy from France who was so keen on being a "booster" for the American palate.

Everyone knows that Thomas Keller's kitchens are among the cleanest kitchens, even people who worked for Thomas back in the eighties in New York. You'll ask, "What do you remember about Thomas Keller, when he was at Rakel?" One of the first things everyone will say is, "He was always cleaning." When the Bocuse team practiced, they generated a lot of dishes. Adina would clean up and sometimes Timmy would do it, but, I gotta tell you . . . often, if the team was doing a practice or whatever, Roland would jump in and clean—get right in the sink and wash dishes. It was a touching gesture from someone who didn't need to be doing that at all and could have stayed in the corner working.

Right before the team flew to Lyon, Roland cooked them dinner at the Bocuse house. It was a beautiful thing, and they were all touched by that. When I describe his dissatisfaction, I don't want to make it seem like that's entirely the case. Just that he was up-front about the things he thought should have been different. It wasn't by any means an adversarial relationship, and I hope I'm giving it the proper balance. He was on a mission, and I didn't fit into the mission. Up until the point where I didn't interfere with that, he was just about as gracious and supportive as anybody could be. But then, there was that little zone of time where I think he felt that my . . . presence . . . I don't want to say my *existence*, but my *presence* was at odds with the *mission*. It was as simple as that. It's like I said before, like they say in *The Godfather*: It was just business, it wasn't personal.

SUSAN: *It's not my intention to spin it any other way, although I am biased, in his favor. I was one of those CIA people in the eighties who worked with him for only one month, yet he left an impression that's lasted a lifetime.*

ANDREW: He is indelible! I got lucky; I got this great shot of the team in the window right after they put their platters out: Tim, Adina, and Roland. I framed it and sent it with a thank-you note to the key people who helped me with that project. I heard from, maybe, two or three of those people. One of the notes I got was from Roland: *This is really well done and thoughtful of you.* That meant a lot to me, because he wouldn't have said that [laughs] if he didn't mean it. I didn't dwell on the disagreements that were happening, although did mention that the sabbatical didn't happen. Roland sent a note, saying he appreciated that I had been honest, didn't brush anything under the rug. That meant a lot to me, too. He's an uncompromising guy. The upshot to that is if you screw up, you're gonna hear it, and if you do well and he approves, he's not blowing hot air. His positive feedback meant a lot to me. I'm sure I would have heard, otherwise.

The Director: The Art Institute of Seattle

Hard asses make good training.
–Dave Megeins, CMC

In the mid-eighties, Roland Henin was wooed away from the CIA. For several years, he worked in culinary research and development for major Oregon corporations. Living in the western US offered another perspective in this new world that prompted the inception of the 1988 ACF Western Regional Culinary Team. Soon, Chef was enticed once again, this time to found a culinary program at the Art Institute of Seattle (AIS). An opportunity to create his own program, in a land surrounded by ocean and Pacific salmon? Henin grabbed it.

Chef spent over three years at Art Institute of Seattle, until political values clashed. Goals of the college shifted from product-driven to profit-driven models. Henin had to battle over basic pedagogy such as practicing actual cooking skills to develop one's craft versus simply watching videos, suggested as being a sufficient teaching method for preparation in the industry. Henin's integrity won, again. He left AIS in early 1996 and entered the next phase of his career, which sustained him until retirement.

Dan Thiessen

Executive Director at Wine Country Culinary Institute

It's nice to be back in my neck of the woods.
I'm back to who I was meant to be.

DAN: It was 1995 . . . I was the sous-chef at the Coeur d'Alene Resort. There was an ACF Mystery Basket Competition in Spokane. I had never competed before. At the time, I was twenty-two years old and just returned from Europe after graduating from the CIA, in 1992. I worked in Switzerland for three years, in Zurich, and then Interlaken. This was my first competition, and Chef Henin was the Kitchen judge. [We laugh] I got raked over the coals on Henin's critique. He busted my chops for not making cracklings with the duck skin. I didn't know who he was or what was going on.

The next day, Rod Jessick, my executive chef, called me into his office. When Chef hired me, he would only let me work there for one year and then expected me to move on to other opportunities: "We're going to learn as much as we can from each other, and then, you need to be somewhere bigger than Coeur d'Alene." Anyway, he called me into his office and reminded me of that conversation. This was a month away from the end of the year and he says, "I just got a phone call from your next employer." Roland had called Rod to ask about me. He was looking for an instructor for his new team at the Art Institute of Seattle. One of the things he viewed from the kitchen critique, after beating me up, was that for a twenty-two-year-old, I had a good command of fundamentals, the things schools don't teach people anymore. That was beaten in my head at the CIA and, of course, for three years in Switzerland.

All I had was Rod saying, "You've got a Certified Master Chef saying he wants you to go work for him. You better go work for him." So, that was the deal. I went and interviewed with Roland and said it would be a great opportunity to be part of. I got to be there from the ground floor: building lesson plans around the curriculum and teaching knife skills on the third floor of the school, before there was even a kitchen built. It was a tremendous opportunity, so I jumped at it. At the age of twenty-three, I moved to Seattle and was the first full-time instructor on Roland Henin's team to open up the school. That's how Roland and I met.

Chef became a mentor in my life. From the beginning, I was kind of like his little protégé. He wanted me to get into more competitions, and I also coached our competition team for the students. He encouraged me to try out for the Culinary Olympics and arranged it so that I went and worked with Chef Franz Popperl for a week. He and Franz had been on a team together. Chef Franz was a master of cold food and could get me to a point where Roland could finish my training. I hadn't had a lot of cold food experience at the time. I was a hot food guy. So, I went and spent a week with Franz and went on, gaining a ton of experience.

Henin has this incredible ability to have a frank almost blown-up conversation and then get over it and move on. In my experience, the European chef will push until the American shows their backbone. They will push and run over you until you give up or you finally make adjustments, so you don't get run over anymore. We developed a positive friendship, both fiery and supportive. He used to *love* coming into the kitchen and giving his critiques. Most times, they could be pretty brutal. There is a time and place for these critiques, and we would have a lot of conversations about that. When we focused on the students, we could speak our own personalities and get through it versus attacking each other. In this way, we were able to work well together.

Roland excelled at goal-setting: listing the steps you need to do, to get what you want to achieve, envisioning yourself ten years from now and what you wanted that to be. You had to backtrack and build forward, so the steps you take today were in the right direction of the goal where you wanted to go. Of course, there are sidetracks—life happens—but you don't just all of a sudden create success; it takes practice and discipline and critiques.

When I sat down and said, "Okay, here's where I want to be in ten to twenty years," I found that I was halfway to *not* matching up with where I wanted to be. Some people chose the competition path under his tutelage. If that's what they truly want to do, then all the power to them. It's just not the path I chose. It was time to change my trajectory. He did not like that, at first. He saw me as a protégé, but once he got over it, we were able to move on. And, now he wants to go hunting with me. I'm afraid of him shooting me. [Laughs]

When I said to him, "You don't have what I want," he started screaming and yelling and told me to get out of his office. Three days later, we're having coffee, talking about what we're gonna do next. The deal is, you bet he will chew your tail off, but on the flip side, he will joke about it later, might rip you a little bit: "Has the scar tissue healed yet?"

When I worked for him, I went straight from being a sous-chef to his instructor, never had my own kitchen or team, so I left the Art Institute to become chef at the Space Needle. I worked positions in Seattle and owned a restaurant in Bellevue before moving out to Walla Walla in 2011. I grew up about ninety minutes east of here. This was an opportunity to get out of the Seattle rat race, get back home and start a family. I own the ranch where I was raised, and we're buying a small farm. It's nice to be back in my neck of the woods. I'm back to who I was meant to be.

I was raised on a cattle ranch. We raised about three hundred mother cows. I always worked on the ranch and on my uncle's farm—they farmed about 15,000 acres across the border, into Idaho. My parents used to visit this restaurant about once a month, 3-Mile Inn, three miles up the river. In the eighties, it was basically the only game in town. We became friends with the restaurant owner, Skip. One night, Skip, being a smart-ass, said "You know, if Peewee over here ever wants a *real* job, he can come on over and work for me."

"Will I get paid?"

He says, "Well, of *course* I gotta pay you!"

"Perfect. I'll start next week."

On the ranch, your payment for chores is called "room and board." So, I started working at the restaurant when I was fifteen, washing dishes, busing tables, and cooking omelets for Sunday brunch. By senior year, I was the lead line cook, doing a little bit of everything, working fifty hours a week, while going to school. I'd get out of school at about 3:00 in the afternoon, drive up to the restaurant, and work until eleven at night. I'd work Sunday brunch, too. I was working my tail off.

I was fortunate as an only child. My dad said, "Listen. We know you like this culinary thing, and we want to support whatever you want to do." They knew I wanted to be a veterinarian and also go to culinary school. He said, "You've worked in a restaurant. You know what that's like. Why don't you spend a week with our vet, work on-call with him, and see what you think?" So, I did. After a week of being a veterinarian, I said, "All right, dad, I'm going to culinary school."

There were thirty kids in my senior class. Small town. My dad told me, "Listen. If you don't leave now, you'll never leave, but you can always come back. You're getting luggage for your graduation, and I expect you to use it!" I graduated from high school in 1990, got on an airplane for the first time in my life, flew to New York, and went to the CIA . . . bit of culture shock, to say the least. I graduated from CIA in April of '92, and on June 15, I landed in Switzerland.

The first guy I worked for (Skip) said to my dad, "If Danny's serious about this chef deal, he needs to go to chef's school at the CIA, and then he needs to go to Europe." I spent the last two months at the CIA in the Resource Center looking for jobs in Europe. At the time, Euro Disney was opening up. I interviewed with them and they offered me a job, but they could not guarantee me where I would be working. They were only filling requisitions. The guy said, "You're not going to know where you will work until you get there."

"So, what's to say I'm not gonna work at a hot dog stand at the front gate?"

"Nothing. We're sending over a number of people that they need. They decide on where you go."

I thought, *Okay, that is not what I want to do.*

Literally the next day, I was in the Resource Center, and this Switzerland job popped up. I sent them my résumé and two days later, got a response. That's what started the deal. The first practicum visa was for a year and a half, and then I had a nine-month visa. That was my tenure over there.

When I met Henin, I had a lot of youthful confidence and ego, but I had some chops in me, too. Coming straight from that European kitchen for three years was like putting gasoline on the bonfire. Over there, I don't wanna say that it's better, but there's a different intensity than with American chefs. This was back in the early nineties. America had some chefs who could compete at that level, but were not compared to the Europeans. There were a few of them, I think . . . I don't want to tick anybody off, but we were definitely not on a level playing field with Europe.

In the early nineties, the Artisan-Slow movement was nonexistent in the United States. Over in Europe, it's how they live. Most Americans don't grow up in that culture; unfortunately, if we're ever going to learn it, we've got to work with somebody who will teach it to us. As culinarians, it seeps into us. Those of us who were raised on a farm or ranch have the great fortune of being raised around agriculture, but there are not a lot of chefs who come from a farming background. Usually it's the other way around; chefs start understanding where their food comes from and *then* get into farming.

A few years back, we were discussing the Bocuse d'Or. His perspective: "It's funny. Americans always wanna beat the French. They ask for my opinion, and I tell them, 'You gotta be American.' Don't go with the focus of beating the French; you've got to represent your own food. You've got to have conviction around what is the definition of American cuisine: do the research; have conviction; and cook from your own soul."

SUSAN: *What life lessons persist?*

DAN: Your greatest learning opportunities are from *bad* experiences—not only from your own mistakes, but also seeing mistakes of other people. Henin may not deliver the message in the way you want to hear it . . . but *what he's saying is* *absolute truth.* There are times I didn't like that, but those were opportunities for me to learn the message he was conveying *and* also challenge my reaction to *how* he was conveying it. We don't want the truth, but we need it, you know?

I learned respect for the themes! During critiques, he'd repeat, "There's no *team*! You have no *team* in your menu!"

The poor kids were like, "Team? We *are* a team!"

We're like, "No, he's saying *theme*. He just can't say the, *"th."* You have a *team*, but you don't have a *theme* in your menu."

No matter how long he's lived in America, he'll never give up his French accent.

Henin's got that habit where he goes to shake your hand and feels for those callouses. He wants to know: *Are you a real chef, or are you a kitchen chef?* He still does that! Whenever I see him, he's like, *All right; let me see your hands . . . how much time you been spending at the desk?*

Maybe it's so important to him, because he gave up so much for his craft. That's the downfall of Roland Henin, and it's one of the things I considered, when working toward the Certified Master Chef title. One of the most difficult things—one of the most painful things—I've ever said to the guy was, "Chef, you don't have what I want. You're a Certified Master Chef, but you've sacrificed everything in your life for that!" He's one of the greatest CMCs out there and probably that ever will be, as far as what he's been able to accomplish in his career, but that comes at a cost. Now he's retiring and winding down. He wants to fish and have someone there fishing next to him. He's got Joni (his wife), all his friends and colleagues.

For a long time, he was "Old School French." About the only time he's not Old School French is . . . ah . . . never. The man *fishes* Old School French: he's got his lures lined up with the water temperature and the ideal fishing conditions and numbers on the boat for where you put your fishing pole. He's got *mise en place* in his fishing boat. It drives me nuts. He's just like that all the time, and . . . there are times where that's good and times where you gotta be able to kick back and relax. And, he can relax today. I don't think he could have years ago, but he can relax today. Finally.

SUSAN: *What's your relationship with Chef these days?*

DAN: We touch base all the time. He wants me to take him hunting, for bird, deer, and elk. He's probably one of the oldest men in history to go through the hunter-safety education course. Two years ago, he got his hunting license. He's going to start coming over about once a month, because he wants to see this part of the country. I want to get him around the students here. At the school, we have a Hot Food Team for the Junior ACF Culinary Competition. I'd love to have him come over, offer some critiques, and do some judging. If I can get Henin to critique my Culinary Team, heck yeah I'm gonna jump on that opportunity.

SUSAN: *Here you are, back in competitions . . . full circle?*

DAN: One of the best ways to learn real-live cooking is through competition, so I need to provide the opportunity for my students to compete. Where else are you going to get the critique of all these judges and the type of practice and the one-on-one workings with the coaches? In a classroom, you're one of twenty. In a team, you're one of five, with three to four instructors giving you their opinions. As you look at ratios and immersion, there's no better way!

In competition, you see all these teams trying to do their rendition of a classical dish . . . you can't cook it ten different ways, but you can see it cooked from other people ten different ways. What better way to learn than by seeing all the other interpretations? It teaches about discipline and *mise en place* and to be able to be *critiqued*—to be critiqued is a skill set—to be able to take that and come back for more! That's a tremendous way to learn.

See, here's the deal . . . my students know that, just because it was not *my* path, doesn't mean I don't try to provide that opportunity for others. I can't pick who's going to be successful, who's going to be the rock star in the kitchen. I have to provide the opportunity for everybody to blossom into that, if that's what they want to do. Just because I don't want to compete anymore, doesn't mean that none of my students do. That's the beauty of our business; it's not cookie-cutter. Everybody has the right to express their deal. Even though the Culinary Arts is an individualistic art, it takes a team to do everything.

John Fisher

Chef Instructor, Renton Technical College, Retired

In this business, you can't let outside interference make your judgments.
It's not about going to work from nine to five.
You've got to live, breathe, and eat your profession.

JOHN: I got interested in cooking as a young person, around ten years old, from my aunt, a great cook from Old Country in Italy. She got it from her mother. I learned a lot about Italian food, a lot of great recipes. She taught things you wouldn't learn from an Italian chef. I always wanted to be a chef.

I met Roland Henin around 1992, through competitions. We went to Salish Lodge for a tryout. He was emphatic about the classics and made sure things were carried out in a proper manner of execution: butchery first, with the rest falling into place within the timeline. The final critique was somewhat comical about certain items, like placement of food and styles. Chef gave me a lot of grief over how I was dressed! I dressed appropriately, as far as my hat, starched top chef coat, etc. I had on gray slacks. They were starched and creased, looking good, but he didn't like that too much.

Chef's way is the only way. Some of his associates shy away from him because his critiques are incredibly intimidating, but then a lot of them will warm up. Some of the younger students burst into tears and fall to pieces under the pressure of his critique. The professionals appreciate his critiques, in that they see another side of the cuisine and presentation. The first time he ever judged me was in Spokane, Washington. Chef says, "I am teetering on this gold medal."

I asked, "Why are you teetering on it?"

"Because you're wearing those gray slacks."

I got the gold medal. He doesn't just give those away.

Chef judged me several times in competition. One time in a Portland competition, my time was up. I began putting my food up in the window, and the tasting judges were saying I was late! Right next door to the competition, there was a timer for some security system that had a ticker tape. Roland sees that I actually have about three seconds left, so he goes up and tears up this ticker tape and brings it up to the judges. They honored the tape! He wrote the start time on there, so it was handy. He saved my bacon on that one.

I assisted him in one of the National Conventions. He was doing this sea-food dish with mussels. I was getting ready on the set and checked to see if the mussels were there. They weren't to be found. Chef was not a happy person. We went down to see the guy who had showed them to me earlier and the guy said, "I don't know where they went!" Chef Henin was ready to kill him! I said, "Chef, don't do that. We'll find something." We got a hold of somebody—I think it was Atlanta Fish—who smoothed it over. The fish market was not far from convention center. A guy went down and picked them up. He was there in thirty minutes, so we had about forty-five minutes left to prep. Henin was, uh . . . agitated . . . to say the least. He has a way of speaking French when he should be speaking English. He'll roll his eyes! If he looks over his glasses at you, you're in trouble!

SUSAN: *What did Chef Henin see in you?*

JOHN: Persistence, wanting to do the best I can. A few years down the road, in 1996, I went to work for him at the Art Institute in Seattle. I was the second instructor he hired, after Dan Thiessen. Our interview was pretty comical.

"You wanna go to work for me?"

"Yeah, I'd like to work for you, Chef. I could learn a lot and contribute quite a bit."

"Well, here it is." He handed me a few sheets of empty paper.

"Where is the syllabus, and where is the subject matter?"

"Here's the Title Number. You do it."

We were running this program for the first year. I said, "Chef we only have a month to prepare. Who's gonna be teaching this?"

"You wanna teach it?" I already had a full load, running the A la Carte restaurant. Long story short, I ended up working doubles with no weekends off, for seven weeks. Chef approved the courses, but relied on me to get it done.

Chef always liked to talk down to you, and after a while, he quit doing that to me. Roland and some lady were at a convention. My wife and I sat down with them. Roland proceeded to talk down to my wife. He didn't know that my wife is also opinionated and wouldn't take any crap! They were toe-to-toe; it was really good. One thing they argued about was the gray slacks! She was emphatic about having them starched and pressed. They were gray khakis . . . he must not have liked that "relaxed pant"—I don't know. My wife still comments on that, but ever since then, they've gotten along.

SUSAN: *Is anyone as big a hard-ass as Chef Henin?*

JOHN: Me, at times . . . like when I was at the Edgewater, we were loaded with banquets, had the dining room, the coffee shop and all that. I was talking with the sous-chef and told him, "If you want to go on to succeed, you're going to have to do this, this, and this. What you're doing now is just not working." I had both the lead line and sous-chef's attention. The general manager was there. I had his attention, too. I said, "You're going to need to rise to the occasion; otherwise, you're not making it."

After he quit crying, he said I was absolutely right. He was going to get back on track. A lot of it was from outside influences and family stuff. I said, "You got to put that aside." That's hard to do. You have to focus on what you're doing at the time. Especially in this business, you can't let outside interference make your judgments. To be successful, it's not about going to work from nine to five. You've got to live, breathe, and eat your profession. If you don't, you're not going to be good at it.

SUSAN: *Can "Chef" and "Balance" co-exist?*

JOHN: Roland sends me a Christmas card every year. I send him one, and we stay in contact. We haven't been fishing yet, but keep talking about it. I think Chef is a bit of a loner. Oh, he's got many colleagues. I may be wrong, but I feel that because he's always working, he doesn't have a lot of close friends, other than a few CMC guys . . . no one you'd see on a weekly or monthly basis. It's the same for me. I don't have a lot of friends, per se, but I have a lot of colleagues in the culinary field. I never had time, and he's the same way.

I look back at raising a son and not having a lot of contact throughout his life, other than bits and pieces. When people are playing, you are working. It makes me feel differently now, wanting to rectify all those years. My wife and I have been married thirty-four years. When I started teaching, I'd get home at 3:00 in the afternoon, and she'd say, "What the hell you doing home?" There's a lot of payback in family. They accept what you're doing, but at the same time, there's gonna be a lot of resentment. One of the positions I had was vice president of Food Quality. We had six restaurants, four were fine dining. I was working eighty to a hundred hours a week easy, for about six years. It finally broke me. I had to take a time out, get something different. I was successful, but wasn't successful as a husband or father. I've given back a lot to the people in the business. It's time I give back to my family.

I stop teaching at Renton Technical College, after the fall semester, January 1 [2016]. I'll still be involved in the apprenticeship, keep that running. Will want to bang some pans a couple days a week, possibly do some studying, and keep an eye on the program. We're moving to the coast, Ocean Shores. That area needs a lot of work. Tourist season comes along and everybody's freaking out, trying to hire people. They can't find anybody who has blood flowing through their veins. It will be fun to go and do consulting, mentor some of those places that need work: *Will work for wine and fishing worms.*

Brian Williams

Chef/Owner, Big Wave Café Manzanita Oregon
Senior Vice President, Le Cordon Bleu North America

*Chef Henin looked him in the eye and said, "Taste everything you pre-
pare. The meal needs salt." I couldn't stop laughing . . . his message was
still consistent, twenty-six years later.*

BRIAN: In 1988, while a student at Western Culinary Institute, I had the honor
of meeting Chef Henin the hard way; I cooked a meal for him. Chef Henin was
at the campus to work with Chef Franz Popperl on preparing for the Culinary
Olympics in Frankfurt, Germany. I was in the capstone class, A la Carte. The
school had a chef's table right next to the hot line in the kitchen and the day
Chef Henin visited, I was the class sous-chef. Chef Henin was seated with Chef
Franz Popperl and Chef Michael Spina. Chef Popperl had a bit of a dark reputation for being critical, but our class chef instructor warned us—Chef Popperl
couldn't hold a candle to Chef Henin when it came to being detailed about
food. Needless to say, I was a nervous wreck.

As tickets flew in from a busy restaurant, I kept watching for the chef's table
ticket. Once I had the chef table ticket in my hand, I communicated the order
to the stations, gathered the different items at the pass, plated them, sent the
dishes out to the chef's table . . . and then watched them look at the dishes for
any signs of pleasure or other. Chef Popperl looked up at me, made eye contact,
and waved me over, asking, "Are you proud of the dishes?" Of course my answer
was "Yes," even though inside I was dying. Then Chef Henin began to share his
thoughts. He pushed the food around with his fork and then, looking up at me,
began to break down the plate from construction and technique, to his final advice. "Always taste everything throughout the course of service." Chef Roland
provided feedback on the vegetables, starch, and protein. Chef Roland was very
serious on his feedback and went into great detail. "The dish is all right, but it
lacks salt." I thought that as a student Chef Henin would give me a pass, but I
was wrong. The look of disappointment in his face is one I will always remember, and while the feedback stung, his advice has never been forgotten.

To this day I always not only taste the food myself, but train my cooks to do
the same. A year ago, I hired a cook from Delaware North and asked him if he
had any "Chef Henin stories." Of course he did. He had prepared the crew food

at Safeco Field in Seattle and Chef Henin came by and tasted everything. Chef Henin looked him in the eye and said, "Taste everything you prepare. The meal needs salt." I couldn't stop laughing . . . his message was still consistent, twenty-six years later.

SUSAN: *Why was he drawn to mentor you, and vice versa?*

BRIAN: I believe Chef Henin took me under his wing due to my passion for the kitchen and culinary education. In all of our conversations, Chef Henin has a style that goes into great detail. As our relationship moves into the third decade, I believe it is my skill as a fisherman that keeps bringing him back to my restaurant. Chef Henin loves seafood, and as I am the chef of a seafood restaurant, we have a lot in common.

Chef Henin is still very consistent in his observations, as he provides me detailed feedback on the appearance of my restaurant from the outside, the entryway, my service staff, the meals he orders, and the kitchen. My entire team lights up when he surprises us with a visit. They take in all of his feedback as if it were dessert.

In a lot of ways, how Chef Henin is in the kitchen is how he is in life. I was salmon fishing with Roland out of his home port of Ilwaco, Washington. From the moment we met—early that morning—until we said good-bye, he was laser-focused on catching fish and committed to every small detail. Upon arriving at his boat slip, the first thing I noticed was that, even though his boat was several years old, it looked brand-new. As we loaded the boat, I quickly learned he had a process for everything . . . even loading and getting on the boat. Everything we had packed down carefully passed from the dock to the boat in a methodical way with nothing being passed until the last item was put away in its specific place. There was no rushing this process. Once in the boat and heading out into the river, Chef Roland gave instructions on where we were to sit, where we were going to fish, and the role everyone would play on the boat. I found this very similar to his *mise en place* before meal service.

Fishing started out slowly, but Chef Roland never lost focus in directing us to make small changes in our technique: we changed bait; we changed the water depth; we changed our trolling speed. These changes worked, and we started to hook and catch fish. Chef Roland has a very specific way to handle fish from the moment they are gently laid on the deck. From his soft blow to the head with a club, to cutting the gills to "bleed" the fish, everything was done swiftly, as if it were a dance. Once these steps are completed, he tied the fish to a short rope and hung it over the side of the boat to allow water pressure to completely bleed out the fish. I had never seen this done before, and I am not sure I would do it again.

In the Columbia River, there is a problem with sea lions eating your salmon as you fight them with rod and reel. We had that problem. Chef Roland directed us to put the reel in "free spool" and let the fish swim away while still hooked, explaining that the fish is faster than the sea lion. We did as directed and chased the free swimming salmon for a few minutes until clear of the sea lion. The fish was then fought and netted and then Chef Roland began his fish-handling steps. When he pulled the short rope from the side of the boat to hang the fish in the water to bleed out, we quickly learned that the sea lion had made away with the salmon we caught earlier, hanging over the side. I was disappointed until Chef Roland stated in a matter of fact way, "Sea lions need to eat, too . . . *C'est la vie.*"

After a long day of fishing, we headed to the dock, and then Chef Roland's process of unloading began . . . very similar to the boat loading process, except now we had to clean and scrub the boat. It reminded me of cleaning the kitchen after a long day. Being exhausted and tired was no excuse for anything less that perfection. Within another ninety minutes, we had the chef's boat cleaned and were ready to take everything we had packed on the boat earlier back up to the car. I was excited to head home, eat, and go to bed; but remember, this is Chef Roland. Instructions were given to meet Chef at his fish camp a few miles from the marina.

In Chef Roland's backyard, I found him with a cutting table set up, a knife and equipment bag, running water, and an opened micro-brew. As someone who has fished all his life and cleaned fish, this was an eye-opener. It would have taken me fifteen minutes, tops, to gut and filet the four fish, but I was about to get a whole new perspective. Chef Roland gently reached into the cooler and removed the first fish and gently placed it on the table. He then started the process of scaling the fish and rinsing not once, not twice, but *four* times, talking about the process as if this were a lecture at the CIA in the famed Seafood Kitchen. By the time he was done cleaning and fileting, we were over twenty minutes into just one fish. Just when I thought I had seen everything, Chef Roland produced a role of cheesecloth and cut about a four-foot long section and began wrapping the fish before placing it into another clean iced cooler. When he was done with the fish, it looked like a swaddled baby.

SUSAN: *Compare your mentoring style to his.*

BRIAN: My mentoring style is a mirror of Chef Roland's. As does Chef Roland, I have a list of non-negotiables. It starts with very clear communication of expectations. At a minimum, we expect work ethic, effort, positive body language, high energy, good attitude, passion for the craft, being coachable, doing extra, being prepared, and being on time. From those basics, it moves on to attention to detail and taking pride in your work. Leading a kitchen is not really different from that of a culinary school instructor. You are always teaching and coaching. Often this requires repetition over the same method or technique. It is more than just having the cook learn the technique; they need to understand *why*—the importance of doing it over and over, never taking shortcuts

I am the luckiest one in this book, as my relationship with Chef Roland went from mentorship to friendship. Chef Roland is different from so many people who have come and gone in my life. I found him to be so loyal over the years, and that is, indeed, a very rare quality. My wife Carol often gets excited when she brings me the mail and shows me another handwritten letter from Chef Henin. In today's modern age of technology, who takes the time to handwrite a letter, let alone do it a couple of times a year?! I enjoy it when one pops up in the mailbox—not social media, not email or instant messenger. Really, who does that!

Our relationship has shifted from seeing each other at meetings and conferences over the years to spending time having a meal together. It doesn't have to be fancy or fine dining. Some of our best meals are in small towns like Ilwaco, Washington and Astoria, Oregon, at little hole-in-the-wall restaurants. Chef Roland is not a food snob. Doesn't matter what it is, but if you are going to do it, do it well.

If you have never been fishing, it can be quite boring . . . but not with Chef Roland. I get to sit in a boat for hours, just the two of us, and often Chef Roland and I just talk. Believe it or not, it is rarely about food, but about family and life. I value the time I get to spend with Chef Roland, as it is both insightful as well as an opportunity to learn and see inside the man who has accomplished so much.

The Judge: American Culinary Federation

My nickname for Chef Henin (he has never known about this but he will after this book is out) was "Monster Master Chef Henin." He would give a compliment when your quality of work had his stamp of approval. That was the grand prize (compliments from a great, yet crazy, Certified Master Chef). Do not ask him a stupid question without expecting to get a monster answer from him. That was his way of caring for you and wanting you to do your due diligence before wasting his time. I always loved his answers. Most recently, I had emailed him to ask him about Spinach Subrics mentioned in the Escoffier book. I emailed him a picture of the version that was solely my interpretation of it. His response: "Do not make me hockey puck next time." After all these years, he has not changed a bit but you cannot help but to admire and love the man.

—Alex Darvishi

People who don't compete are average. Average, according to Chef Henin, is the best of the worst and the worst of the best.

—Scott Steiner

Jill Bosich

Chef/Owner: Cowgirl Cookie Co. and Chef Instructor: Orange Coast College

You're getting beat up with a velvet hammer.

I competed freshly out of culinary school, having been exposed to this cool thing called the "Culinary Competition" through the American Culinary Federation. I stood back on the sidelines, helping and assisting, then convinced myself to enter my own show. Chef Henin was one of the first judges I ever encountered. Here he was, this tall Frenchman. You hear about these intimidating European chefs. I'm not usually intimidated, but I was inspired, and I thought, *Who is this guy?* He was friends with so many chefs in my region, like Raimund Hofmeister, Larry Banares, and Jeffrey Mora. These guys were on their own culinary team who went to Germany and competed in the 1988 and 1992 Culinary Olympics.

Chef Henin always got asked to judge. He was brutal but honest, and gave good direction. I was struck by that in a positive way, like *wow, you're getting beat up with a velvet hammer.* I first started competing in 1991—a window of time when people like Henin were still somewhat competing themselves while coaching other guys. There was a lot of energy and interest; competitions were going on all over the place. You'd show up in Los Angeles or Arizona, or Nevada, and you'd see these guys, either judging or competing. In 1988, they were all close because of the Culinary Olympic team and the Western Regional team. In 1992, Chef Henin was an advisor for Team USA, yet still had a big influence with USA West Regional team. A lot us younger people doing small local competitions had access to these guys, this incredible group of chefs and Master Chefs who were active and made themselves available.

I recall him being hard on me, thinking, *Why was my critique so rough?* Then, the award ceremony would come up: Jill Bosich, Gold Medal. It was just his way of . . . the velvet hammer. He sensed talent. I see that now. That's one of the reasons I respect him so much. He beat me up with purpose. You don't see it in the moment, because you're young. In 1991, I was twenty-one years old, trying to figure out the industry, learning about classical cooking, and linking it all together.

His persistence led me to try out for the Olympic team. I saw their videos. That team was fortunate to have a tremendous amount of sponsorship. They traveled all over the world and documented their experiences on being on Team USA. In one of the videos, Henin said, "This is the first day of the rest of their lives." I had been apprenticing for chefs Larry Banares, Brad Coles, and the members of the 1992 Olympic team (which Henin advised). After working with these guys, seeing the videos was profound. It provoked me to try out for Team USA myself. In 1993, at the American Culinary Federation National Confederation in Orlando, there I was, twenty-three years old, naïve and green, but so motivated. There I was, trying out with thirty or forty guys; I think I was the only woman. I never would have thought I'd be ready in such a short amount of time. There are chefs who try for years. It's sad. Maybe they don't have the guidance, support system, or access to the right people. I was blessed to have the chance to be polished by people like Chef Henin.

Because he was an advisor in '92, they used Henin as a floor judge in '96. The Orlando tryout was just one phase; we had to go to the National Restaurant Show in Chicago for the second phase. He patrolled the kitchens, marking what we were doing. He made sure we didn't have an abundance of waste. He comes up with his clipboard, looking at me with his face, his Henin look.

"Where's your trash, where's your waste?"

"Right here, Chef." They were in these little bins I labeled, *usable waste* and *non-usable waste*. "But there's nothing in them."

"Well, there's a little bit, you can see what's there . . ."

He looks in all my trunks, coolers, and equipment, lifting lids, rifling through all my stuff, overturning everything, not believing me, claiming I was hiding trash and venison trim, and finally saying, "Wow, you did well."

Ha-ha, I'll never forget that. You're so nervous, in the middle of a National Restaurant Show. There are thousands of people watching you, in a fishbowl kitchen. You don't dare hide anything nor do something that's not on point.

We had around seventy different ingredients and had to incorporate more than half into our menu. It was a challenge, because the ingredients weren't immediately compatible: venison, Arctic char, and red cabbage. I received a massive venison leg that wouldn't fit in my pot. Red cabbage with venison would be enjoyable, but red cabbage with Arctic char is incompatible. You had to think through what they gave you. It was challenging being younger in my career, having to think on your feet. This was during the dawn of reality shows like *Chopped* and *Master Chef*. People now have that mindset of thinking fast on their feet, but back then, it was just intense. You're looking at those ingredients, and they don't seem appetizing together. That's the challenge of the Mystery Basket; they want to know that you're going to put the venison with the cabbage, versus the Arctic char. These are decisions you have to make in a quick moment.

We only had to do several portions. It wasn't like we were serving fifty people. We had to butcher what we needed and return the rest. That venison leg was huge, and to get that size of a protein was daunting. We needed some of the bones to make stock and then, sauce. Had it been leg of lamb or something conducive to our number of portions, it would have been less challenging, but this thing was *massive*. That was the victory—those curve balls. They wanted to know that you weren't going to keep the entire thing, because it would have been wasted. I guess that's what he was looking for in the kitchen. *Where's your waste?*

Competition presentation weaves well-prepared, technically executed food, taking "concept" into consideration: *Where was the food grown? What season? If it was a rabbit or deer, what might that animal have eaten? What would have been in that environment?* The '92 culinary team adopted a vision of holistic experience around food and preparation: what foods naturally go well with particular cooking methods; which foods came from the environment that the animal lived in. If nouvelle cuisine was born of that era, then this had a distinct look and feel to it, as well. The foods and presentation style of the nineties were designed in the Culinary USA '92 team. A lot of people copied it, because it was beautiful—food that not only looked good, but tasted great.

You know this big craze now, Farm-to-Table? Local sources? They were already taking that into consideration. The Western Region is so fortunate, with access to food. Chef Henin was from the Northwest. We weren't East Coast; we were the West Coast. The West was always known for being more edgy and daring, less traditional. We had so many influences: Asia, the Southwest . . . bright, flavorful cuisine. Team USA used these concepts. Whether chefs were running country clubs or more like Thomas Keller, on the forefront of a retail side, dealing with customers versus hotel chefs who were more in the back, Henin had a broad brush.

Once he was arguing that there are not five mother sauces. He was arguing that *espagnole* sauce was not a mother sauce. His argument was so sound, we left the room believing that everything we've ever known about the five mother sauces—béchamel, velouté, *espagnole*, tomato, and hollandaise—was wrong. It was like he was rewriting history. He can argue it till he's blue in the face. One time hanging out with Hofmeister and Henin—it's one of those things you probably shouldn't put in a book—they were so upset with one of the culinary team guys. They called them those "bronze medalists." *Those guys can't earn anything better than a bronze medal.* They were so competitive. I'm like, "I never want to earn a bronze medal." Ha-ha. Don't say I'm a bronze medalist!

SUSAN: *How does your mentoring style compare to his?*

JILL: My mentoring style is true to how he was with me. I'm just as tough on my students, in a general loving way. I nurture, but also drive home the point and leave people hungry, wanting more. I tell my current students that I'm not an answering machine, I'm a provocation machine. I will provoke them to get the answers themselves. That's how you learn best, and that's what he did for us. He'd coach you along, trail you along just to the point where you wanted to know more and then that became up to you. At first people get frustrated, but then recognize, *Wow, she's leading me down the right path. It's not like she's leading me astray.* People respect it. They know you're not misleading them. The velvet hammer . . . I'm telling you, that is the ultimate thing. The hammer wrapped in beautiful velvet.

My students need to structure their questions in a way that tells me they've already thought of what the possible solutions are. If they're close, then we'll have a conversation, and I will guide them. If they show me that they haven't tried, they know I'm done. They might ask me if the texture on a dough is where it should be. I'll ask: *What does it feel like? Describe me the texture. Do you recall my dough's texture, when I did the demonstration?* They'll say yes, and I'll ask if their dough looks close. They'll say it's too dry or too moist. We get to that answer together, but I don't tell them specifically, because they don't learn that way. That's how he is. Socratic.

I recently saw him while judging at an ACF competition. I had a moment to break away to ask around *where's Henin, where's Henin?* It felt so good to see him. Wow, you haven't seen someone in so long, your mentor. He's helped so many people. That's when he told me about the book, and I said of course, whatever I can do to be a part of it. I just adore him. Thank you so much. He makes me get teary. He's such a cool dude.

Susan Ettesvold

Community Nutrition Advisor/Chef, "Eat Smart Idaho," University of Idaho Extension

Anyone who came under Chef Henin has that same set of tools,
if they were willing to accept them.

SUSAN E.: We met in 1990, when I tried out for the 1992 Team USA Apprentice Team at the ACF Conference, in Portland. That is the most poignant moment to begin with. Tryouts consisted of a big written exam and two Practical exams [A "Practical" exam is a hands-on test of culinary skills which assesses ability, versus a written test which assesses only knowledge]. I made the team, and we had eleven practice sessions at Disney World, Epcot. He was there for each practice. Although my role was *sanitour*—glorified pot washer and floor mopper—at each practice session, he had something for all of us apprentices, even when it came down to washing a table.

I started washing a table and he kindly stops me in the middle of it. "Please allow me to show you how to do this correctly." I thought, *Oh my gosh, here is this Master Chef who is showing me how to wash a table. He shouldn't even have these tools in his hand!* Right? He got all of us around and started washing this table, explaining each step. I thought he would start and then let me finish, but he continued from top to bottom. He got down on his hands and knees, covering every nook and cranny. That table hadn't seen that attention since it was made. I don't think anybody had ever seen those parts of the table. He spent thirty minutes impeccably cleaning this table, explaining each detail and why we needed to do that. That has stayed with me forever, and I pass that on to my own students.

Now as a working pastry chef, all my crews have that same lesson—*from-top-to-bottom-explain-why* lesson. It was bigger than sanitation; that was an obvious first. It was about attention to detail, doing a task all the way and correctly, the first time. He had that same kind of attention with every little thing we did. We weren't competing; we were there to wash their pots, melt their chocolate, and do their *mise en place*. It started with us. Our role was just as important, because it would follow through with them. He gave us validity. Anyone who came under Chef Henin has that same set of tools, if they were willing to accept them. When I pass that lesson on to my students, it takes some time to drive it home. Most young people just blow it off, but some people take that to heart, and I can see that later in the jobs they have.

SUSAN: *What is your mentoring style?*

SUSAN E.: "Everyone knows something you don't." That's something I like to impart. Nothing I teach comes from me, because there have been mentors. At FENI—Foodservice Educators Network International—we come together and share ideas for teaching. All your classmates are teachers. Chris Kottke, a chef from Kendall College, held a class on teaching paste. I teach in Idaho, and a lot of the students here are not necessarily versed in flavors, haven't had the opportunity to try new things. Using Chef Chris's lesson, I teach them to build their flavor library. Once you understand how food behaves and you have that flavor library, you become more skilled.

In my first year teaching, I realized some students here hated certain foods. Why would anyone go into the culinary world if they weren't a complete foodie? I never understood, but thinking about the food library, maybe they hadn't had the chance. On the first day, I have everyone stand up and raise their hand. They take an oath: vow to taste everything, at least once! It's not my invention; I saw another chef do that in a cooking class, but it works well for my two years with them. When they say, "I don't want to taste this. I hate this," I say, "Oh, have you tried it?" "No, I haven't." "Well, then, you made an oath!" I've never had anybody back out. It's amazing how many things they haven't tried. It's Idaho; they've tried dozens of potatoes. In their career, a flavor library contributes to their being indispensable because they can come up with something on the fly.

Chef Paul Kasper, who recently passed away, was a pastry chef in Lake Tahoe. He proctored his final Practical, an eight-hour exam, in his sixties. He had this clipboard, taking notes on my exam. At the end, he asked me what I had learned. I said, "A ton!" There were so many mistakes and great learning opportunities. When I finished talking, he flipped over his clipboard and said, "This is what I learned from your exam." How could this sixty-year-old pastry chef possibly learn from me? He said, "You never stop learning. You'll never live long enough to learn everything you can, in pastry."

A few lessons I pass on:

1. Set the bar high! I have arguments about this, with students. They don't understand why, in Twin Falls, serving lunch to a crowd of math teachers, they have to do it perfectly. They can work however they want when they leave school, but while they are here working with me, they are doing

their best and serving it like it was going out of a three-star restaurant. I
think they remember that, when going to work. They don't have fine dining in this area, and they report back, "Oh man, you won't believe how
they do this!"

2. Indispensable is good: know all those little things and think ahead with
   what the chef is doing. *I know Joe because every time I turn around, he's ready
   with that tool I need, or I can count on him whenever I need a shift covered.* If
   you become indispensable, then someone will call on you for that special
   job.

3. *Cook until it's done.* Students constantly ask, "How long do I bake this?"
   I'll say, "Twenty minutes to check." There's never an exact time.

That lesson started in my apprenticeship at the Bonaventure. In my first week,
I burned two #10 cans of Blue Diamond almonds—two full sheet pans! That
was bad. The Bonaventure has 1,500 rooms, eight restaurants, and banquet
space for up to three thousand people. We made all the bread, pastries, and ice
creams for everything, including the room service, and the restaurants—everything! There were no timers in the kitchen; you just had to sense it. Whenever
I asked the chef, how long, he would look at the one clock on the wall, and he
would always say that: *Twenty minutes to check. Ten minutes to check.* I had to bake
the almonds again. I stood in front of the oven, waiting for them to bake and
smell and . . . I didn't do that again!

Timing is everything—not so much in other industries: one second or minute
can change everything. In my first job, I worked in a bakery with a carousel oven.
I worked in the middle of the night with the cake baker. He had a full oven of
sheet cakes, and I was trying to get an idea of how long they would bake. He'd
say, "Two more turns." I just couldn't get it, that it would go around the oven
one more time . . . and in one turn, it would be done. *Really?* One turn? Or two
turns? You can see this? Now, I get it!

I bake off a batch of *palmiers* and ask the students, "When do you think they
should come out?" They always choose by looking at the golden color, right? I'll
pull some out—enough for all of them to taste. Then, I bake them until they are
done and have them taste both. They smell them, pull them apart, taste them—
the whole difference. Just because something is "golden brown" doesn't mean
you're going to enjoy the flavor at all. It may not even have any flavor! They get
so excited when they learn it! They have this understanding of what good flavor
and aroma is. They can see it, then. I love seeing that lightbulb turn on.

It's a small town, and after students graduate, maybe because I had someone like Chef Henin take an interest in seeing me move forward, I feel like I have coached each one of them. I'm using the word "coach," because we're talking about Chef Henin. That's part of your role as an instructor, to be a coach. I build relationships and follow where they're working. They send me pictures. It's fun to see. Over twenty-five years later, Chef Henin continues to coach and encourage me. Perhaps even more profound is Chef Henin's kindness. To this day, his lesson is the importance of staying connected. He makes the kitchen feel like family.

Randy Torres

Chef Instructor, Oregon Coast Culinary Institute

Chef had this regalness about him. It made me want to be like that—command that respect, when walking into a room. I don't necessarily want people to be terrified when they hear my name, but I definitely want them to say "whoa."

RANDY: Chef Henin was judging culinary competitions in our area. He was known for being, politely saying, *to the point.* As a first-time competitor, you hear stories about some of these chefs, so when you hear that Chef Henin is going to be there, you work a little harder to make sure things are at their best. At that point in his career, you prepare for the worst and it pretty much comes. At the time, you don't know what it's for. I see it now, in the later parts of my years. We're told to focus on the positives, but the positives don't always help us grow; it's the negatives that help us grow. That's part of the approach with chefs like Chef Henin; he focused on the negatives, to help us become better. I've followed in his footsteps and become a judge now myself, and I tell you, if we talked to competitors the way that Chef talked to us then, they wouldn't deal with it now. I think the people have changed. However, I tell people these stories, and I'm so glad that he talked to me that way, because I think that was the best way for me to learn. Maybe that was just me as an individual, maybe I'm a little hardheaded or something, but definitely you can appreciate the honesty. You appreciate, if we dare call it, *enthusiasm,* to make a point and *teach* somebody about this great world of cooking. At the end of the day, even if you walked away with a lower score than you hoped, to even *get* something—a bronze medal with Chef Henin in the room—you knew that it meant something. For me, it's about getting gold, and it's going to mean a lot with him in the room as a judge. He's not giving it away, by any means.

I guarantee you, those days you weren't winning any gold. At those times, and this is me sounding old, but back then, it was a lot harder to get gold in competitions. Everybody gets a trophy now, and we try to be more encouraging. At least that's what we're told, because the average person is different. I've been teaching now for a solid ten years. Classes when I started were way different than classes of today. What's happened over the years is evolution. As we age, we mellow. Knowing Chef Henin now, I make fun: *Chef, if I had done that same thing, years ago, you would have been a lot tougher on me.*

Initially, as an instructor, you want to right all those wrongs, to build that perfect employee. You think, *These students are going to go out and work.* Nowadays, many culinary students just want to learn to cook. They have no intentions of getting into the business, so the question I give my students to ponder on is: What is culinary school for, now? Is it restaurant training? Are we teaching people about working in a restaurant, or are we teaching people about cooking? It may sound funny, but those are two different worlds. Teaching someone how to cook is different than teaching people how to write a balanced menu for hundreds of people, or how to make this in a quick fashion, because you have to serve hundreds of people. There are different thought processes to how you approach culinary education now, because your average student is different. Ten years ago, I'd ask how many people want to be an executive chef, and almost everybody would raise their hand. Now it's the other way around, maybe two or three people. The rest of them say, "I want to be a food writer," or "I want to own a little boutique counter-type store, but we're going to do a small amount of food." You might have some, "I just want to write a book," and you might have some say, "I'm just here because I like to cook." It's an expensive hobby. So, that's changed me. It hasn't necessarily caused me to mellow, but I have to handle each student a little differently. We still approach it from a professional standpoint, but it may not be as hard as it used to be. Then we get into the Student of Today, the younger generation. Society basically tells people, "Don't be uncomfortable for a second." People won't stand to be uncomfortable, especially when they're paying to go to your school. They don't want to be uncomfortable or made fun of. They don't want to be yelled at, or they'll just go somewhere else. We're all fighting for the students, so we have to bend a little bit.

SUSAN: *It's not the same CIA it was in '83, ha-ha.*

RANDY: I was a young Latino boy. My parents are of Mexican descent. I'm third generation in the United States, grew up in a small community in Southern California, not influential with high-end cooking. When I went to culinary school, it was vocational work to get a job in a restaurant. I never thought of doing world-class competitions or going after being Certified Master Chef or becoming an Olympic champion . . . anything like that. When I was in culinary school, the instructor there was an avid competitor and started putting out the usual *volunteer for this or that.* I never got involved in the beginning. I lived about forty-five minutes from my school, so was like, "I have to get home. I don't have time for that." One day it hit me that I should get involved. I went to a culinary show and got hooked. I helped people with their competitions, then competed in my first show and have been competing ever since.

SUSAN: *What attracted you to Chef Henin?*

RANDY: I had my, whatever I like to call it, my awakening—understanding that this career is more than *oh, you're cooking, and you're going to a kitchen, and you're working.* Cooking is a lifestyle in its true profession. You connect with other people and do more than the norm. When the competition thing came around, I was so attracted to Chef Henin, because of those qualities. It wasn't just about a person who could cook, because at this point, I had never seen the man cook. His reciting information from classical recipes to techniques, knowing things line by line . . . you could never get there, to his level. His being a Certified Master Chef . . . at that point in my career, Master Chef was an unachievable goal. There were only like fifty-something Master Chefs: *Oh my God, I'm just this young Hispanic kid. I could never do anything like that. You have to go live in Europe. There's no way.* But I was intrigued. I'm not a person who, even if it feels unobtainable, turns my back. I continue to embrace and go after it and at least associate myself with it. Whenever Chef Henin was judging, I wanted to be part of that show. I chased the gold medal for some time. I won one with a team, but I wanted it personally. I was in what they called "The Silver Bump"—you're just about there, and it was always close. Chef had this regalness about him, in how he carried himself. It was this energy coming from him that made me, in turn, want to be like that—command that respect, when walking into a room. I don't necessarily want people to be terrified when they hear my name but I definitely want them to say "whoa."

As far as him? He'd laugh and say, "I'm not attracted to you, what are you talking about?" As my career went on, he saw enough of me. A lot of people in this business come and go: do one show, get their medal, and you may never see them again. I kept going, and trust built: *Hey, this guy has been around, he's taken enough beatings, he's got enough silver medals, bronze medals, a few gold, this young guy knows what he's talking about.*

How do you know when you're a chef? It's not a title where someone comes down and knights you; you just know. Chef and I were at a conference. He'd brought some people he was coaching, and they had their platters displayed. He said, "Chef Torres, I want you to give these guys a critique."

I smiled, "Chef, what can I tell them that you haven't?"

"You're one of the younger guys, an up-and-comer. I trust you."

That was one of the greatest experiences of my career and my life. You feel like you've done things right, paid your dues, and someone trusts you well enough to give feedback to someone they're working with. I can only hope it was because of years of my hard work and persistence. I had also been involved in coaching students myself, in culinary competitions. It's easy to say you truly love something, but when you see how many people stick it out, it ends up being a small percentage of the people that start.

I was in a Hot Food competition and set up my table, which was on wheels and mobile. You don't ever think of doing anything with it at the beginning, moving that stuff around. I left the tables where they were. I was working inefficiently, so when it came down to the critique, Chef just ripped into me. "You're being stupid. You could have moved the table, brought the table way over here, put it close to your stove, then you don't have to move around, wasting steps." I'm a heavyset guy, need to go to the gym more and lose weight. He says, "I know you need to work out, but this is not the place!"

I tell people that story and they laugh or cringe and say, "He talks to you that way?"

I say, "Yeah, but it's coming from a good place, and guess what? To this day, I never forgot it."

When instructing a competing student, I'll say, "Hey, let's see if we can move that table and make it more efficient." That's where we miss out on, in today's PC age: *Don't raise your voice, and be polite.* People don't always respond well to polite.

I bring only certain students to him. I wouldn't waste Chef Henin's time bringing someone I didn't think was going to make it. We had a student, Reilly Meehan, preparing for the *Chaîne des Rôtisseurs*, the annual young *commis* competition. Reilly won the national and was on his way to the international competition. "Of all the people I'd like you to cook for to prepare, I want you to cook for Chef Henin."

He's nervous, because I'm telling him the stories. Reilly's cutting butter on the paper, and Chef is giving him a bunch of crap.

"Why would you ever do that? That's so dumb."

I told Reilly, "Those are the little things that someone like Henin will see that nobody else will see. Nobody else will even think about. Whether or not you think it's important, people on his level do. All these little tidbits separate the good from the great."

He mentored Reilly for that competition, gave us the extra push, and Reilly won the international Santa Rosa series. To this day, to my knowledge, he is the only American who won that competition. Chef Henin jokes with me later and says, "Of course, the only reason he won is because you guys came to me."

"Of course, Chef. There'd be no other reason why."

I've been in pursuit of the Master Chef certification: took the CMC exam in November 2014, completed the eight days, and finished the last part. I didn't get enough points, so I have to retake it. We were discussing the retake and for Chef, it's not just discussion, it's full-on illustration. He's grabbing things and putting them on the table and using things as examples. At his age—I've met plenty of people, and dare not name any names, but you get the toned-down approach: *Yeah, well you could do this or that, and would probably be okay.* It's much more subdued, canned, or generic. He goes into the teaching, and to a certain degree, I go back to being that young student again. *The master is talking.*

The first time I competed on an international team, they were bringing Chef Henin in to give us a last review. It was one of our big practices before going to Germany. Here I am, getting ready. I'd been on the team for a couple years now, on the international team as a professional. So, now he's coming back into my life. *They're bringing the Big Man back.* The guy is basically going to tell you how bad you're doing. To a certain degree, you feel confident. You see the refinements you've made over the past couple years. Still, Chef Henin is going to capture things. Sure enough, he comes in and asks, *Why are you doing that? How come you're doing that?* At that particular point as a professional, as a guy who's been doing it for a time, it's harder to take. By all means, you're always respectful and never going to argue with him. You listen, say, "Yes, Chef," but in your mind, you're a little bit like, *Really? I just worked on that for like two years and all the other chefs here are fine with it. Why all of a sudden is it not right?*

But then, you sit back and you remember who you are talking to. You remember the difference this person makes, so you go out and you make changes. You have that same feeling of—it's not fear by any means, because you know nothing is going to physically happen to you, you're not in danger—but you know your professional reputation is on the line. Someone can see through things that others can't see. You gotta be ready for him, do your best and go to bat. Sometimes you hit the ball, and sometimes you strike out.

Our mentoring styles are hard to compare. He's a European-based chef, and the thought process is different from how American-based chefs are, but I always keep him with me and the thoughts he has instilled. When I coach my culinary teams, I tell them: *I'm not here to be nice.* This is not the classroom. In the classroom I'm nice. I have to look at the positives. On the culinary team, we focus on the negatives. Focusing on the negatives is what is going to make you better. Compliments kill. They really, really do. Chef Henin only gave you a compliment when you truly deserved it. There wasn't any kind of courtesy compliment just to be nice, just a compliment if you did it right and knew you did it right. No, he's not going to be nice. I follow the same approach, and through that, positives will arise. You get your students ready by making sure they understand it's coming from the right place. It's never easy when someone keeps bringing up the negatives: *You did that wrong again. You did that wrong again. You did that wrong again.* He focused on making us better by telling us what we did wrong, not necessarily what we did right. He made us better, didn't just make us feel better. Modern mentoring is always looking at the positives. Just looking at the positives and complimenting somebody hurts them later, because life is still life. If you don't focus on the negatives to achieve your goals and be your best, you'll never get the other stuff that goes along with it.

That's kind of how it is. Students will make something and walk around, going to the different offices. The untrained culinary people, the assistants or secretaries will tell them how great it is. *Oh, that looks beautiful!* That's fine, but I just don't ever want a student to get the wrong idea. Let's face it; they get enough compliments in their homes.

"I bet your mom or boyfriend or girlfriend or wife or husband all say you're a great cook, right?"

They're like, "Oh yeah. Everybody's excited about it."

"Well, they're probably wrong, because if you were, you wouldn't need to be here. You're here to learn how to cook *professionally.*" People may have differences of opinion about food, of course, but professional cooking versus cooking at home are completely different worlds.

I rarely compete myself anymore; it's my students. It's that legacy in passing that on and watching my students grow. We just got back from the Culinary Olympics in Germany, where Chef Henin was part of the US culinary teams over the years. One of my students on the US culinary team was onstage getting their medal. I mean, wow! I'd done that: gotten up on stage, gotten my medal, and blah blah, but to see one of the people you've trained . . . wow! What a great thing. It's that circle you want to continue building. They're the ones who keep me going on that kind of stuff. They keep me sharp. You always hope they're going to be better than you.

What I love about Chef Henin is he's still there. He might be there in a smaller arena, but I still saw him at the most recent convention. He's not just there like an old-timer hanging around. He was there managing a booth for his company, Delaware North, walking around, shaking hands, discussing food, and giving people crap, being a part of things. That stamina of still showing up and having a presence is something a lot of us won't get to, for many different reasons: we don't take care of our health or we don't want to go anymore. There's a lot to be said about seeing someone who continues to fight the fight and be that presence. It's inspiring.

The Big Catch

Chef was strictly food—not payroll, not HR, not the babysitter, not the shrink. He was the chef.

—Kevin Doherty

Over a hundred years ago, on the corner of Delaware Avenue and North Street, in Buffalo, New York, a young business is born. From its humble beginnings grew a humble giant.

It all began with a simple idea based on a foundation of service. In 1915, brothers Marvin, Charles, and Louis Jacobs took the first step toward realizing the American dream of their immigrant parents by establishing a modest popcorn and peanuts vending business in Buffalo, N.Y.

Through hard work, dedication, and innovative thinking, that small business has grown into one of the largest and most successful hospitality companies in the world. The arc of our story spans generations and industries, but threaded throughout has been the kind of insight that's allowed us to see into what fans crave, travelers need, and people desire. It's been a century, in other words, of anticipating the next big thing.

At 100 years, Delaware North now celebrates a three billion-a-year industry, spanning the globe from the United States and Canada, England, Australia, Singapore, and beyond. The legacy endures today through Chairman Jeremy Jacobs—a son of one of the founding Jacobs brothers—and his three sons, Jerry, Lou, and Charlie, who are all company chief executive officers. In 2015, we celebrated the entrepreneurial spirit of the Jacobs family and ushered in the next century of dynamic growth and success.[1]

After eighty years, Delaware North (DN) executives decided it was time to make a major change. They invited Roland Henin to interview for the position of corporate chef. He was met with some resistance. *Why hire a French chef, some big shot CMC? Who needs that crap? People don't pay attention to the food. They're here to watch the game, roll the dice, or hike a canyon. Who cares if the food is gourmet standard or classically prepared?*

This was 1997, and back then, they may have had a valid point . . . but it turns out, people *do* care, and they *do* pay attention. Food is emotional; it anchors an experience. One of the Jacobs sons, Jerry, saw the future mission: bring the company *up*. The face of foodservice in these organizations—sports arenas, casinos, airports, and national parks and resorts—was changing, and Henin was hired to make that change.

When Chef Henin was hired to revolutionize the foodservice industry at DN, he understood the resistance, and he also understood that change was worth the

---

1   From Delaware North, www.delawarenorth.com, accessed May 2017

fight. This sentiment was summed up with Henin's trademark wit and candor (and butchered English) in his home run comment to Jerry Jacobs: *Jerry, I don't want to help keep knocking on door to get business. I want them to knock on my door.* Bringing this concept to DN was not revolutionary to Henin; it was business as usual. He was the man who would shepherd in Jerry Jacobs's mission.

"I thought when we hired him that he was an excellent choice, but Roland has proved to be flat-out the best chef I've ever worked with," said Bruce Fears, DN president in 2003. "With Chef Roland, it is all about the food, not about him or his attitude. I know it sounds clichéd, but he has taken our company to the next level."

Chef Henin's mission was to establish a foundation: develop the fundamentals of classical techniques and make sure DN executive chefs knew *how to cook and how to teach cooking.* The vision behind the mission was to instill a value—have chefs and cooks *care* about the mission. This was a much tougher sell. The culture of high volume and shortcuts begins at the bottom rung and pervades. In order to achieve his mission and vision, Chef Henin had to infiltrate their kitchens, into the nooks and crannies of each soul.

Sounds romantic, but how does one do that? One must travel a lot and constantly and be with one's people. That is what Roland Henin has done for the past twenty years. Until recently, Henin traveled over two hundred days per year visiting each facility and collaborating with not only each executive chef, but also their brigade. The advantage to this methodical approach is to have access to his mentees. These chefs, in turn, become the mentors for the next generation. The vision is about more than training chefs; it is about creating values. Culinary arts will be the next wave! Chef Henin believes if you invest in employees and invest in cuisine, you invest in your own future.

When faced with expansion and promotion, DN chooses to hire internally. Investing from the inside has pros and cons. It may be more difficult to develop chefs for certification, but in the long run it benefits the company. Executive chefs know their staff's strengths and limitations. The staff knows company culture, so there is less of a learning curve. Hopefully they repay the investment with loyalty and remain with DN, but if they do choose to leave, they have DN to thank. This good extends into their next venture.

SUSAN: *Why are there so few Certified Master Chefs (and Certified Master Pastry Chefs)?*

RGH: No one in the system is investing much in their preparation. In this business, you are always a teacher. You teach, coach, and groom your people. When I taught, I did okay. I was rough around the edge and demanding, but this is what you do in your daily life—constantly teach people. DN is privately owned. This company is one of the best to invest in its people to prepare chefs for certification. This exists very little in our business. Most want a quick return on their investment. As far as I know, there is no other company, organization, restaurant, other than DN, who offers this kind of preparation, Practicals, and events for chefs. Even the CIA doesn't do that [for their chefs]. They may offer the certification tuition and ACF membership fees. If you pass the tests, you will proctor in the future. DN gets it back—an investment in themselves.

The industry is notorious for not doing much. When you ask somebody to pay for your ACF membership or to go to the conventions, they bark, "BLLA-LAAAYAYAYAYYYAAHHH!!!" DN is a model that should be used more often. If our industry did, we'd have more Master Chefs. Everyone would be teaching, from left to right.

SUSAN: *Were you the catalyst for DN?*

RGH: I think, to a certain extent, yes. I was with DN for twenty years. At the time I came, people thought, *What, a Master Chef? What do we need a Master Chef? And, a French one, at that! We are popcorn! We are peanuts!* Yes, it was a popcorn-pretzel-beer company. But since then, the face of foodservice in these venues has changed tremendously. In the last ten years, the customer wants good food. In the park, they want healthy food. They go there for the pure air and the exercise, and they don't want to put garbage in their body. We've moved to more local, sustainable, organic . . . more *what's good for you.*

There are a lot of things we've changed in the past twenty years, and it wasn't that easy. Don't get me wrong, it was a constant battle, but I could take it. I had wide shoulder and thick spine and hard head and I didn't quit. I didn't lie down when I was beat up by all those people who wanted the short time, the short-term vision of *we want the return today, we want the number today–this week, this month. We don't care what's going to happen in a few years; we want it now.* You can't blame middle management—they are paid to protect the "bottom line," and in fact, they receive bonuses for saving money, so it's in their best interest to not invest in the long-term development. Sure, it's been a battle with the middle management, but the top people are always behind me and supportive. The big guys upstairs running the show realize that in the foodservice, they have to come up to snuff to what is happening in the rest of the world. That is why, twenty years ago, somebody hired me to realize, *hey, we're going to need that kind of help, if we want to be ruling to where we want to be.*

I developed a culinary council. The food and beverage departments from every area would get together and discuss our food programs and our challenges. How can we unify? Their food was just terrible, so we improved that. We eliminated the free lobster and crab legs, which are expensive. It doesn't do much. We made better food.

I developed some regional chefs, administered mandatory training and then, certification. The first thing I did was to develop sanitation class. In these restaurants, we had the food-borne illness . . . visitors got that everywhere, all the time, my God. We held sanitation class for four hours at a time. We had to pay the chefs and cooks for their time in class. We also needed people to fill their shifts—extra labor. I had people against me because this would cost. The general manager, the president of Yosemite, came to me and said, "What's the return on the investment?!"

I said, "I can't tell you until you tell me how much the return is when we have somebody who is sick, and we have to take them to the hospital, or we have to comp them food and lodging. What is the suffering of those people worth? I mean, it's not pretty. It's not nice, and it's painful!" These people don't deserve to be treated this way! They deserve to have good healthy food.

What's the return on the investment? It's true, it cost money to educate . . . we'd have to pay those people for mandatory training, so we had thirty hours by twenty-nine chefs in the first training session on sanitation. Calculate thirty hours by twenty-nine people . . . that's nine hundred hours at whatever they made, fifteen to twenty-five bucks an hour. That was a lot of money over a period of time. *What's the return on the investment?*

The return on the investment was that, through education, we basically eliminated food-borne illness on our property. We have one now, one in a blue moon, a mistake . . . somebody left a sandwich in the back window of their car, and then they ate it, or the altitude or the alcohol got them sick, but not our food. The middle management, they were not receptive. They didn't think like that. *What do you need sanitation class for? Chefs just want to get out of work.* They didn't realize it cost them more to have people sick than it cost to educate. They'd ask, "Can you write policy?"

I say, "No, I cannot write policy. That's not going to affect anything like this. We need to *educate*. We need to teach them to understand what they must do to not make people sick: cool down your stock and sauce; bring back to a boil, when you reheat; wash your hands, and all that kind of stuff."

The first month I was in Yosemite, we had suspected food-borne illness at least half a dozen a week. Aaah, God. It was terrible. People were sick. It was sad. We had to change that, and the best way was education. It took some doing . . . but now, everybody is okay. Everybody is on board.

SUSAN: *Sometimes management will fight all the way but then give in and even later, glorify it!*

RGH: Jerry wanted to advertise the certification, so he could market over the competition: *all our salaried and sous-chefs are professionally certified by the ACF.* It's a big deal! Sure it costs money [laughs]: they have to take class; they have to do the Practical. But it's going to be a big plus when you go to advertise. It took a helluva time for middle management to accept that. It was okay because I was strong . . . I could kick butt when it was needed. There is still a small remain of that kind of thinking, but gradually, most are seeing the meaning of that. Their numbers are better because they don't have to spend that money on fixing things that had been done badly: we don't have to pay all those fees for doctor, flying to a hospital after the park clinic . . . *comping, comping* . . . avoid a lawsuit, all kinds of things. We effectively eliminated all food-borne illnesses in our national park. And now, the chefs and sous-chefs are also becoming better culinarians!

It took some doing to change the concept. The staff in the park, especially a park like Yosemite, you have all kinds of people. They are not cook, not food people. They are mountain climber, rock climber, or they are trying to escape something or whatever it is. Doesn't matter. Your staff is not always qualified, so it took some doing to change the concept of getting more professional people. We got better staffing too, instead of just hiring somebody who was driving by or running out of gas. We would hire them because they were handy, but they were not what we needed. When I first implemented the Practical for all the salaried chef positions, HR said I was never satisfied. The test took four hours of cooking, and only two out of five would make it. HR would say, "We can't get people good enough for you!" What can I say? It's your job to get them. I test them out, but they say I was too demanding in the Practical. That's still part of the fighting, you have to go against, in your own town. You know what I am saying . . . wide shoulder, thick spine. It all worked out okay.

The Corporate Chef: Delaware North

If I questioned Chef, "Am I doing it right?" He'd respond, "I don't know. You tell me."
—Chris Matta

When you have a chance to meet Yoda, you better go and say hi.
—Peter Afouxinedes

Even if you're one of the best, there's always something that you can learn.
—David Coombs

Henin is brutally honest. Honesty is to help you move along. If you don't want to learn and grow, don't ask.
—Mark Mistriner

Percy Whatley

Vice President, Food & Beverage, Delaware North Parks & Resorts

Chef Roland explained that I should proceed with caution; advancement too quickly could be detrimental. Looking back on that part of my career, I was far from ready!

PERCY: I met Chef Roland in May of 1998. I had just returned to Yosemite after my two-year culinary program at the CIA and a brief few months of employment in Lake Tahoe directly after graduating in October of 1997. I was hired back in Yosemite as junior sous-chef at the Ahwahnee Hotel. I was twenty-nine years old when I met Chef, who had been hired as the corporate chef of Yosemite. I did not know the name, but having recently come from culinary school, I was certainly well aware of what those three letters, "CMC," at the end of a chef's name meant.

My first kitchen encounter was a few days later. I was serving pork tenderloin for the nightly special with tomatillo *verde* sauce, sweet potato purée, and sautéed summer squash (why can I still remember this nineteen years later?), and he gave me a quick demo on plate presentation before the staff pre-shift. It was a mellow encounter; he was just doing his mentor thing, and this continued every time he walked into our kitchen. There was always something he could and would show our team, a little nugget of learning, on any given day.

I was interested in being ACF-certified that first year. He walked me through the process of the application and verified that I had my certification "packet" complete. This was back in the day where all you had to do was apply and take the written exam; there was no cooking practical exam as part of the process. The only level you had to cook for was the CMC. I breezed through the written exam, signed the application, and was good to go as Certified Sous Chef (CSC). He took notice of my desire to continue to learn and grow and move my professional life forward. He gave advice on what it means to develop oneself in a profession. If you needed your car fixed, would you go to the shop that had the sign stating certified mechanic on duty, or would you go to the next shop that had no certifications? The choice is easy.

Fast-forward a year-and-a-half later, to August 1999. I had the opportunity to take over as the executive chef of the Wawona Hotel, a small, seasonal hotel twenty-five miles to the south of Yosemite Valley, and I seized it. I had my first child on the way and needed to further my career and compensation, as life dictates at times. Chef Roland explained that I should proceed with caution; I was not fully prepared for this step, and I should continue to learn cooking at this stage of my life. Advancement too quickly could be detrimental. I shrugged this off, thinking about my family and money from a promotion. Looking back on that part of my career, I was *far* from ready, and if I were to run that kitchen now, it would be completely different! I offered fine dining in a place that was not built for it and the guests were not expecting it.

During this time, I moved to the next step in the certification process, Certified Chef de Cuisine. In 2003, I had the opportunity to return to the Ahwahnee as the executive sous-chef. In 2005, I was honored with the appointment to executive chef. This was another step in having to overcome the "Roland G. Henin hurdle." He did not want me to take this step . . . he said I was not ready, again. Our organizational chart does not give him that ability to flatly state the answer "no"; this decision lies in the hands of the property general manager. I was supported by the GM, but not by Chef Henin. This, again, is another scenario where reflection clarifies. I was not ready, not by a long shot. Those first two years were very, very difficult. I simply worked my ass off to overcome my weaknesses. I took Dale Carnegie classes for leadership. I competed for my first time in 2006. I took classes at the CIA Greystone, and worked hard to achieve the ProChef Level III certification, as well as ACF Certified Executive Chef (CEC). By 2007, I was in much better shape, able to build a great team around me and finally able to get my head above water.

In late 2007, Chef called me on a random day. He stated that he was given the opportunity to coach the Bocuse d'Or USA team. Gavin Kaysen was a regular guest chef at our Chef's Holidays, so I had a lead on what this competition was all about. Especially now that chefs Thomas and Daniel were involved, things were going to change in that arena. During this call, Chef Henin encouraged me to apply to compete. He told me I can cook, and I deserve to be a part of this. I was so honored by this compliment and he certainly recognized my journey over the last couple of years. Maybe it was all of the extra effort that I took in developing my skills over the course of the almost ten years we had worked together. In November 2007, I was called by the Bocuse d'Or USA and selected to be a part of this amazing competition. Now is when things get pretty interesting. . . .

I had three months to prepare for the competition—not much time. Chef Henin came for a couple of practice sessions to observe and offer insight. On the first session, he blasted our performance: fish was overcooked; garnishes were garbage; flavors did not stand out; shitty, shitty, shitty! This was my first experience of an angry Chef Roland. I wasn't sure how to handle it; all this time we had worked together, this side of him never reared its head before! Next session, the same thing: "No! Not good enough! You have to think about the *message* you are trying to tell the tasting judges! What is your food trying to *say*? What cooking are you doing to make the flavors better? You don't have it right!" And off he goes, without any more words of wisdom. He was not about to answer those questions for you, no spoon-feeding . . . no sirree. *Perplexed* is a good description of the emotional reaction, when these encounters occur with Chef Henin. It takes your breath away, and the best medicine is a healthy reflection.

Without spending too much time on my 2008 Bocuse experience, I was a disaster. It did not go well. Do I look fondly on the experience? Yes, in some ways, but there was a lot of unfinished business. I didn't truly "get it" until I failed miserably and reflected on the experience.

In 2009, I reapplied to the competition and was selected again. Armed with a better understanding of what could be accomplished in that little kitchen and with the given equipment, I set out to do things at a higher level. When Chef Henin made himself available to observe a practice session, I was absolutely welcoming to the idea. It was no different, even though my food was at a higher place; his reaction to it was the same low-level miserableness. *Is it good enough?* I was armed with a few answers this time, but that sent him into a frenzy. I spent a lot of time over the last two years researching platters and presentations of previous high-level practitioners of Bocuse d'Or, in Lyon. When I brought this up, he did not even want to hear it. Angrily, he would say "Why do you want to do what has already been done?" Oh my! How deeply true was that? Where does he get this wisdom? And why don't I have a shred of it, after *twelve* years working with this man? That interaction set me up to achieve the Best Meat Presentation for the Bocuse d'Or USA competition. I was inches away from the podium, but also proud of this prize. It showed that I was finally "getting it" . . . a little.

Over the course of the next two years, I continued to pursue competition efforts in the ACF arena. There was talk about a formal Delaware North nomination to support pursuit of the Certified Master Chef exam. I knew I would be supported if I showed interest; I just wondered if I could succeed. This exam is nothing short of unachievable to almost 90 percent of those who take it. The formal agreement came in 2011 and my three-year roller-coaster ride on the Roland G. Henin Express began. This journey was full of surprises, tears of both joy and frustration, more perplexity, laughs, quiet despair, sleepless nights, happy esprit de corps moments, and respectful soul-jabbing.

Chef Henin always signs the annual Christmas card, "In Good Cooking." There is nothing more important than that statement as it relates to my friend, colleague, and mentor. I would not be who I am today without some of the influences he has bestowed upon me.

William Bennett

Executive Chef, Corral de Tierra Country Club

*We worked long hours into the night, just goofy-tired. I couldn't get
enough of it, and thought, If this is what professional cooking is,
I want more of it! After working with him that day, I would go anywhere he told me to go to do anything he told me to do.*

WILLIAM: I took a job with Delaware North in 1998 at a conference center,
my first job as an executive chef. I got a call from the GM, who said the company
wanted to send me to New York for an important dinner. Their corporate chef
was going to be there, a well-known French-trained chef. I said, "Wow, that'd be
kind of fun." I was excited; this was my first experience where a company "flew
me out there"—paid for my flight, meals, and everything. I would help do a dinner for about 450 people in Niagara Falls, at another kitchen that DN operated.

I had never met Roland or had experience with a chef of that level. That
weekend was the hardest, most high-pressure cooking that I had ever done up to
that point . . . and [laughs] probably even since. It was the only time in my life,
cooking in the kitchen, when I was so nervous and stressed and freaked out that
I was just holding back the vomit. I thought I was going to throw up for a good
half an hour.

Chef was super intense. We spent three days preparing for the event. All the
problems that could happen when you're doing an event in a new place where
you've never been, with people you've never worked with, happened: people
didn't show up; ingredients didn't show up; there were all kinds of issues, from
lack of facilities to equipment, and he battled through every one of them. The
night of the dinner, we had more people not show up. It was a huge event, with
fireworks and a huge tent overlooking the Falls, and a separate tent for dessert.
Two kitchens were attached to the main tent.

The night of the event, staff didn't show up, and we didn't have enough
chefs. He came to me. "You're going to be in charge of one kitchen, and I'm
going to be in charge of the other. Come with me, right now. I'll tell you what
I want and how it goes." He put me in charge of one kitchen that plated up
around 250 of the meals; simultaneously, he would be on the other side of the
tent, plating up on his side. It was the most exhilarating thing for me to have
the guy pick me out of the four to five other chefs who were there and to have

responsibility. From that day on, working with him in that capacity, he invigorated me toward being more of a professional chef and challenging myself.

That night was frantic. The beef Wellington in the oven wasn't done yet at the time of service. He had to decide on whether to serve the salad now that he was planning to serve after the beef. He ran through the kitchen with the towels flying and saying, "Salad salad salad now! *Serve the salad now!*" Just running through and everyone was looking up, like, *Who the hell is that guy?*

We switched gears and had to change the whole thing around. My stomach was turning, I was sweating and shaking, and I was thinking, *How am I going to get this done? This guy is crazy!* He put so much pressure on me and I had just met him four days ago! It pushed me to my absolute limits—showed me what I am capable of and what it takes to do those kinds of things. From then on, after working with him that day, I would go anywhere he told me to go, do anything he told me to do; I was like . . . probably one of his best soldiers, to be honest. I still feel that way. If I ever have an opportunity to work with him again, I'd drop what I'm doing.

Some guys were put off by his intensity. The closer you got to him, the more intense it was. They were like, *I better keep my distance, or else he's going to make me do things that I won't be able to do,* or, *I don't want to do that much work.* We were working about seventeen hours a day. I loved it. I would have worked nineteen or twenty or twenty-four. And he was there with us the entire time. He didn't say, "Here's a list—do it, get it done, and I'll see you in the morning." He was the last guy to leave the kitchen. He was the first guy there in the morning. To watch a guy in his sixties work full-tilt over twelve or fourteen hours a day . . . he could do twice as much work as me, and I'm half his age! Everything he did was spot-on. If this sixty-something guy can stay on his feet and work to this level, there's no reason why I shouldn't be able to. People would complain and I'd say, "Your feet are tired? Look at *that* guy. He's twice your age. I'm sure his feet hurt. His back is tired and his knees hurt, and he's not going to stop or slow down. Or complain." I thought that was the best thing ever. I guess it showed in my enthusiasm, my respect for him, and my work. He saw that in me that, of all the people there.

I think back and wonder, *Why didn't we just bring in more people? Why didn't we buy a different product?* It's that uncompromising commitment to doing it the right way . . . at literally *all costs*: you don't sleep; you don't eat regular meals; you don't get a phone call. You are there for the one single full purpose, and that was different. The seriousness of it was different for me. I liked that single-mindedness—*you're going to get the right product, no matter what. You're going to handle it the way it needs to be handled, no matter what. If it takes one hour or ten, it is what it is.*

That's what you're here for. He was real clear about that. Some people didn't want to put in the effort and commitment to work up to that level.

SUSAN: *How do you think the night went, then?*

WILLIAM: We served a French-style meal: an appetizer course, then the meat course. After the meat, it's traditional to eat your roughage—your greens to wash everything down—and then move on to the dessert. He planned to serve beef Wellington, followed by the salad course, with these delicate little greens all stuffed in these little Parmesan baskets that [laughs] you had to make, one-by-one. And the meat, with a propane oven, outdoors, didn't cook as fast as it should have. In a dining room with four hundred–plus people waiting, it was going to take another fifteen minutes to finish the beef, and then it should rest and everything. So even though the menu was on the table saying, "beef first and then salad," he switched it around, in order to make sure that the beef was properly cooked, to assure the quality of the food. This required putting the hot plates away, getting the other plates out, and resetting the entire thing for ser-vice—ten minutes of frantic running around. With the available staff we had to plate up that night, he kept two-thirds of them and threw the derelicts at me. He put me to the test, seeing if I could get it done. I thought, *Why does he have, like, twelve people, and I have seven?* He would run through—and I mean, literally run through this massive tented dining room. He would run through the kitchen, saying, "LIKE THIS! LIKE THIS! LIKE THIS!!" Not screaming in a bad way, but vocal and loud. He kept coming through there, while I was watching the plates and checking on everything. He's running through, barking these orders out, and I'm saying, "Yes, Chef. I got this. I got that."

There were some culinary students there from NFCI. Chef and I are yelling to each other, back and forth, and this girl—she didn't look real serious about anything in life—turns to me, and says, "Who is that asshole?"

I said, "Hey, hey, *hey*! He's in charge! He's a Certified Master Chef! Watch your mouth. You gotta show some respect, here."

She says, "I don't care *who* he is; he's an asshole!"

"Well . . . you're going to have to learn how to deal with these people, if you're going to want to be a decent chef, someday."

SUSAN: *I guess that's why I'm interviewing you, instead of her.*

WILLIAM: From then on, whenever there was a DN event that required atten-tion, like if they were looking to gain another contract, he would set up these elaborate meals over the course of a few days. It was like a big long meeting with the DN people. He would fly out there and invite this team, and I was lucky enough to be one of them. You go out there, cook with him, and execute these meals. We'd show up someplace where we'd never been before, go in and assess the kitchen. We did a lot of cleaning, scrubbing, and organizing. He refused to work anywhere that was dirty, messy, and unsanitary, so we spent half of the first day cleaning and scrubbing: the floors and walls; inside the refrigerator; the prepping tables; behind the tables; the shelf underneath the tables we were working on. We cleaned everything that we were going to come in contact with— completely scrubbed and sanitized and straightened up. That's how we started.

After a couple of these trips, you learned the procedure and how he liked things. We would get flown into wherever—Florida or Ohio or New York. We'd land and connect, get the menu going, and get the stuff in the kitchen. We were like a military operation. We'd walk in and these cooks would be there. They didn't know who we were, and we didn't know who they were, and we'd say, "Hey, I need you to come over here, clean this and clean that," and they'd say, "Who the hell are you? You're not my boss!" We would basically command the kitchen and the crew. You're working with this guy who is a world-class level chef, and you show up at a place with guys making food who didn't know culinary operations—a bunch of stoners on their summer job at Jones Beach. In twenty-four hours, you'd try to turn them into something acceptable to a Certified Master Chef.

SUSAN: *What impressions stand out?*

WILLIAM: He loves the camaraderie of the kitchen. At the Asilomar Conference Grounds, these older Portuguese cooks had been there for about forty years. These guys never had much professional training, but they'd been cooking their entire lives . . . they had these cooking *instincts*. Roland became friendly with them and absolutely loved this one guy, Eddie da Silva, the chef of the kitchen for many years. When things got computerized, Eddie couldn't do the things they needed, so they hired me as the chef to come up in this new company while Eddie "the rock" stayed on. He had the history and knew all the visitor's preferences.

I wasn't sure how Roland would handle those guys . . . he'd come in and they'd be a little sloppy and he'd jump all over them. Instead, he immediately recognized how special they were. He'd call and ask, "How's Eddie? How's Roberto? How are my buddies down there?" Maybe because he was French and they were Portuguese . . . they were working in another country. They talked a lot about the food that they grew up with and their kitchen experiences. He couldn't get enough of hanging out with those two Portuguese guys. It was another side of him: he could be so demanding, but then super friendly.

He is such a humble guy! It's funny . . . that first weekend, he mentioned Thomas Keller. I was trying to be up on the food world. Thomas Keller had opened a restaurant in Napa Valley that was getting attention. People called him the best chef in the United States and here this Roland guy I just met tells me, "Oh, I gave Thomas his first job and was a mentor to him." I was like, "Yeah, right. Sure you did." [Laughs] I thought it was a joke. *Thomas is the best chef in the United States! What are you talking about? You gave him a job, like he was a summer cook? What?*

Then my wife and I go to this bookstore in Berkeley. *The French Laundry Cookbook* just came out, and I bought it. I asked my wife if she would drive home so I could look through it. I am flipping through the book, and in a beginning section, there is this whole paragraph where he is comparing Roland to Zeus. I read through it and jumped up out of my seat. "Holy crap! He keeps talking about Roland! I just worked with him two weeks ago! Look at this!" I turned to the index, and under "Henin" there are multiple pages. It kind of hit me at that point, like, *Wow. He really did do all these things with Thomas Keller. Look at all these other things he's done for all these other people.*

He never hangs his hat on that stuff, never puts it out there: *Oh, look at me. I'm a big chef.* He never talks like that. Especially now, where everybody wants to get their face in front of the camera, his work speaks louder than the publicity. Years from now, when he's not around, people will look back on him and say he was more than he ever let on . . . it's that business of being humble and not just trying to get all that attention. I handle myself the same way. If one day I am the best cook in the world, I'm not going to put it on a billboard and I'm not going to have people address me that way. He's a one-in-a-million kind of guy, but he'll never tell you that.

When he told me about Thomas Keller and I didn't believe it, he just shrugged it off. Then when I saw the book a couple weeks later, I realized he's a lot more than he'll let on. Nowadays, all chefs want is all the attention. It's annoying. I treat it the same way, when his name comes up.

"Oh, I worked for Roland for a while."

"Oh, geez! How was *that?*"

"It was the best time of my life. It was the best cooking I ever did."

I had those four years with him, and it's more than most people are ever going to get to be around the guy. It meant a lot to me, but I'm not going to toot my own horn about it.

He can be kind of gruff when you meet him. If you don't play ball and do things correctly, you're gonna get the horns. One time, he flew a bunch of us out to an event. There was this new DN chef, and Henin liked to take the new people to these things. They fly us all out there and put us up in these hotels, feeding us and everything. The first day on the job, this guy unrolls his knife roll, takes his stone out and starts sharpening his knives. Roland's looking at him, and I could tell, *Oh boy. Here we go.* He went up and asks the guy, "What the hell are you doing?"

The chef thought he was going to impress Roland. "Oh, I always like to keep my knives sharp. I want to make sure they're nice and sharp for today."

Henin just lit the guy up. "Do you think I flew you all the way across country so that you can stand here and sharpen your knives?! That's something you should have done, before you got here! You're not prepared! Put that away!"

The new chef says, "Chef, my knives aren't sharp." The guy was arguing with him a little bit, and they went at it. When that's going on, you just keep your head down . . . [Laughs]

This was a treat to be able to come out here and work with all these people. You should be better prepared than that. When you see that happening, you make sure everything you're doing is right and everything is in the right spot. You don't want to be the next guy on the chopping block. So everybody went back to their respective jobs, and about two months later, he was just gone. I imagine they had more than that one run-in.

SUSAN: *Compare your mentoring style to Chef Henin's.*

WILLIAM: I don't operate the same as Roland, in the kitchen. I'm a little bit mellower as a person, probably a little more patient with people. Let's say I peeled a tomato. He would come over and say, "This isn't a peeled tomato."

I'd say, "What are you talking about? There's no peel on them."

He's like, "No no no . . ." And he'd scrape the peels, themselves! He'd scrape the back of the peels off with his knife, and he'd show me this little bit of red on the edge of his knife and he'd ask, "What is that?"

"What is what?"

"What's that, on the knife?"

"It looks like tomato."

He'd say, "There you go. Exactly." And, he just walked away.

I thought, *What is the guy telling me? I don't understand this.*

Then, I had to go approach him and say, "Chef, I don't know understand what—I want to do this the right way, and I don't understand what you're getting at."

He said, "What was on the knife?"

"It was tomato! Obviously!"

"You're right; it's tomato. Is the tomato supposed to be on the knife or on the tomato?"

Probably on the tomato.

You would have to figure it out on your own. Maybe I am more forgiving and [laughs] maybe give people more chances . . . but when you're in the kitchen, *being* the chef in the kitchen, everybody should look to you, respect you, and know that you're the hardest working guy in the kitchen. You can handle any job. I've washed dishes side-by-side with Roland. I've swept floors, scrubbed rusty pipes in the walk-in refrigerator. Just because you can cut a filet and cook it to temperature doesn't mean you're a chef. Leading by example is huge. When I do something, I'm trying to do it my best *and* better than yesterday.

SUSAN: *You mentioned your wife. Do you have children?*

WILLIAM: I have two girls, twelve and eight. I tell my younger daughter, "You met a famous chef one time. He was holding you in his arms, and you pooped all over him."

He was holding on to my daughter, saying, "Oh, she's so cute!" This and that, and I heard this loud rumbling.

"Uhh . . . Chef, I think you need to give her back to me. You won't like what's going to happen."

He holds her out like she's a hot potato.

Once, we had trouble. I was talking to him. "She's not sleeping much, crying at night . . ."

He says, "When I had my son, I used to open the bottom drawer of the dresser. We put the blankets in there, nice and soft. At 6:00 at night we put him in the drawer and close the drawer. At eight in the morning, when we want to get up, I open the drawer."

It was like, "*Whaat?*" [Laughs]

He says, "You can't let the kids run your life. You have to do what you need to do. They need to oblige."

It was one of those Roland parenting suggestions.

I'll sum his philosophy up with something he'd often say: *You did well today. Pat yourself on the back, but don't pat yourself too hard, because you probably could have done it a little better.*

Ambarish Lulay

Department Chef, Hospitality and Tourism Management, Purdue University

You do that task from start to finish, and you do it well,
and you apply it to everything. I always want to do my best
when he's around—or even when he is not around.
He is the VOICE IN MY HEAD, and he will be, forever.

AMBARISH: We're talking about Chef Henin . . . one of those all-pervasive topics, where you don't know where to stop and you don't know where to begin!

I was a culinary student at Kendall College around 1999, cooking for a dozen people at the home of the dean of the college. A gentleman walks into the kitchen. I did not know who this person was. I was in that space where, *I am a fearless student and know everything about everything.*

This gentleman walks up to me and asks, "Do you need any help? I can chop some parsley. I know how to chop parsley."

I thought, *Oh my God, it's one of those guests who want to know everything about the kitchen.* I'm like, "No, I'm okay, thank you."

He had the meal, and everything was good. He gave me a card, which said *Roland Henin*. I put the card away.

The next day, I am talking to a couple of my instructors: "This guy walks into my kitchen and he wants to chop parsley . . . it was strange. He gave me his card, and it said *Roland Henin*."

The instructors were both sitting down, and they both stood up.

"Chef Henin was there?"

"I guess. Do you know him?"

The stories came out when he was an instructor at the CIA, so I realized that he was somebody special. I met him a couple more times. Chef told me to call him after I graduate if I would like to work for Delaware North; instead, I went to work in Europe. When I returned, I still had not called Chef. Then, an opportunity came—chef de cuisine at the Ahwahnee Hotel. I flew out there to do my Practical test. I didn't realize Chef Henin would be watching over my shoulder for five hours as I cooked. By this time, I had learned enough about Chef to know that I was terrified.

I meet Chef in the lobby at 7:00 a.m., and he wants to sit down for breakfast.

"Oh, no, Chef. No breakfast."

"What, you don't eat breakfast? How are you going to start a good day?"

Little things like that were strange at the beginning: Chef Henin looks at our profession as a *holistic* thing. It is a profession that consumes you, if you do it right: *How are you going to have a fruitful day in the kitchen if you don't sit down for breakfast?* His discipline translates into everything: what time he goes to bed; when he wakes up; all those little things. HOW DO YOU ORGANIZE YOUR LIFE? We haven't even talked about organizing your cooking station or your *mise en place*. It's about *what kind of personal qualities it takes to be a decent quality chef.* That's when I started thinking about these things. When you're a young cook, you are reckless. You work hard, put in fourteen, sixteen, eighteen hours a day, and you stay up late at night. You don't think about these things. Chef is right there to remind you about all these things. So, in my formative years as a cook, he was already an influence.

I managed to pass the Practical. Chef laid out a detailed review of the test, and there was an HR interview afterward. Me being me—you know, stupid—I said during that interview, "What is there left to interview? I have just completed a cooking test with Chef Henin! If you look at those notes, it will tell you everything about me, and what I can cook, and what I cannot do." We had a little encounter there; this was obviously not the right thing to say in an interview, but not many people understand him unless they are in the field or they work with him.

SUSAN: *How did he influence you?*

AMBARISH: The basics are the basics. Fundamentals don't change. Before you start a project, have your prep list done. Before you encounter your day, have a priority list. During that period, I worked on traveling DN projects. Chef would fly down for the Bracebridge Dinners—eight traditional Christmas Dinners hosted by Ahwahnee. They are a four-hour theater performance accompanied by a nine-course meal. Chef was always responsible for the fish course. I would make certain that Chef had his *commis*, his setup ready and recipes in order, because the first thing he does when he comes in is test the recipe.

Let's say we are making lobster terrine. By this time, I knew the format. No, I should rephrase that: by this time, I did *not* know the format. Chef comes in, and I pull out the recipe.

"Here is the recipe we are thinking of making."

He makes a couple tweaks, and he says, "Okay. We got to make a test."

"Oh. Can't we just make the terrine?"

"No. If you're going to go ahead and make eighty lobster terrines, shouldn't you test one first?"

Thank God for this. We test one. We fix the mistakes. We make another one. By the third terrine, Chef approves. We sit down for a few hours and create an elaborate prep schedule for the next few days. We will make eighty terrines: lobster, poached gently, split open, and cleaned; filled with a mousse of lobster roe, wrapped in spinach; roe mousse went into the middle of a scallop mousse studded with lobster claws; the whole terrine was set in a mold lined with thin strips of Nantes carrots from a local farm in Madera, California. It was amazing. We multiplied the recipe, tracked the production schedule, and went through the whole process. Three people worked eight hours a day for six days just making sheets of spinach leafs: stemming the spinach leaf; blanching the spinach leaf in perfectly boiling water; shocking it in ice water; dabbing all of the liquid out of the leaf; laying it down flat, on a twelve-leaf by twelve-leaf square, so we can perfectly wrap the lobster in it, all of the leaves going the same way. When the terrine was done, it was close to perfect.

Until then, you could have asked me what "perfect" means, and I would have given you some cocky answer. It's one of those elusive things, but when I saw it happen, I was able to identify it. Working with Chef, you break everything down into smaller, manageable units, you do each one of those units perfectly, and you are going to get an end result . . .

When Chef came down for the holidays, we would slice the tenderloin of beef, a traditional main course. In feeding four hundred people, four lines would put up one hundred plates each. Again, everything perfectly organized, because we have done this dinner for years, and we have a system. Chef adored the system and was so pleased to come down and work with us. It was a pretty large event! It consumed about thirty days' worth of our lives and also mixed in holidays including Thanksgiving, Christmas, and New Year's Eve. It was one big stretch, and we loved it, to say the least. We're all suckers for punishment, aren't we? That's why we meet people like Chef Henin, because, we are suckers for punishment.

We were invited to cook at the James Beard House, in New York City: the executive chef from the Ahwahnee, Chef Roland, our pastry chef, and me. We did a California menu—heirloom tomatoes and things like that. This was late fall and we had wonderful produce available to us, so we had it all shipped out. We prepped our food the day before at a catering company. This kitchen was full of people—being New York City, it was elbow to elbow . . . but nonetheless, we were prepping. Chef was over there in the corner. He wasn't too excited about the quality of the lettuce greens we had now, after shipping. He proceeded to shock those lettuce greens in ice water and go through each one—de-stem each one and make sure they were perfect for this party of 110 people. He spent quite a bit of time doing that!

We were in the other corner of the kitchen, prepping constantly. In California, we have the Diestel Turkey Ranch. We made turkey roulades for our main course—organic turkey breast, pounded and stuffed with a turkey sausage with dried fruits and nuts. I went by the textbook! We were cooking at the Beard House, a once-in-a-lifetime opportunity. I prepared the roulades in California, wrapped in Saran Wrap and tied in butcher's twine. The butcher's twine is tied at about an inch and a half apart. They were cooked *sous vide*. We would finish them off last-minute with whole butter on the grill to a nice, golden-brown color on the outside and then slice them.

Our day started at the farmers market and then by 7:00 a.m. we were in the kitchen, spending the entire day prepping and making sure that everything was organized, racked up, and ready to go. Seven thirty in the evening comes around. Chef is getting antsy, because he wants to go to dinner. He's picky about sitting down and eating when you have long days—again, that breakfast thing. He wants everybody to stop prep at a decent time, sit down, and eat a proper meal, always with a salad. There should always be a salad in there. But, when you're in the zone, just hammering away at a list, that's the last thing on your mind.

I had just pulled out those turkey roulades. He looks at them and says, "These are not tied tight enough."

I'm looking at the clock. It's a good fourteen hours into the day. "Okay! I'm going to re-tie them."

He says, "What? You're going to re-tie them *now?*"

I found myself saying, "Yeah. Absolutely. Tomorrow is our dinner. These roulades are not right. I'm going to re-tie them, right now."

He stood there, and he watched me for the next hour and a half as I re-tied those twenty roulades and got them as tight as they needed to be. I removed all the twine from before and got new twine on there, an inch apart (or half an inch apart . . . I can't remember now), but they were re-tied and they were tight. This time. As I look back on this now, I think, there are a lot of times when there is no compromise. If you want to do something right, it doesn't matter what time of the day it is or how many people are coming to dinner. If you're going to do it right, you're going to do it right, no matter *what*. At any cost. You got to do the best you can at that point in time. These lessons are right there around the corner, but sometimes we hide behind our work and choose not to notice them. After ninety minutes, he says to me, "You could have saved on twine. The way you were tying it is inefficient. If you had to tie more, you would have wasted a lot of twine." I was cutting the twine to the desired size and proceeding to tie it in a sort of basket. *But he waited until I was done.*

Yes, I learned . . . that was my second chapter of working with Chef. We had a wonderful time at that dinner. The next day, we were working in the James Beard Kitchen, a wonderful place. Chef is poaching eggs, which is, again, a treat to watch. He's got his poaching station all set. We brought in farm-fresh eggs from California, with beautiful marigold-colored yolks that were absolutely delicious. The eggs are all cracked into thirty bowls, as he's going to poach for 110 people. We had a *commis* who would poach the eggs, but Chef was excited to poach them. We set up the station: eggs cracked in bowls and a pot of water, eight to eleven inches deep, with vinegar.

"How much vinegar?"

"Until the water smells like vinegar."

These are things you learn in school, maybe, but to put them into action each time you do something . . . that is what's important, no matter how small the task. His poaching water is the perfect temperature, and his ice bath, and then, all set? The station is ready to go? Yes, Chef!

He starts poaching those eggs, one at a time. "Where are the shears?" Shears! There are little wisps of egg whites that come off those eggs. He wants to trim those so that all the edges are round and matched perfectly. You can just visualize him standing there, poaching the eggs and trimming the albumen so that they all look perfectly oval. Then, he lays them on a towel. These are things that make him who he is. He is the product of all these little things, done perfectly. That's his philosophy, and that's what he lives by. The quote that comes to mind is by Fernand Point: "Cooking is an accumulation of details done to perfection."

SUSAN: Did you have dinner after you tied the roulades?

AMBARISH: We *did* have dinner! I believe we did have plans to eat at Momofuku that ended up being closed for a private event. We ended up eating a quick dinner at a corner bistro in Tribeca, and then afterward went to Bar Boulud to try some pâté and terrine. It was definitely a wonderful night, no doubt, but I was not leaving that kitchen without re-tying those roulades.

SUSAN: It says something that he stayed there with you.

AMBARISH: Uh-huh! I'm sure it was some kind of test. There always is a little bit of a test in there, isn't there. What are you going to say? How are you going to respond? All he expects is the correct response. After working with him this long, I thought the right thing to do would be to stay behind and re-tie those roulades. It was something perfectly under my control that I could fix. There was no other way, but it wasn't always that easy. You learn to have a good set of eyes, where you can see your own mistakes. You can self-critique and you correct. He always said, if you can see things in a critical manner, then you're going to start to fix those mistakes. He allows for mistakes, but if you're making fundamental mistakes for the level at which you are, it is unacceptable.

Conversations didn't come about easily. Working with Chef, if he received the respect he deserved—if you were the person who would put your head down and do your job—then you have the privilege to have conversations. If I am working with Chef, I am not talking. My nose is to the cutting board. My eyes and ears are open and my mouth is shut, so I can understand direction clearly, whether it's verbal or nonverbal. [Laughs]

Chef being in the kitchen makes it a better place. I always want to do my best—the way it should be done, the way I was trained. I don't want to take a shortcut when he's around, or even when he is not around. He will always, always be the VOICE IN MY HEAD, because we need that. We need that internal check. We get lazy sometimes, and there is no substitute for good hard work. When it comes to doing something well, there is no compromise. You see Chef wrap a pan in plastic wrap and label it, and you go, "Wow!" It's such a simple task to take a pan of food, wrap it in plastic wrap, label it, and put it away. You do that task from start to finish, and you do it really, really well. You take that formula, and you apply it to everything. Chef is the voice in my head, and he will be, forever.

Colin Moody

Executive Chef, Monterey Peninsula Country Club, Pebble Beach, California

Nice to meet you. Don't fuck up.

COLIN: In summer 2000, I started as a sous-chef at Asilomar Conference Grounds. In my first week, Chef Bill Bennett said, "We're going to a Rice Counsel Conference at Greystone. Master Chef Roland Henin is going to be there." I said, "What's a Master Chef?" I get off the bus that took us to the CIA and see him. Roland Henin is a pretty intimidating figure. I'm tall. He's taller. Chef Bennett introduces us. Chef Henin extends his hand and says, "Nice to meet you. Don't fuck up."

I had no idea what it took to be an executive chef. Chef Henin put together a proper sequence for a chef to become a leader. He had a path for each of us. He had a hundred different chefs under him . . . I don't know how he kept track of all this. He led us through ProChef training at the CIA, which took up to a year to prepare for. You have five Practical exams and a bunch of written tests . . . a real butt-kicker. He had us over-train. When we went in there, we were ready to do twice as much cooking as needed. They actually had us back off with what we were putting together.

What was truly telling about how Roland trained us for this is, we had another group who was sportservice, and they were also doing this training for five days. They were trained by a corporate chef. Roland Henin was on the parks and resorts side. I think 60 percent of them failed. Only one out of the nine of us failed. His training, while rough, was effective.

One thing I enjoyed about Chef Henin was that, for his age—and around this time, he was in his fifties, if not sixties—he'd throw down twelve hours right next to all these young kids, like it was nobody's business, just tear it up. I mean, he was relentless. He was nearing the end of his career when I dealt with him. We were doing an event for the general manager's conference. I had two guests chefs come in, and Roland Henin, of course. By the third day, these guys were just exhausted. They'd always come in late. Henin's favorite thing to say was, "Good afternoon." Even if it's seven in the morning and you show up two minutes after him, it's *Good afternoon.*

SUSAN: *What did Chef Henin see in you?*

COLIN: That's a good question, man. I was shocked that he actually called me back. [Laughs] I was one that . . . I would question him more than a lot of other people. I showed him that I wanted to learn. I was a little more humble than most, at the time. Like, *I don't know anything! Please, teach me.* I was receptive, but at the same time, strong-willed enough to say, "Hey, I don't think that is a good idea." I would never say things to placate him, more like a straight-shooter. When you're doing these events, he doesn't want to waste time with a yes man. He appreciated that I was able to learn and be moldable, but if I didn't like something, I'd call bullshit. The other people who Chef called in were the same way: *Whatever you want me to do, I'll do it, but also, don't micro-manage me. Just tell me how you want it done or let me do my thing.*

Henin called on a short list of people who would travel around for DN events. We'd take the Red Eye, make some magic happen, and then fly out. He was the scourge of a lot of general managers at different properties, because he knew the way to run an event, while they all had their own ideas and itineraries. He was stubborn, saying *This is how we're doing it, because this is how the food is going to taste best. I'm in charge of food.* They'd have to rearrange their event and timing to bend to his will, because he was the Master Chef. I can't tell you how many of these GMs went to the head of the corporation wanting to get this SOB out of their properties. It was crazy for a chef to have such impact on a GM and a company. We were always stuck in the back of the kitchen. He was the guy who stood up for the rights of the chef, to honor the food.

Once, we were doing a bid on a property, going up against the Wolfgang Puck operation. All the higher-ups are there pitching, and we fly in to do a food sampling. There was some hiccup with how the higher-ups wanted to present versus what Roland wanted to do. They came around to me to be the middle-man. I said, "I'm not going against Henin." They wanted people to come in with platters and set up right in the conference room. Henin had me do an ice carving of their place, with everything all arranged in the other room. He wanted the potential clients to walk into the room and be blown away. It was a huge setup, just incredible. We destroyed the opponent.

His respect for other properties . . . we're going in as guests into other people's kitchens. After we turn out a fourteen-hour day, we put it back better than it was before. Teaching that respect: no matter how much time you put into something, you still have to do it the right way. Not just, *Oh, I'm tired. I'll do it tomorrow* and walk off.

Chef Bennett did a similar event with Chef Henin at the top of Niagara Falls, a high-end luncheon for senators. It was off-site—there was no kitchen. Bill told me it was *the* most stress he had ever felt in his entire life, and he's the guy who doesn't get stressed out. When I took over his position and was going to do that event, he told me, "Good luck with *that* one." We did five hundred people at the top of the Falls: appetizers and dessert, in one tent; fish and entrees, in another tent. Right when I got there, he says, "You're in charge of appetizers and desserts. Here are two chefs from sportservice." He took all the guys I was used to working with off to his entrée tent. He was like, "All right, make it happen." I drew the maps and organized all the prep that we needed to bring onsite, etc. They didn't have anything up there. It was probably the most intense thirty-six hours of making sure everything was perfect. During those many crazy events, over my seven years with him, I came to realize from Chef Roland that no matter how far "in the weeds" we were, or when other people dropped the ball on something crucial, or in the moments we thought to ourselves *There's no way in hell we are going to pull this off,* we kept telling ourselves it wasn't a question of *if* it was going to happen, but *how* it was going to happen.

SUSAN: *Any funny stories stick out?*

COLIN: Once at the CIA Greystone campus in Napa, we were doing a Mystery Basket cook-off, a televised event. Four chefs competed. A little background information: Roland was doing the interviews with a satellite feed. When he's in a hurry, he can't convert to English right away, so he had a French translator helping out, which created a little delay. As the dishes came up, he described them. A few dishes came out, and then this one guy from Yosemite thought it would be cool to do a purple potato cannoli. He had these sheets of purple potatoes that he fried like a cannoli, and then he piped mashed potatoes into it. He presented it with two lamb chops "frenched" on either side and then stood the purple potato cannoli straight up! It basically looked like a dick and balls. Which happens. It's funny; they've done studies on brain stimuli and found that food and sex affect the same area of the brain, so you see phallic presentations sometimes or . . .

Anyway, he gave me a stern "Henin" look and said, "That looks like a dick and balls!" He told me to take it to the table, away from where they were filming. He continued speaking French into the headset as the interview proceeded. One of the production assistants sees the plate and says, "This is amazing!" and proceeds to take it over and set it down in front of Henin, who is turning around just as the camera is about to pan onto this "boner" plate. With the French-English translator delay, he just goes, "Whhhooaaa—!" His face is all red. Just before the camera comes filming all the plate presentations, he quickly pushes the cannoli over, so it doesn't stand straight up.

SUSAN: *Wow [laughs] . . . that story truly sticks out!*

COLIN: Chef can take it. He is a true innovator.

We have a big event, the AT&T—a big golf tournament hosting tens of thousands of people. My sous-chef and I were planning how we're going to structure this thing. We kept getting stuck, like it was beyond our scope. Then I remembered the time at Niagara Falls, how we had to structure that remote, and suddenly everything came together. I used the Chef Henin's framework and superimposed it onto this event. It came together seamlessly. Just from doing that one event with Chef Henin, it created the blueprint for how we organize our events. The AT&T is in our fifth year. It's an incredible event and brings us new members.

The more I reflect, the more I understand the depth of what I have learned from *El Tuci* [Toucan] . . . . some of my South America cooks called him that because his big red nose reminded them of that bird. He'd always build the team. Even if it's been a crazy-long day, he'd bring us together for a beer to strategize for tomorrow. When I'm at work, I'll step back and look at the situation instead of getting myopically focused. I don't have all the answers. That stays with me to this day.

Mary Burich

Former Public Relations, Delaware North

Cooking is an act of love. And you don't measure out love.

MARY: I heard Roland Henin's name often after joining the company in 2000. At that point, he was based in Yosemite. I had heard about this larger-than-life figure, a Master Chef who was an informal mentor to many of our chefs. We became fast friends and colleagues who worked well together. As you can imagine, he had incredible publicity value for the company. He was always so generous with time, in terms of interviews and cooking demonstrations. He'd get involved with charity events, cooking meals, and so forth.

SUSAN: *What are some stories you remember?*

MARY: So many . . . a lot of funny moments. I accompanied him and other DN chefs to the Culinary Olympics in Erfurt, Germany, reporting back to the states about their progress and helping them with props, printed menus, etc. I was also the designated driver because they had been up nights on end. Another time, he and I were in England, and I will go to my grave owing him for this . . . a media opportunity where he ended up preparing this wonderful meal in a borrowed kitchen with no help. We then hailed a cab and loaded the food, heading across London to the radio station at about 9:30 p.m. Needless to say, the radio people were in their glory. I don't believe we ever received much in the way of publicity; they were probably just looking for a free meal.

I was setting up an interview for him with one of our industry parks, and the interviewer said, "I am always impressed when people can learn a second language *and* can be funny in that second language." I had never thought about that, but that impressed me greatly. Chef has a huge mastery of the English language and the culture. He wasn't born or raised or trained in it, but he is definitely an American true and true, in so many ways.

Chef and I were out at a culinary competition in Las Vegas a few years back. We walked through the tunnels of the hotel to the Food Hall, and so many young chefs would stop us. He was like a culinary god! They would stop and say, "Ahh, Chef Henin" or "Ahh, Chef Roland!"

The young chefs would go on and on. "Are you judging?"

When he wasn't, they'd say, "Thank God!"

And he'd laaaugh!

He enjoyed that reputation that he had. I knew him in a different way. I got off easy because I was not judged by him. We had this symbiotic relationship. I wasn't a chef; therefore, I was never subjected to his evil eye. In fact, I would tease him. He'd be cooking something and I'd taste it. "Does anybody have any ketchup?" And he'd laaaaaugh. I'd tell him about things I'd made, and he'd say, "Good! Good!" He'd try to get me to make something else.

Roland served Laura Bush when she was First Lady. She would take a yearly vacation with some of her female friends. One year, they chose the Yosemite High Sierra camps, and Roland was their chef. He'd travel ahead by a half day and cook for them. So many stories . . . he'll tell you who was wonderful and who was a pain in the neck. If you asked him questions, he'd say, "Are you writing a book or working for the cops?"

He lives to fish—absolutely loves it. He's given up so much of his life for cooking and creating magical experiences for everyone else, but fishing is the one thing that will put a glimmer in his eye. His standard joke is: *Wanted: A good woman with a boat. If interested, send a picture of the boat.*

SUSAN: *What impressions did he leave with you?*

MARY: One of the gestures I recall . . . this was years ago, and it so impressed me. In the early years of knowing him, we had a group come to Buffalo—about ten chefs from Delaware North properties all over the country, doing an event, which Chef was leading. They prepared at the sports venue near the DN Headquarters. While he was in town, I got a couple of interviews going, including one with the local business paper. We wanted a group shot of all the chefs to use in our marketing material. One of the younger chefs came in and had forgotten his toque [chef hat]. We were feverishly trying to get one from our supply management. Nobody could find one just lying around. We couldn't find one. Right before the photo was snapped, Roland took off his toque and handed it to the younger chef. He never said a word. That young chef suddenly appeared with a hat. We were able to Photoshop a toque on Roland, but the gesture was not lost on me. I don't know if anybody even noticed it, except maybe him and the younger chef. For him to give up that hat—a symbol he had dedicated his life to earning and wearing—to someone who was so much younger, so much his junior. That's how he is. It's a side I don't know if everybody sees. *What a metaphor,* I thought. *A gracious, generous, and powerful gesture!*

Also . . . be true to who you are. He never lived with any regrets. He was who he was and made no apologies. It wasn't always easy taking that road. He's demanding with his protégés, but most of all, with himself. His stature is such that he didn't have to fly all over the world and do the things he was doing. He could have an endowed chair at CIA. He could have been a celebrity chef. He could have easily done all of those things, but he loved to teach. I never heard him say, "Gee if I had to do it all over . . ." We often talked about gambling, because DN had a gambling division. I would say, "Ahh, wouldn't that be nice—to win the lottery or hit it big at the slot machines." Henin would reply, "You make your own luck." He is a self-made man.

His ability to give back is what fulfills him. He used to say, "The younger chefs . . . they'll be here longer than me, and they'll be better than me." I don't know if the latter is true, but he certainly taught as if it was. Shouldn't that always be the ideal goal of the consummate teacher? To have your students be better. Because if you go into it saying, "You'll never be what I am," then from the get-go, you're not giving it your all. He went with the feeling, whether he believed it or not, and I choose to believe he did: *they can be better than me.* So he gave them everything he had.

I had the privilege of speaking with Chef Keller on the phone. He said, "So many chefs have that story about standing at grandmother's knee or their mother's knee. I don't have that story, but Roland was that for me." Roland is everything to him, but it's a relationship that Roland will never abuse. As you can imagine, Roland is often hit up with, *Oh could you get me a reservation for tomorrow night at the French Laundry?* Sometimes he would say yes, and sometimes he would say no. It usually had to do with not so much the person who was asking, as much as how much of a burden that would be on his friend and if he would be comfortable asking. If he wasn't, he would say no. A phone call from him would have resulted in the fulfillment of whatever request that was being asked on the other end, yet he just simply wouldn't abuse his power.

He said something, and I don't think he realized how quotable it was. I was complaining to him, when we started to do those two books.

"How come you chefs, all you do is cook, and you never have any recipes! Don't you have a file of recipes that you pull from?" And then I found out that, no, nothing is written down.

He says, and here's that quote: "Cooking is an act of love. And you don't measure out love."

Larry Johnson

Executive Chef, Busch Stadium/St. Louis Cardinals

If you don't call him, he figures you're a genius.

LARRY: I was interviewing for the position of executive chef for the Balsams Grand Resort. The Balsams runs an ACF accredited Culinary School Apprenticeship program. Dan Hugelier, a Certified Master Chef and good friend of Chef Henin's, recommended me. Driving up from New Hampshire was a four-hour drive. I thought I was lost, and then realized I still had an hour to go. *What the heck am I getting into?* I was a little late, getting sidetracked on how to enter the property. Once I got there, Chef Henin, as straightforward as always, says, "I'm glad you were able to join us. You got ten minutes to get ready for dinner." Right away, I knew he meant business. We made dinner, and he was going through the whole Practical format, which he had sent to us twenty-four hours in advance.

He looked at me and said, "Chef, you might want to breathe. It's okay."

I was extremely uptight, and he asks, "Are you nervous?"

I said, "Absolutely!" It's not that I lack confidence, but I want to make sure I do well.

"Okay, we'll see you tomorrow for breakfast at 7:00 a.m., sharp."

That evening, I thought, *Wow. This is not your regular Mystery Basket kind of stuff. We're going back to the old days of truly going into a formatted kitchen.* He is one of the most classical chefs I know. The joke in the industry is—it's not a joke, but an admiration of—are you working with Chef Henin? You better have your butcher skills in check.

We meet up for breakfast, and Chef says, "Are you hungry?"

"No, Chef. I'm good."

"You gotta eat. You need your energy." Then he asks, "How did you sleep?"

"Did not, Chef."

"Good. Then you're ready for it."

We got into the Practical format. The Practical would complete around noon, and my flight left at 4:00 p.m. The distance to the airport was three and a half hours. I was rattled toward the tail end and mentioned to Chef that I had to leave a little early.

"Well, you should do more!"

"Chef, I'm more concerned about making that flight." He didn't know what time my flight was; he just thought I wanted to leave early. Even though I did everything I was asked to do, of course I could have done more.

He said, "I know you won't be able to present it, but at least do all of your courses. Wish you well and safe travels."

This was a working Practical where you cook for a kitchen judge (Chef Henin) and four tasters, typically: General Manager; Food & Beverage Director; Catering Director; and Director of Operations. That is the standard now, for DN: all salaried sous-chefs and executive chefs go through this, like certification, except that you have a Mystery Basket. You create similarly to the ProChef or CSC tests. It follows the ACF outline: you have thirty minutes to set up your station; you have X amount of proteins presented to you; after 1 hour, those proteins go away, and you may not go back and grab any of the former proteins. All the proteins that you select must be used. You have one *commis* who is not allowed to do any knife skills, cutting, or cooking; he or she is basically there for washing and menial tasks.

It's pretty intense. I did a Practical during my apprenticeship and thought, *My God, we're back to square one, here!* It was great. Anyone who had done a certification Practical feels comfortable, and that's what I love about what Chef has done. It's not this whole foo-foo confusing thing where you set up candidates to fail. He gives you all of the tools and information and says, "Call me if you have any questions." If you don't call him, he figures you're a genius.

SUSAN: *Was Chef intimidating?*

LARRY: His stature is such that, if your cooking skills are subpar, then yes, he can be extremely intimidating. If you think your cooking skills are better than his, then you're kidding yourself. The goal should be that you want to become as good as he is. From the day I met him until today, the common thread has never changed. I admire that consistency in the relationship. You're not trying to feel these highs and lows: *Oh my God; what is he thinking now?* He's pretty straightforward and classical: *Use your head.* Just because you learn something in the classroom doesn't mean that's all there is. There is more behind it. That is what we always refer to as "the width of knowledge." Wisdom is width of knowledge, over time. Knowledge is what we've learned: today, yesterday, and tomorrow. But, the *wisdom* is what you learn *about* the knowledge, over time: what has succeeded and what has failed, all meshed together.

The younger generation wants to go fast—not like how they did it in the old days. For certain things that you learn in this industry, it's repetition that makes you successful—repeating and tweaking and making sure that you can do a dish for five people, and that dish is just *rock star*. Now, when you need to do it for five hundred, can you make that dish? That's when you scratch your head, "How can we make this happen?" Some dishes can duplicate and some cannot. That's where the challenge comes in, and that's where the *wisdom* comes in.

SUSAN: *What is your personal background?*

LARRY: A Cuban-born native, came to the United States, and grew up in New Orleans. I've been in this business thirty-five years. Started in 1982 at eighteen years old, trying to help my mom pay for college, and honestly, I fell in love with it. I worked for a hotel in New Orleans. What a great time and place to grow up and be in the food industry, in New Orleans. I did my stint downtown and ended up at the apprenticeship program at the Intercontinental Hotel, a five-star, four-diamond hotel at the time. I encountered my first 100 percent French chef with his "very calm" temperament (which I say facetiously).

I always grew up with structure! My mother instilled this in me. In that hotel, I learned classical structure. Our cookbook was Escoffier. It was a dream. There was a pallet of Escoffier books, and Chef handed them out, saying, "This is your recipe book, and this is our code!" At that time, I was young, naïve, and wanted to learn, but I heard some of the other sous-chefs saying, "This is ridiculous! Who *does* this?" I worked with some phenomenal chefs, like Paul Bocuse. Charles Chavant from La Provence was also there, plus a lot of old Escoffier-style chefs who instilled in us respect and integrity of a brigade—no man is left behind. No one is too good to wash dishes, unload a pallet, or help their comrades. To this day, it's one of my fonder moments. It's difficult trying to teach that now, because the work ethic is totally different. Some guys still have it, so you can't just make a broad stroke. You always look for that little gem . . . that gleam in someone's eye, when you know that kid is gonna get it.

I went through convention hotels, country clubs, and eventually ended up at the Balsams. I've been with Delaware North for ten years; Balsams for three and a half years; NFL and Buffalo Bills for three years; and now I'm in St. Louis with MLB and the Cardinals for the past three years. I've always had a sound résumé, and I think that's one of the things that Chef likes: *This kid sticks around, no matter how rough it gets.* That's uncommon now, where people last in a company for two or three years.

The luxury we have with DN is that we're so big and diverse that you can make an entire career in one "flat" or umbrella. Delaware has four major identities or segments: Gaming, Parks & Resorts, Sportservice, and Travel/Hospitality.

Within those identities, there are multiple units, which allow an individual to get well-rounded with all these places. You could do ten or twelve years in sports-ervice and then do ten or twelve years in national parks. I'm an old believer that you should never leave a place prior to three years: the first year, you're learning; the second year, you're starting to give back and make an impact; the third year, you start to build your benchmark, so that you can progress to the next level and develop your next layer of culinary instincts. When we stop springing out of bed and can't wait to get to work . . . then it's time to move on. It hasn't happened yet, so that's good!

SUSAN: *Utilization is something that comes up a lot . . .*

LARRY: He's always asking, "What would you do with that?" You tell him, and he'll sit there and listen, but then he'll offer another option. You sit there and go, "Wow. I'm an idiot." I was working on a product for Practical, a poached pear. I peeled the pear and threw the peelings away into my food scraps, then put the pear into the liquid, so on and so forth. At the end of my full run for certification, he says, "Why would you not put the pear skins in the poaching liquid?" I said, "Chef, I thought it would turn the liquid bitter." He says, "There you go, over-thinking. Why don't you just try it?" The next time I did it and the intensity of the poached pear flavor was like ten times . . . not that you were serving the skin, but the skin added more flavor. It was not bitter, but so divine. Simple! Plus, that's one less item in your scrap pile that became food trim you cooked with. Same thing if you butcher chicken: you roast the whole thing; roast the chicken skin with the chicken fat to brush your chicken, versus olive oil. Use everything from that item; it's all there, to fortify the stock, etc., without adding fifty-five ingredients.

SUSAN: *What was his impact on your life?*

LARRY: His dedication to the integrity of our business: if you call it a roast chicken, make sure it *is* a roast chicken. It may sound silly, but when you put something on the menu, make sure it is prepared that way. If you say "sauté," make sure it is sautéed! Make sure there is caramelization on it and color. When my guys are putting menus together, they send them to me. I ask them to walk them through and will question, "Why are you thinking about this? What is your final outcome? You can't skip certain processes. If you don't have enough time to cook a velouté sauce, don't call it a velouté!

Chef pushed me for certification. Our company standard is to be certified within three years. I had a hard time meeting that deadline, due to work and volunteering for company events, but he never let up. "It is your career, for you to benefit, personally. You have to make this happen. How can we support you? We won't ask you to do events in those crunch time months before certification." He helped me approach the GM to create a timeline they understood. He got them involved, so that they had ownership. We all reap the rewards and they get to say, "Our chef is certified!"

One of the things we did in Buffalo . . . it was brutal. Chef was on a mission. We went through a whole year of doing a tour around the company with the Jacobs family, with different parties, and so forth. I looked at my sous-chef as we were driving back and said, "You may want to let your wife know that you and I are going to be in bed together for the next ninety days, because we are going to get certified. We need to get this monkey off our backs." Everyone supported it—the GM, Chef Henin, all the upper management. Chef says, "You guys keep thinking I'm the bad guy, but if you give me just ninety days, I can stay off your hit list, and yours will be the only unit in this company with three Certified Executive Chefs."

Chef came in and mentored us. He treated our Practical as competition. "You guys are coming in as professional chefs. You're not just going to pass. You are coming in as a brand—Delaware North—as your own integrity and your own name." Chef suggested a competition package, including a personal history, menu, and seasonal concept, a grocery list and dietary needs. It listed all your cooking and cutting skills. It highlighted all the items and provided pictures, making sure the recipes were spot-on. We did not skimp on products. It was a spring menu, and we had morels, ramps, and fiddleheads. Finally, there was a section thanking the judges! That way, there was no question of, *Did he do this or do that?* We set the tone right away. That was the first initial contact with the proctors, when they asked if we had our menu. They remarked, "I guess we know who we have to watch." They said that in a positive way.

After our Practical, a judge approached me and asked, "Who the hell taught you to do this competition stuff?"

"Chef Henin."

"Please tell Chef Henin that it's hard for the rest of the world to keep up with you guys, the way you represent. This was ridiculous food for a three-hour window!"

That was the peak of our day. Chef is right. If you fail on one little thing, everything else will carry you. Thanks to Chef, the monkey was off our backs. It was the best beer I ever had, that afternoon.

Scott Green

Executive Chef at Orchard Park Country Club

Is it good enough? Think again!

SCOTT: For the first twenty-two years of my life, I couldn't figure out what I wanted to do and kinda failed out of the four-year school. I had been doing this "cooking thing" all along, so I decided to go to culinary school at Indiana University of Pennsylvania. That's where my career started to take off. I went to a four-star resort in Phoenix. Then 9/11 happened. I moved back to Detroit and ended up working for Delaware North. After six months, I was chosen to be the personal chef for the owner of company, Jeremy Jacobs Sr.

SUSAN: *After six months, you became the personal chef to the owner of the company?*

SCOTT: I had been cooking since I was sixteen, you know, the whole story . . . starting out as a dishwasher, then a pizza cook. I cooked during college—went to a four-year school for the big book of degrees, and it just didn't fit. My girlfriend said, "Hey, you can cook. Why don't you try that?" I went to the one-year school to get my bases down, but being in the business for several years helped. I went to the Wigwam in Phoenix—a giant place that had a bake shop, butcher shop, fine dining, casual dining, and a country club. I learned a lot there, and I worked my tail off, making [laughs] about $7.50 an hour. You could work a hundred hours a week, if you wanted.

Then 9/11 hit and it crushed the tourism business, which is a lot of what they did at the Wigwam—it's a destination place. After I returned to Michigan, I saw an ad for a sous-chef at Comerica Park with Delaware North. I wasn't a sous-chef, but the chef gave me the job. For six months, I ran my own restaurant. At that time, Jon Perrault was a corporate chef as well as Chef Roland. He ventured more into the aesthetic things—layouts, etc. He saw me and thought I would be a good guy for that personal chef position, so I went down to the Jacobses' house and I tried out for three weeks. I was nervous, going into a billionaire's house . . . well, he was not quite a billionaire; he was 890 million at the time. The next year, he was a billionaire.

SUSAN: *[Laughs] No pressure.*

SCOTT: Yeah. That setting was nerve-racking and I had my doubts. People were coming from all over the country to cook, also interviewing for the job. They selected me. At the time, I was seriously thinking about turning it down, but decided to take it and stuck with it for about five years and then carried on to a different part of the company.

During that time, they had this thing called a Chef Summit. I was young, maybe twenty-six, but Chef Roland wanted me to go out to the Napa Valley summit. I was nervous about meeting the guy: CMC . . . *who is this? He's French . . . has a funny-sounding name.* Being unsure of myself, I flew into Sacramento. I had my luggage, walking out, and there's Chef Roland with his giant minivan. He was the most gracious person I ever met. Being a guy of such a high stature with the company, and, basically in the world, he made me feel at home: "Heeey . . . I hear you are the great chef Scott who is working with Mr. Jacobs." I was quite shocked, to tell you the truth. It was like meeting a movie star who was treating you like a normal guy. I'm going in like, there's this mythical god of cooking . . . *who is this guy? This mentor to Thomas Keller and Emeril Lagasse?* He was still just one of us, a cook at heart. It made me feel like part of the team. It was like being in a locker room, with all the chefs talking and the camaraderie.

Chef Roland and I were part of the 2008 Delaware North Culinary Olympic team. He saw that even though I was young and green, I had the work ethic and the vision. We trained for ten months, and it was stressful. [Laughs] He'd fly us all into the Balsams Resort—fly us into Manchester actually, and then drive four hours to wherever the heck it is. We're driving up in the van—me, Kevin Doherty, Ambarish Lulay, Rolf Baumann, and a couple guys working as *commis*. We're driving and driving and Chef is giving us the precursor of what's gonna be going on the menu. We got our templates ready to go for the week: our platters, the THEME, the *teeeeeme*, what the *teeeeme's* gonna be . . . we heard about the theme a thousand times! We drive up to the Balsams in the middle of winter. There's no one else around. This place, it's like *The Shining!* The rooms are kind of scary.

We're all new to the thing, doing cold platters. As accomplished as we were, we were novices walking into this. Chef Larry Johnson, the Balsams chef at the time, set us up in this butcher shop to work. This room is maybe ten feet by eighteen feet with a big butcher block in the middle that we all work out of, so Chef can see what we're all doing at the same time. On the last day, we started at midnight and had the platters done by nine in the morning. Chef Roland comes down around 3:00 a.m. One of the *commis* is messing around with the gelatin and Chef rides him a little bit. The *commis* bumps Chef and spills his coffee. After the coffee was spilled, it was downhill for the rest of the day. Everybody got yelled at. He set the tone for what was needed in the next ten months.

He knew what buttons to push: some people need more coddling, while some people you just need to ride. He'd send out a picture of a platter and write: *Is it good enough? Think again!* (That picture is up in my office now.) When we made sturgeon mousseline, it was *sturgeon*—no substituting out another white fish. The judges may not know, but *we* knew we did the right thing, weren't faking anything. You could see it: from the first platters we put up, to what we accomplished at the Culinary Olympics.

En Gelée. That was the biggest thing. He makes you do research first, then tells you a little bit how to do it. I made a mushroom and salmon *en gelée.* I know what I'm doing . . . do all my *mise*, get my gel set, and have it all together, first laying the mushrooms down, all in a line. I line my salmon, then more mushrooms, then the condiments, and then I start pouring the gelatin, pressing it down and putting it together. I wrap it up, let it cool and set. I start cutting it, but stop. "Chef! It didn't come out right!"

He says, "Chef, you didn't pay attention. You didn't watch what you were doing. You didn't follow the instructions, as I said."

He makes me melt down the whole thing, pull it all apart, and separate each little tiny mushroom. I have like five different kinds of mushrooms in there. I pull it all apart, rinse off all the mushrooms, get them all re-seasoned, get the salmon out, pick all the gelatin off of that, and re-season the salmon. Then, he shows me how to build it. He gets a standard two-inch hotel pan. He gets the ice. He puts the bowl in the ice. He puts the plastic wrap in there, and then he starts building it, one by one. He puts more in there. He methodically puts everything in and says, "You have to do it like this." Then he steps aside, and I do it. I'm putting mushrooms in, and salmon in, and gelatin in, and he says, "Do it faster! Do it faster!" I keep going and going and he says, "Oh! You're a mess!" I have to break the thing down again. Then he shows me, straight up, how to do it. He does the whole thing, and *then* it makes sense. I now understand why you do things a certain way and in a certain order. We let it cool and set and then we slice it, and it is a beautiful terrine. I learned why he had me make it several times—so I would understand why he had to take the extra steps to get a beautiful finished product.

SUSAN: *That seems like classic Henin.*

SCOTT: Here's another classic. We did a high-end gala for about 250 people at the Albright-Knox, an art museum north of Buffalo. I believe the exact event was called *Panza*, based on the art collection. We set up a tent in November . . . in Buffalo. We had no idea what the weather would be. I've worked in places with three inches of water on the floor and you're plating up in fifty-degree weather.

These high-end galas tend to host a lot of vegans. Chef Roland takes on the challenge of the vegetarian meal. Duck and steak are the main meal options, and he's got this vegetarian chop. All the meals were pre-ordered, but then everyone starts switching plates, and now everyone wants the vegetarian chop. Suddenly, he's doing the most out of everybody.

There were fifty of these plates, and they looked exactly the same. He did it in small batches, over there in his little area with another person helping him. I went over to help him out, because he was getting very busy. The entire time, he's in this zone, his cockpit. He's sautéing the carrots, with shallots. Then he tosses in the green beans. He turns around and starts plating. Everything is going in the same order: he's got the shallots and carrots down; he's got the green beans down; he's got the veal chop down; he's got the sauce down; he's got the mashed potatoes down; he's got the *accoutrements* down on the plate, and then BOOM! Then the next plate.

And to the next plate. And the next plate. And the next plate. Then he turns around and prepares more carrots. And more shallots. He cooks more green beans. Everything is in small amounts for five to ten orders, so everything is hot and fresh. I'm over there helping him, and then . . . I don't know how old he is—no one knows how old he is!—he's probably well in his sixties, and he's boxing me out of the kitchen!

I'm like, "Chef, I'm trying to help you, here!"

He says, "Okay, do this, do that!" Then he's yelling at me, "Hurry up! Speed it up! You're too slow back there!"

He's hitting me on the back, and I'm like, "Here you go, Chef! Here are some more!"

I'm cooking and cooking and going, and he keeps going, methodical, methodical, he just keeps going, and he's putting these plates up, one after one after one after one, the exact same way. He has the same motions of how he puts the carrots, and how he puts the greens, and how the chop is placed, methodically every time—a machine in an assembly line.

I watched Chef when he was training chefs Percy and Kevin for the CMC test. I went out to Buffalo a few times to help out and be part of the critiques. Chef Henin would break down each piece of food on their plate:

"No, no, the spinach, you need to clean it, you need to wash it. You need to make sure the stems are gone from it. There's a stem here. You got a little bit of rust on

this piece of lettuce that needs to be taken care of. You can't have those mistakes. This sauce, here, you can see the beurre blanc has a slight little break in it. You can't have that for a CMC test. You can't have these kinds of mistakes! Your THEME! Your THEME! What's your THEME for this menu? This doesn't match with the THEME that you're doing. This plate here, out of the five courses, is an outlier for the rest of the things you are doing."

He'd break you down like that, right down to the carrots on the plate . . . and help you understand, *this is what's wrong and this is how you make it right.*

When he was a young chef in France, he went to watch a team event. There were fifteen teams in this kitchen and he watched all of them. One team was working hard. They were running here and there and they looked busy, like they were doing all this work, and getting all this stuff accomplished. Then, he saw this other team, in the corner. It looked like they weren't doing much. They were standing in one place. They didn't move around a lot. There wasn't a lot of motion. He looked at it. He thought about it. The team that "wasn't doing much" was actually more productive. They were organized down to what steps they were going to take, which *commis* was doing what, and what they were going to need. They had their *mise en place* arranged with all their pots and pans, so they weren't running all over the kitchen during cooking. It showed in the final stage, and don't quote me on this, but I think the team that was the most controlled won, while the team that was all frantic, their platter wasn't up to snuff. That was a lesson to him as he was growing up: make sure you are organized. I took that to heart. When I do a competition, I don't want to be moving around. I'll work right there, do the turning and twisting, and that's it—no moving around in the kitchen like an idiot. I see that in the workplace, too: first plate vs. final plate is completely different. You do more, more, you practice . . . you practice a dozen times before competition. Chefs who are more organized stand right there, not running around. They work, do the project, BOOM. Do the next project. I am amazed what I am able to accomplish in an hour's time.

I had a sous-chef who wanted to take the CSC exam. I said, "Chef Roland is coming into town next month. Here are the things you need to learn. Chef will come and take a look at what you do. You have a month to practice."

And he's all, "Oh, yeah. I'll get it done . . . I'll fluff it."

I'm saying to him, "You can't fluff it. It's gotta be right. You've got to know what you need to do."

Next month, Chef comes for a three-hour practice run. Chef is watching this sous-chef, not saying a word. I didn't get any precursor from Chef from what this sous had been doing, what his training was or how far he'd come along. Chef is writing his notes. He's got one page . . . now he's got two pages . . . and I'm thinking, *Oh, boy. This is going to be rough.*

The sous finishes, he's plating his food . . .

I don't think Chef even looked at his food. Chef could *tell*, from the moment he started, that this guy wasn't prepared. The guy was young, maybe twenty-five. You can't fool Chef; he knows. He tears into the kid with the biggest rant I've ever seen Chef on, in my entire life. It didn't stop for like twenty minutes: how unprepared, how unskilled, and how embarrassing this was. I thought the kid was gonna cry.

The kid needed to understand what it takes to be a chef in order to do these Practicals and get these certifications. He rode the kid . . . "You need to get this written out, you need to get your head clear, you need to get more mentally involved with this, and be more prepared, in order to be a professional." Chef knew that the guy needed to be berated, and it helped him, immensely.

The guy said, "Chef, you're right. I've got to spend more time on this, focus on that . . ."

Anyway, the guy took his CSC exam and passed with flying colors. Not a problem, because he understood what it would take.

"I was trying to fluff it. I sandbagged it. I thought I knew more than I knew."

Chef was like, "Nope. You don't know anything."

I was ready to go crawl in a hole, because this poor kid . . . I mean, whoa. But Chef always knows what buttons to push, and in the end, he's right.

Everything Chef does ends up being a life lesson. The way you put your pants on: how would it be more efficient to get ready in the morning? Packing for the Culinary Olympics was [Laughs] . . . "Oh, no. You have to do it like zees. We take zees out of zees. We put that here. You wrap zees three times." Packing for the Culinary Olympics was a day-long process. We'd ask, "Chef, shouldn't we plan on bringing more? What if we make mistakes?"

"Don't make mistakes!"

SUSAN: *Anything else to add?*

SCOTT: Roland Henin is not going to let people change his mind on how he thinks things should be. He sticks to his guns on what he believes in. He makes recommendations, and a lot of the times, you see that the recommendations aren't followed. And you go, "Well, why didn't we listen to Chef? Why didn't these things happen?" In the end, you find out that he's always right. He would say, "This guy is no good for the company, he's gonna create problems for you, later down the road." You'd see the guy promoted and then the problem would happen down the road, and the guy would get fired.

He pushed education, with DN: "We gotta develop these chefs. We gotta build up the talent." Working in a corporate setting, people are always looking for ways to cut costs, but you've got to spend money to build and retain the business. Everything Chef ever said to me . . . in the end, he was always right, no matter how wrong I thought he was. [Laughs] I don't know how, but he always is.

Jon Wilson

Executive Chef, Ralph Wilson Stadium

He acts like a normal guy. He doesn't push it in your face.
Someone once said to him, "You made Thomas Keller famous?"
And he replied, "No. Thomas made me famous."

JON: I started with DN in 2002, at the First Niagara Center, home of the Buffalo Sabres. When you saw Chef walk into your kitchen, standing up tall, you'd scatter like cockroaches. When I first met him, he asked me if I knew what the "M" meant in CMC. I said, "I don't know, Chef." And he said, "Mean." Then, in 2008, they sent an Olympic team over to Germany. That's where I got to see the other side of Chef. He brought Chef Rosendale out, and Chef Handke came out to compete. The stuff you learned in one month preparing for the Olympics was like two years of doing it in the business—the research, the practice, everything.

The company invests a decent amount of money in us, professionally. We have a budget each year for professional development, and we go to Chef and say, "This is what we want to do, and this is how we want to go about it." I tell ya, he's right ten times out of ten. It gets a little frustrating at times . . . but if he tells you you're ready, you're ready. He won't send you unprepared.

When I was preparing for my certification for executive chef (CEC), he came in and helped me practice. Some people would talk to you, like "This is terrible. This is what you need to do." He was different. He'd tell you, "This sucks, and here's why." If you blow him off, you can chalk it up . . . but if you listen to his critique, he's a tremendous help. I just did a Cold Foods competition. I'm going for my ProChef II. Chef Henin says, "Your garde-manger is pretty shaky. You're going to have to do a couple competitions." I wanted to try a Cold Food, figured I'd get a medal and prove to Chef that I could do it. I sent him a photo of the platter and within an hour he emailed back. He must've written for about two hours, tearing the platter apart! At the end he says, "That's enough for today. I'll call you, tomorrow."

I'm in Buffalo, he's in Seattle . . . he kicks my ass from three thousand miles away! He'll say, "Send me all your work." Then he'll call me and say, "Are you ready to talk? Yes?" And we go, page by page. He says, "You know what you gotta do, all right? We'll talk, tomorrow." When somebody at that level is so interested, you want to try that much harder!

Whenever doing a Practical, you utilize the usable waste and separate it from the non-usable waste. The proctors come through and look at it. After one of my practice sessions, Chef came through and said, "Look at you. You have all this usable vegetable, all this usable fish, all this usable stock. Why don't you put it on the damn stove? Instead of just sautéing with butter, you could deglaze with the stock and have less waste than you're telling me you have. Use the damn waste!" It was one of those lightbulb moments where you say to yourself, *Why didn't I think of that before?* A lot of times when you're going through the process, he comes back and says, "You could have done this so much easier than you've done it." He waits until you've done it before he says anything. That way, you learn.

SUSAN: *Why do you think he had me call you?*

JON: I think he sees that I'm sincere. I'm not just chasing the money or the titles. I'm a Certified Executive Chef, and I'm a sous-chef, and I'm going to stay in Buffalo. You see a lot of guys with DN that say, "I wanna do this, and I wanna do that." They talk big, but they don't spend the weekends and the nights and the holidays practicing and researching and traveling. I think, once he sees that level of commitment . . . I mean, if you just show up for one practice, *yeah yeah yeah.* He acts like a normal guy. He doesn't throw it in your face. Someone once said to him, "You made Thomas Keller famous?" And he replied, "No. Thomas made me famous."

SUSAN: *What other stories come to mind?*

JON: I have three. First one was earlier this year, when I was competing in Madison. Chef said, "Send me your menu." I was making applesauce, and he said, "Put the type of applesauce you're doing [on the menu]."

I said, "Chef, I'm doing Red Delicious apples."

He said, "I'm sure the apples in Buffalo are delicious. But, what type of friggin' apples are you using?"

"Chef, I'm using Red Delicious."

He said, "Oh, okay." Then, he went right to the next line, like nothing ever happened.

After I competed, he called me. I was in the competitor's lounge, and he followed up, like he always does.

"Well, how'd you do?"

Because I was in the lounge, I whispered. "Let me take the call out in the hallway."

He said, "What are you, sleeping?"

"Well, no, Chef. I've spent thirty-six hours competing, and I can't really talk." I said I hadn't read the critique yet.

"Well, call me as soon as you get your critique."

So I read the critique and called him back, and he says, "What do you think about your critique?"

"What do you think I thought about it?"

And he says, "What did you expect them to give you, roses?"

Henin always asks for five bucks, whenever he answers a question. If you're looking at something, and he doesn't tell you, he'll say, "You want me to tell you, you owe me five bucks." Once, I wrote him a letter, and I thanked him for his help, and I put five dollars in an envelope. I put it in his briefcase, before he went on the plane, and I drove him to the airport. I didn't hear from him . . . didn't hear from him. The next time he was in town, I said, "Hey Chef, did you find an envelope in your briefcase?" He looks at me stone cold. He says, "Did you think five bucks was enough?"

Last year, he called on January 13, which happens to be my wife's birthday. He asked, "Do you want to go to dinner?"

I called my wife and said, "Hey, Chef's in town." She's met him a couple times. She knows him.

She says, "Yeah, go ahead. Bring me something home from the restaurant."

We were eating and afterward, I went to order and the kitchen was closed. Chef asks, "What, are you hungry? I didn't feed you enough?"

I said, "Chef, it's my wife's birthday. I have to bring her home something and now the kitchen's closed.

He went off, "Your wife will not be pleased. Don't think you're getting anything from me tonight."

SUSAN: *Anything else you'd like to add?*

JON: It's funny . . . because Chef always swears, but then, when you hear it in his accent, it doesn't sound so bad.

Chris Gould

Chef-Owner, Central Provisions

I went through the practice feeling pretty good.
Then I read through the notes and I thought, Wow! I was terrible!
The stuff he said to me brought me to tears,
but he was only doing it because he wanted me to win.

CHRIS: I met Chef when I was about nineteen, just before graduation from the apprenticeship program at the Balsams. Delaware North had just taken over management there. The Balsams was heavily into competitions. I had stayed late, working intensely on some competition stuff, and he walked into the kitchen. I didn't know who he was. I was young at the time and didn't know anything about Delaware North or the management side of it.

He came in and—he is obviously a *big* presence—I was fairly terrified. We talked about what I was working on. In the next couple months, I got to know him a little bit. I'd see him when he was around the restaurant. Then, I entered into a competition—the ACF Junior Chef of the Year or the Culinarian of the Year—and he coached me. I had won the regional competition in Columbus, Ohio, and trained for national competition in San Antonio, Texas. He coached me one-on-one and taught me a lot about timing, proper French technique, etc. We spent *months* training. Not many people got one-on-one time with him.

SUSAN: *Why do you think you got that time with him?*

CHRIS: Before I met him, I was working on my own accord. After everyone would leave the restaurant, I worked on my own time, practicing for competition. I think now, me being a chef in my own right, if I saw someone doing that, I would spend the time with them. That would motivate me to put all my effort into somebody, if they're putting all their effort into it.

Once, during a competition practice, he wrote me a note that I have saved. It was our last practice before the nationals, before he had to travel west for a few weeks. I was meeting him in San Antonio for the ACF convention. For our last practice, we did a full run, like it was the actual competition. He sat there and took notes the entire time on stuff I did right and stuff I did wrong. I went through the practice feeling pretty good. Then I read through the notes and thought, *Wow! I was terrible!* He had three full pages of notes, mostly stuff that I needed to work on. Afterward, he went through the whole list of every single thing, for ninety minutes. He just beat me up over it, beat it into my head. If I did it like that, I would never win. This was the stuff I needed to work on in the next couple weeks, so that when I met him and did the competition, I would win. So, I practiced and practiced and practiced all that he had written down. I did a full run by myself. I went out to San Antonio and won the competition. The stuff he had said to me brought me to tears, but he was only doing it because he wanted me to win! For example, in properly poaching my Dover sole, I didn't add the *cartouche* over it. Little things like that made the difference between doing it properly or not. He says, "If you practice all of this stuff, and you do all of this stuff right, you will win." I did, and I did!

In recipes, I would write vinegar as "vin." He'd say, "*Vin* is wine! You don't abbreviate vinegar as *vin!*" To this day, I don't abbreviate vinegar. There are so many things he taught me that I instill in my cooks: basic cleanliness and *mise en place.* He was huge on station setup, making sure it was neat, clean, and organized, at all times. When I worked with him for that year preparing for competition, it was all about timing and organization: when you do this; when you do that; how long it should take; and proper techniques like properly boning a chicken or poaching a Dover sole.

SUSAN: *What got you to the Balsams?*

CHRIS: I started washing dishes in high school, as a summer job. Part of the job was making salads and stuff like that. I enjoyed that part, but didn't like washing dishes. At the end of summer, the chef asked me if I could come back the next summer, and I told him only if I could be on the line, because I wanted to cook. He said okay. The next summer, I worked on the sauté line, not knowing how to cook at all . . . but the chef trained me. I enjoyed it and excelled at it. I did that for two summers. When I was figuring out where to go to college, I wanted to continue cooking, so I applied to Johnson & Wales, CIA, and all these places. My chef was a graduate from the Balsams and said I should check it out. I went up there, applied, got in, and was there three days after I graduated high school. The apprenticeship lasts three and a half years, so I was there from 2002 to 2005. I met Chef Henin in 2004.

SUSAN: *How did he affect your own mentoring?*

CHRIS: He is passionate and unrelenting, but also *fair*. He holds people accountable for what they do. He won't go after people and yell at them for no reason; it is always to make them better. It was not just a personality, like, *I'm a chef and I'm gonna yell at people, 'cause that's what I do.* The reason he's spending the time teaching or even yelling is because he wants to have the best out of that person.

I take that into my philosophy. I only hire cooks who have that drive. A lot of cooks these days grew up on the Food Network. They think being a chef is glamorous, where the opposite is true: it's a lot a lot a lot of hard work, persistence, and training. Chef personified that. He would be there after work at 2:00 a.m., working on kitchen training. It wasn't in his job description to do that, but he wanted to help me get better. I do that, too. Even if you're hard on somebody, if they sense *why*, then they'll do anything that you ask them to do. They might not understand exactly why they're doing it, but they understand that what you're doing is going to make them better in the long run. That's the biggest life lesson from Chef Henin. If they don't understand that you're doing it to benefit them, then they are going to resent you for it and they are not going to want to do it. But then, you also need to find that *right person* who wants to work that hard. In that way, the mentor and the mentee kind of find each other.

Beth Brown

Chef Partner at 45 Surfside Bakery & Café

I would ask, "What do you think?"
He'd say, "Ehh, it is your life."
He'd walk away and I'd think, All right, I'm going to redo this.

BETH: I did my apprenticeship program at the Balsams. We had our Annual Culinary Symposium where chefs come in and do demos. This was around 2005, the year before DN took over, so I met him as a chef, not my employer. There was a hubbub of activity about who he was. All these apprentices and recent graduates were going around the kitchen. Thomas Keller had described him as Zeus, and that's such an accurate statement. Without even standing next to or working near him, just his stature alone. . . . He came up to me while I was cutting whole chickens. I had all my chickens on ice and I'm cutting, and I remember him coming up to me. He asked me how long I'd been cooking and I told him I just graduated. I was so nervous, just cutting chickens. . . .

Soon after, DN took over management. Chef came up, doing a dinner for the Jacobs. I was his *commis*. I still have the menu tucked away. We served braised monkfish. Some *mise en place* had already been done. Somebody cut a ramekin of chives—uneven, like lawn mower clippings. Chef Henin had his own ramekin of beautifully sliced, even chives. He wasn't mean about it. He showed me the chives on the table and showed me his and said, "We'll use these. These are nicer, huh?" I said, "Oh yeah, right."

That stuck with me. I taught at the Boston Cordon Bleu for years and would tell it to my Foundations classes. Here's a man who took pride in something as little as slicing chives. I was a recent graduate and could use my knife, but wasn't so skilled then. I practiced slicing these beautiful chives. I now show my students that you take care of the little things. It's all about the details.

Chef Henin recruited me to help test recipes on a couple of DN cookbooks. Chef says to me, "I could write cookbooks, take all the profits, and buy a Corvette, but that's not what this is about. It's about teaching the next generation of cooks." He would say, "You're going to be the next generation when I'm gone." Wow, he could be all over, doing anything he wants, and this is what he wants to do. He wants to train me. He wants to train my other mentors, like Percy Whatley and Ambarish Lulay. That definitely resonated. It's something I honor and value. I tell this story when teaching students who have these great ambitions to be rich and on television. It's not about that. It's about passion, and doing it, loving what you do, and passing the craft on.

Recruiting me to work on the cookbooks allowed me to meet so many great chefs in the company. I got to do a little traveling with the books, and I'm kind of backtracking here, but he was one of the biggest influences in my culinary career. I don't think I'd be where I am today without him recognizing this. He took me as a graduated apprentice, lined me up to do the books, and pushed me in the direction to take my first management position. He guided me all along the way.

He also saw that I wanted to be mentored. I know I don't know everything and am open to constructive criticism, which he always gives, of course. That attracted me to him, the fact that I'm working alongside this fantastic chef giving me a lot of opportunities. You keep your mouth shut, you listen and watch. It's not so much about talking, just setting up a board. His cutting board would be next to your board. He was always right alongside you, whether it was four hours or twelve.

The last time I saw Chef Henin was relatively recently. Before we moved to Nantucket, he flew into Boston. "Pick me up at the airport," he said. My husband and I had just a two-seater truck, but we wanted to see him. We'd also just moved to Boston. I didn't even know how to get to the airport, and I'm kind of freaking out, so my husband, Jeff, drove. I'm on the floor of the back of a pickup truck, pregnant with my son. We sit down to dinner and begin talking to him about our move. I had been gone from DN for over five years, and here I am, sitting with Chef Henin, asking him career advice and wanting to hear what he has to say. Just because I'm gone from the company, he's not forgetting about me and moving on. He's still there for me, and that is amazing because in today's world, I mean, sure, you can keep in touch on Facebook, but to sit down to dinner and give advice about the next move means a lot.

He has a lot of sayings—some of which I'm sure are not appropriate to be in print, but two of which can be that I use a lot, too. Anytime he had a cooking tip to make your life easier, he'd always say, "Five bucks. Five bucks." At this point, I'm forever indebted to him. I don't think I could pay him back enough of those five bucks, because he's given me lots of tips! The other one that always made me question is: "It is your life." When you're doing something, and it's the end of your day, and you're tired, and you think it's good enough, and you put it away, I always hear his voice in the back of my head: *It is your life. You do what you want. It is your life.* You hear that voice and hear, *it is your life,* and think, *Well, maybe this isn't the best I can do.* That's what he'd always say if you were working on a project. I would ask, "What do you think?" He'd say, "Ehh, it is your life. It is your life." He'd walk away and I'd think, *All right, I'm going to redo this.* That's how you always knew.

When we were traveling for the cookbooks, I was a lot younger than he was, and I said something about being tired. He replied that he had lived in a hotel over 230 days that year . . . just unbelievable. The man has crazy stamina. He pushed me to do my ProChef. He's the main reason why Delaware North has these chefs. DN is a big corporation, and sometimes when corporations get that big, they tend to lose quality. It wasn't good enough to do the ACF certifications; he pushed you to do the ProChef certifications. He pushes for the ProChef because it's a much more intense and demanding certification. It was a week long, with a lot of written tests and a lot of cooking tests. Being a Certified Master Chef, you have to have your ProChef I, II, and III. It's a normal progression, and he values that.

When I worked at the Ahwahnee Hotel, he would come for the Bracebridge Christmas pageant. We would serve beef tenderloins. He'd come and set up and be in there with us slicing tenderloins. How clean he worked—how neat, clean, and precise . . . an art form. Also, Chef showed his human side. "I'm a Master Chef and people think I can't do anything wrong. They look at me crazy if I'm slicing something and drop a slice of cucumber on the floor—a fucking cucumber!" That's how he talked. "I'm a Master Chef, but we all make mistakes."

I always worked in the culinary field. I got hired as a dishwasher at fourteen, and they quickly moved me to the line. Throughout high school, I worked in different restaurants and the country club in town. I wanted to go to culinary school, but there were things that drew me to the Balsams. I looked at Johnson & Wales. I looked at CIA. Then I went up to the Balsams and absolutely fell in love. It was four years and six externships, and I love to travel. *This is it. This is where I want to be.* I graduated and stayed there a few years. With the help of chefs Henin and Percy, I took my first sous-chef position at the Ahwahnee where I stayed for a while, then ended up transferring again when DN opened up MetLife Stadium. When I left DN in 2011, I ended up in New York City with a catering company. From there, I realized I wanted to have a family and get closer to home, so I got a job teaching in Boston. Recently, I moved to Nantucket with my chef-partner.

I share the same philosophy about cooking, making sure the next generation is learning and instilling the basic fundamentals. I don't know if it's because I'm a woman or a mother, but I tend to be more nurturing. There are times where I think Chef Henin probably made a few people cry. I don't know. That can be off the record. So, I think I'm a little bit, maybe more gentle in my approach. When you're in the industry and you see somebody, you're like, *There's something there. We can make this person better.* You find those people and do your best to show them everything you've learned. When I was teaching, I saw some students go above and beyond. Those are the ones you pick out to help.

Ashley Miller

Executive Chef, Kalaloch Lodge, Delaware North

As a mentor, he was more concerned with how he might have failed us as opposed to how we had failed him.

ASHLEY: I first encountered Chef Henin in 2003. I had finished my externship at the Ahwahnee Hotel in Yosemite and started as a line cook at the Wawona Hotel, located near the south entrance. This is where I met my true mentor, Percy Whatley. Chef Percy was the executive chef at the Wawona Hotel at the time and was one of the most informative, instructive, and kind chefs who I had ever worked with. I've worked with Percy Whatley for about fifteen years; Chef Henin had mentored him.

Chef Henin came for a routine visit to Yosemite, checking in with Chef Percy. I ran into them on the back deck of our kitchen and Chef Percy introduced us, informing Chef Henin that I had recently finished my culinary schooling. I was the only cook at the hotel that had a culinary degree at the time. Chef Henin's response to this was "Very good. It is important that we bring in cooks who have a good understanding of the basic principles of cooking." He thanked me for my service, and I did not see him again for a few years.

Chef Henin's influence through Chef Percy shows. Previously, Percy would offer a couple notes. Since going through the CMC exam, Percy is now more detailed with his suggestions, especially the flow and theme. "How do the items work together on the plate? How do the plates work together as a whole?" With my CCC test, he broke down my menu completely. I probably would have squeaked by, but after the changes he and Chef Henin made, I ended up with a fairly high grade.

In a recent certification test, I was going for a more modern touch, but was all over the board, doing a little bit of Asian and other styles. I sent my menu to Percy. He completely tore down the menu and wanted me to stick to one style. He guided me toward the classics. With my chicken dish, he suggested a chicken *chasseur*. Percy sent me tons of notes, going over where I should make changes. Chef Henin also came out for three days to work with me on this project. Roland reviewed Percy's notes and stuck to Percy's decisions, but also suggested changing simple things like my sautéed spinach. Percy suggested a spinach pancake. It progressed from spinach sauté, to the pancake, to Chef Roland's suggestion of spinach custard, which demonstrates more technique.

There is a lot to be said about collaboration versus your own creativity. You miss things working alone; having that input helps me to understand, *This is where I am lacking and this is where I should go.* The culinary field can be a little bit egotistical, so collaboration can be tricky. I'm always open to constructive criticism. If you aren't, you're going to stifle yourself. You can move at a faster rate of progression, working with people.

I left DN for a couple of years to work outside the corporate realm. Two years later, Chef Percy reached out to ask if I might be interested in returning to Yosemite. They were in need of some sous-chefs. I began working for Executive Chef Michael Gover. That was when I had my first real experience with Chef Henin as a mentor.

I was set to take my CSC (Certified Sous Chef) testing in Chicago, at Kendall College. Eleven DN chefs from all over the United States were training for five days to take the test. Only a couple of chefs were truly prepared . . . it was a massacre. Chef Henin worked with us for the five days prior, but it was too late. No amount of help would pull us out of this mess. I believe only two chefs passed their Practical. I was not one of them. We felt like huge disappointments, not only to ourselves but to the company, our chefs, and to Chef Henin, who had spent time supporting us. After all of that, I overheard Chef Henin speaking with our VP of food and beverage for our parks division. They were more concerned with how *they* had failed *us.* What could they do to prepare us, in the future? There was no backlash. No one scolded us for our poor performance. We were hard enough on ourselves. As a mentor, he was more concerned with how he might have failed us as opposed to how we had failed him.

The best experience I had with Chef Henin came recently as I prepared for my next level of certification—the CCC (Certified Chef de Cuisine). I sent a copy of my menu with photos to Chef Percy. He completely broke down my menu and had me start from scratch. I was heading in the wrong direction and needed more focus to the menu. He mentioned to Chef Henin that I was working on my own and could use some help. Chef Henin is in my region and volunteered to come out and work with me, one-on-one, for three days. I jumped at the opportunity.

When Chef arrived, we reviewed my menu with Chef Percy's notes. He added items that showcased skills that were difficult to accomplish in the amount of time given. He showed me a better way of thinking. I crammed everything into each practice session, trying to get it all done in the allotted time, instead of focusing some practices on doing everything correctly or breaking practices down into sections. Our first practice went way over; the food was looking good, though my station was a mess. Chef asked me if I had ever visited a French bordello, because that is what my station looked like!

We reviewed my mistakes and successes. He pushed me to not take the easy road for a passing grade, but to try to get the highest score possible, in order to test my skills to the limit. I was doing things like pulling all the tendons out of a chicken thigh that I was not even using, to show the judges that I knew how to do it properly. Had I gone in on my own, I would have only broken down the parts I needed. That was another thing they both taught me: you need to cut down the whole thing. Pull out each tendon, whether or not you use it, to show the technique and prepare the product for later use. Chef Henin insisted I put them on the plate, so judges could see I fabricated the chicken. They also both had me fortify the stock before doing the consommé. We broke down the carcass bones for this.

Another mistake I made was how I cut down a chicken, leaving the wishbone. Chef Henin showed me the proper technique for breaking it down, which takes more time, but gets every little bit of meat off the bones: fabricating chicken into small pieces; adding the bones; taking the time, then cooling down; then making the consommé, with the clarifying raft. It was unnerving, having all three judges standing in front of me and breathing down my neck the whole time. They had never seen anyone fortify the stock and worried that it wouldn't be done in time. This was something I didn't have to do, but it looked better in their eyes.

When adding technique, you have to re-evaluate your timeline. Judges rarely see as detailed a timeline as mine. Chef Henin is *very* specific: write out every detail and follow it. During practice sessions, both chefs kept adding things: searing bones and fortifying the stock. Each practice, I'd have to rework the timeline. I stayed up all night to accommodate all the things I had to do. After three hours of sleep, Chef Henin was already there at my desk.

After that training, I broke down completely. Chef has a triangular strategy: Mind-Body-Technique. I was missing all three. You practice for three days, thirteen hours a day, reworking timelines. No one's getting much sleep, and each day adds more work. By the time of the test, you are exhausted, trying to get through it. But then, you discover you were building endurance for the test, all along.

When I mentor, I focus on strengths, and then build up on what is lacking. Lead by example—work hard for your employees, or they will not work hard for you. New people may have a little bit of cooking skill. I move my dishwashers up to prep cooks and teach them the basics. Lead line cooks come up with specials. One of my line cooks is interested in making employee meals simple and nutritious. *Go for it. Try that dish.* Whether successful or not, they are enjoying it, and it keeps them creative.

I've always looked up to Chef Percy. The first time I met him, he was sitting on the back porch . . . he and another chef, Crazy Larry, shucking corn in rocking chairs. Ever since then, Percy has always been there. Any piece of advice, he is always there to help and share, in any way I need. With Chef Henin helping me with the Practical exam, there was an opening. If I had any questions, he immediately responded. I feel a strong connection and bond to him. I was happy to have passed with a good score, but I was even more pleased that I had been given the opportunity to work with such a great chef and leader, and I hope for more of these opportunities in the future. Hopefully, I'll get to go fishing with him soon.

Dawn Hedges; Nick Catlett; Juan Carlos Valdez; Aldofo Calles

Travel Hospitality Team: Food & Beverage Summit Culinary Challenge

I figured we just go to work and grind it out and one day, you run into a movie camera, and then you become famous. Chef Roland brought me down to planet Earth. "Hey, look, kid, quit dreaming and start doing."
—Nick Catlett

DAWN HEDGES, BUFFALO/NIAGARA: My first interaction with Chef Henin was in January of 2016. I received a brief message from the general manager: "Chef Henin is in Buffalo. He's flying back to Seattle and he'd like to meet with you." I asked him what it was in regards to and how I should prepare for the meeting. "I'm not sure, just be ready." Chef Roland flew in and we spent an hour in the office, talking. He wanted to know about my certification, where I was educationally, what my goals were, and how he could help to get me there.

NICK CATLETT, NEW ORLEANS: It was the end of 2014 at the Summit in Buffalo. I just got Chef Keller's *The French Laundry Cookbook*. It was my first Thomas Keller book. I read how Chef Roland was his mentor and taught him how to cook offal, among a bunch of other things. I had wanted to meet Chef Roland ever since. When I saw him at the Summit, I'm like, *Well, here's my chance. We've got something in common: I own this cookbook and he mentored Thomas Keller.* Like a goofball, I went over there and brought that up and we shared a laugh. I think he was laughing more at me than with me.

We talked about certification, culinary acceleration, and my career—things I never thought about. I figured, we just go to work and grind it out, and one day, you run into a movie camera or something like that, and then you become famous. Chef Roland brought me down to planet Earth. "Hey, look, kid, quit dreaming and start doing." That was the beginning. I was nervous as well, but ever since then, we stuck to the rail and now we're reaching for the next goal, a twelve-month plan to ProChef II.

Chef Roland is the standard. He's a classic, and in culinary, that says a lot. We studied from a book that's two hundred years old, and it's still relevant today. With Chef, there's no faking your craft. If you take a shortcut, or you cheat, or you try to make things go faster, he's going to spot you from a mile away and call you out on it. With Chef Roland, there's only one way to do things, and that's the right way, the way it's been done for hundreds of years. I guess I would describe him as a rock. Solid. An oak. He stands true to his beliefs. He encourages us to stand with our beliefs, as well.

We were in competition, on the last day. Chef Juan and another chef were working on this cranberry reduction. I was watching, making fun of how stupid that is, to just sit there and reduce the sauce. Chef Juan goes, "Put some xanthan gum in it." There's probably twenty yards of traffic between Chef Roland and that pot of cranberry sauce, and he stops the press. "If you want to cheat, go home now!" At that point, I was straining eggs, kind of haphazardly. I slowed down and started straining them through a fine sieve. That took me the rest of the day, but we did see how shortcuts end up different than the original method; it may be just a slight difference, but it's there. You can tell in the quality, texture, and the flavor.

JUAN CARLOS VALDEZ, FORT LAUDERDALE: Once we finished the dish and everything was done right, he made us do it again: "Okay guys, make it better now. Let's change this. Let's change that." We're doing the Famous Fish Taco. First, we did it with tempura. Then, we blackened it. Then we grilled it. We changed the tortilla. We did it with a crispy tortilla, with a soft tortilla, with a white corn tortilla, and with a blue corn tortilla . . . you name it. We went through measurements each time, to make the dish perfect. Even though it was a fish taco, it was a perfect fish taco. Now when I do something, I think, *How can I make this better?*

ADOLFO CALLES, LOS ANGELES: I was doing these tartlets—vegetable shells. We put mixed greens in a light shell. He brought in these tools that you can't find anywhere else anymore. As I was making that recipe, he tasted it, and said, "Adolfo, I see you need something else in there." My eyes were wide. He looks at me, smiles the biggest smile. "You need something else." I said, "Okay." I couldn't make the tool work, because the shells kept sticking to it as I was frying them. So, I changed the recipe a little bit. I got a couple of eggs, and added some more herbs, and all of a sudden, it starts working. He comes back and tells me, "You see, I told you, that recipe needed help, but I didn't want to tell you what."

NICK: Preparation is the most important ingredient. Being prepared and having a sharp knife will set you up for success. If you don't have proper timelines, then something can come up and put you off of your game. I'm a competent person, but I had no idea how important that was. Even I could get shook up and embarrass myself. If you plan every detail, no one will be able to shake you.

In the past, we never even got together to practice for these competitions. This time, we had a training week in Fort Lauderdale and a couple days in New Orleans. Another training session was coming up in Fort Lauderdale, when Chef Adolfo and I also had a conference to attend in New York City. I thought, *No big deal. We'll get two days knocked out, do some dishes, and then we can go to this other conference in New York City.* Chef Roland finds out and gets furious. We were on a conference call and I thought the phone was going to explode: "If this training isn't so important then maybe we shouldn't even be involved in it." I'm thinking, at first, *Throw the baby out with the bathwater!* I'm like, well, we've done a good job already, and his point was, if we weren't fully committed to this, then how could we possibly get anything out of it? Our flights are booked, our rooms are booked, and it simply didn't matter; if it was important for us to be a part of this training, we can cancel. Needless to say, I still have a Delta credit somewhere. He's got a way of changing your mind. "Are you *in* or are you *out?*" There's no halfway. All of us know the gravity that is Roland Henin. You are just drawn to him. He's got the answers; he's the key.

We were at the Nestlé plant, where they make their Minor's base, like chicken base. They produce a million different flavorings. You name it and they'll make it, and if they don't make it, they'll get it. We go down, have some fun, have a few drinks and eat. We also do this cooking competition: cook a dish in forty-five minutes using Minor's bases and then declare a winner. Well, this year, Chef Roland and another chef came along. He took over the competition, and now it was going to be on Olympic standards. [Laughs] I, for one, was not prepared for this. My thought process wasn't there. I do get very serious about cooking at serious times, but that was a big lesson: You don't pick and choose when to take your craft seriously. A real chef doesn't treat his craft that way.

We started cooking, gathering our ingredients, and he's walking around, asking questions: "Is your *mise en place* set up? Where is your timeline? What is your goal? What is the plan for this dish?" Needless to say, the Nestlé group wasn't altogether happy. They just kind of got kicked out of their whole deal. Chef would not take this lightly, would not waste an opportunity to learn something and gain that "pressure" experience. They were walking around with their pads and timers, judging us. That was another one of those funny stories if I wasn't the one involved.

DAWN: First and foremost, my takeaway is how limited our resources are, coming from travel hospitality. They only recently created this culinary presence in the airport, having chefs in our unit. Many of our kitchens use "quick-prepared" products. We don't have a lot of kettles, ovens, or space to create everything from scratch. All of us went out and bought several pieces of equipment—pots, pans, utensils. We were accustomed to taking shortcuts. He made us question the integrity of our products: getting the scratch items prepared; pushing back and asking for specific equipment; and making a plan to get the resources we need for quality products, with the support of our management team, in the restraint of the budget.

For a lot of the competition, I was afraid of being called out, but by the end of it, I felt a lot more at ease about being corrected immediately for stuff, especially the "heirloom tomato situation." We were doing heirloom tomatoes for part of our fish taco: get the kettle boiling; blanch the tomatoes; and peel them. I began blanching the tomatoes. They were scored, but I had them in the water for definitely more than five or ten seconds. I had an ice water bath behind me on the counter and the ice bath had been moved on me. Chef Roland called me out right away and asked me why the ice bath wasn't immediately next to it. And, why were there more than two tomatoes in my kettle at one time? There weren't good answers for it; I definitely learned a lesson. After fifteen or twenty minutes, he came back around and said, "I never would have questioned you, if I didn't care. If I didn't see potential in you and didn't want you to know the proper way to do it, I would have never called you out."

My future goal is to pass my Practical, which will be the beginning of March, and continue to do outreach projects. I'm on a project with Chef Henin building an educational kitchen for our local Boys and Girls Club. Looking back at the past year, it's amazing to go from sitting across a boardroom table trembling, being talked to loudly, to just before the competition started, him coming up to me and helping me fix my chef coat, collar, and bow tie.

Although Chef Henin wasn't present during the Practical, his presence was felt all over the Niagara Falls Culinary Institute that week. As I was setting up my station on the first day, I happened to look up at the hood and noticed a quote from him staring back at me. It said, "What is average? The best of the worst and the worst of the best. *Why be average?*"

As I was looking at my final presentation, after the test was over, I realized it was a culmination of conversations and critiques with Roland Henin that had begun over a year ago. I didn't even realize it, until I looked at everything as a whole: the positioning of each component of the menu; recipes; *mise en place*; even the presentation booklet.

Aside from Chef Henin coaching me on technique, menu, and expectations, he supported my mindset in the couple weeks leading up to the Practical. He complimented my progress and appreciated my willingness to work hard to be successful. About a week before I was ready to leave, I told him I wanted to do three more runs before I left. He slowed me down and made me realize I needed to pace myself for the final hurdle. He told me to stop touching food and focus on the little things I needed to be prepared for the week. I was surprised he was telling me to walk away from the food, get rest, and not get burned out from practicing. He said, "Trust me. Do not touch the food because you want to be hungry to do it again when you get there." He was right . . . it surprised me how much I wanted to get into the kitchen and start cooking!

I ended up passing the Practical and am now filing the final paperwork for my Certified Sous Chef certificate. It was a lot of hard work, and although I feel a sense of relief for completing it, it also feels kind of empty. I walked down the hallway after it was over and my equipment was packed, thinking, *That's it? It's over, now what?* Now I turn my focus to the next level of certification. Chef Henin told me to be careful because it can become addicting. I laughed, but once again I think he was right!

So it will be with Henin, too. Mentoring is addicting, and while he may be retired, he will continue. Please keep him posted.

The Fork in the River

Tagging studies have shown a small number of fish don't find their natal rivers, but travel instead up others, usually nearby streams or rivers. It is important some salmon stray from their home areas; otherwise new habitats could not be colonized.
  —T. P. Quinn, Mechanisms of Migration in Fishes

Throughout his life, Chef Henin faced forks in the river. His father died when he was young. As the elder son, it became his responsibility to care for the younger siblings, while his mother found work to support their family. He rose to the challenge, sacrificing the simple life of a nine-year-old. When his mother remarried, he and his stepfather clashed. Roland, then a young teen, favored a social life with his peers. His stepfather would not allow Roland to come and go as he pleased. An ultimatum was given, and Roland left the family home to secure room and board through the pastry apprenticeship.

We might think that moral dilemmas arrive later in life, when our careers are well-established, but young Roland faced such dilemmas before the age of ten. It seems he was born to diverge: *Do I take the easy way, or do I choose the right way? Do I float in the river, or do I choose to swim upstream?* As the river grew more complex and unyielding, his integrity remained constant.

Every chef faces such moments in their career, when they are forced to consider: Do I forsake my values, or do I forsake this situation? If I remain in this role, on this path, will I be true to myself? Sometimes, the answer may be clear, but that doesn't make it any easier . . . especially when the decision creates a fork in the river between you and Roland Henin.

WILLIAM BENNETT: When working with him, it didn't hit me, but looking back now, I was a cook, until I met Roland. That's when I started to become a professional chef—the big turning point. He was the spark that lit the whole fire: the world of good cuisine; the people involved; the ingredients; what it takes, the work ethic; the tools and the training and the staff you're going to need.

The whole time you are around him, he's testing and grooming you to be the next person in line. There was a time when I thought, *Wow. If he keeps pushing me to these new positions, and I'm doing bigger and better things, maybe when he retires someday, I might be able to do what he does.* I'm not going to be him, but just take his position and do these great things. I think we both saw that. It wasn't spoken, but he was grooming me. I think he was always looking to make sure that he's going to build the team up and there's going to be people in place, so that when he's not there, they can keep the quality level up and do well for the company.

My first child was born when I was working for DN in Los Angeles. I was working for a different branch of the company that wasn't under his specific direction, but still looked to him as my leader. My wife was going to give birth right around Christmas. I made arrangements with my GM to take two weeks' vacation then, to be there with my wife, the kid, and everything. He says, "Oh yeah, absolutely. It's the best thing you can do . . ."

About a month before my daughter was born, Roland called me and said, "Hey, I need you to go here and there with me and help with this party."

I said, "Look, that's right about the time that my first kid is being born." I said that obviously, I had to be there.

He says, "No, no, no, no, that's fine. Stay while the kid is born, and then after, you can come and help."

"Well, we don't know exactly when she's coming out so . . . [Laughs] I can't give you an exact date."

My baby is born on Christmas day. He calls me on the twenty-seventh and says, "Okay, so everything's good. I'm gonna buy your ticket."

"Whoa . . . my baby is born, Chef. I got a baby girl."

"Oh, great! Is she healthy? Everything good?"

"Everything's great! Mom's good. Just got home, yesterday."

"Okay, good." And he just went back to talking about how I was going to fly to here and there . . .

"No, no, Roland. You don't understand. I'm on two weeks' vacation."

"No, it's okay. You can get your vacation package and just come back to work."

"No, no, no . . . I'm here with my baby, my family. I want to spend time with them."

"Well, what's the problem? You told me everything's okay. The baby is okay and the mom is healthy?"

"Yeah."

"Well, why can't you go?"

[Laughs] I said, "Look. I don't want to disappoint you, but there's no way I can go. I'm taking the time off. I have to tell you, no."

He was not happy. You just kind of fall out of favor with him when you can't come through. He made a lot of sacrifices to get where he was. Sometimes he expects other people who are like-minded to do the same thing. That was the line for me: "While I'd love to come with you, I'm not going to give up the two weeks I'm never going to have again to be alone with my new baby and my wife."

We keep talking. He's saying, "You said she is healthy. What's the—I don't understand it."

I got off the phone and wanted to cry . . . *Oh my God, the guy hates me now.* [Laughs]

I didn't take the time off to make sure they're healthy; I took the time off to *be there*. At that time, I don't think he understood that.

* * *

I wanted to go to Europe, and he helped me plan out this thing where DN was basically going to pay for me to go. I was planning work in France, Italy, and Spain. He helped me draft a proposal to the owners of DN that if they sponsored me—he hated that word; I couldn't use it because it sounded like we were begging for things—or provided me the means to go to Europe, I would work in these kitchens for free, for two or three years. He was going to set me up with a few chefs over there. I would come back with all that knowledge, and I would basically be like an indentured servant to DN.

There was a big meeting in Yosemite, and I was one of the cooks. I had the proposal and submitted it to the owners. That was on September 10, 2001. The next day, I was in the bakery, early in the morning. There was this little black and white TV that had half a mile of tinfoil coming off the thing, trying to get it to work. There was this breaking news off the TV. It sounded like some dummy in a private plane hit the World Trade Center. The guy in the bakery says, "Oh, you guys gotta see this!" When we walked in, we saw the smoke in the building. We went back into the kitchen and told Roland. He said, "We have stuff to do. You shouldn't be watching TV. Stay out of it, and get your work done." Then the second plane hit the building. He glanced at the TV with us, but we couldn't pay attention to it; we had to keep up at our work.

Everything got thrown to the winds after that. They wouldn't even consider my proposal. Henin convinced me to go with my own money and do the best I could until my funds ran out. He helped prepare me to go. Being a sous-chef for his events prepared me to work in the French kitchen, where things were ten times coarser than with Roland. He saw that I could handle that kind of stuff. I ended up going to France and spent four months over there working. My wife and I went over there, and we basically ran out of money supporting ourselves and came back. Without his mentorship, I never would have even *thought* about going to work in France. Working in a three-star Michelin restaurant in Paris was eye-opening. I was so interested to see how the best in the world run a kitchen. How do they do it? How do they make the food? How is that different than what I'm doing? What do I need to do to get on that level?

I had to find the restaurants. I went to every three-star restaurant in Paris with my résumé. Most of them didn't make it past the maître d'. I'm sure they just threw it in the garbage. Taillevent accepted my résumé and signed me up for a stage—a work-for-free agreement. I faxed Roland some French paperwork about the rules. He signed it for me and warned, "Don't do anything you're not supposed to do, because I'm signing the papers!" I followed in the footsteps of Thomas Keller (who also staged at Taillevent). *Chef Henin did this for Thomas, and now he's doing this for me.* I felt the pride in that and didn't want to let anybody down. I'm no three-star European chef by any means, but having been around Roland and then France, when I do cook, that is my approach. It may not be a three-star meal, but if I can get it to one star today, maybe I can get it to two stars by next year. That's been my goal.

I wish I could have stayed longer. I think Chef was a bit upset that I didn't stick it out, but it's hard when you have a family. The way he's handled his personal life is a lot different than the way I've handled mine. Sometimes he's asking things of you that you just can't . . . and it's hard to tell him no. Once you do, you're kind of on this little shit list for a while. [Laughs] He'll never admit it, but you are.

SUSAN: *The few times he's talked about his son, usually it's in terms of fishing . . . when they go out together, how his son knows everything about fishing.*

WILLIAM: Everything has to do with fishing! At the end of conversations, it's always some sort of fishing. He called me out of the blue a year ago, and he said, "Hey! I'm on the run, but listen. I need something from you!"

"Sure, Chef, whatever you want."

"I need you to [laughs] I need you to send me five pounds of fresh sardine, un-gutted, and I want them ready, right from the bay."

I was like, "*What?* What the hell are you talking about?"

"I need them by Saturday."

"Um, I'll look around Chef, but . . ." The sardines weren't running in Monterey. The only ones we had were frozen.

"No, no, no . . . they cannot be frozen!"

He'll call up, once in a while, with these crazy things. The guy has done so much for you; you don't want to disappoint him. You always want to take care of him, when you can.

* * *

Some chefs choose values of family, flexible hours, etc. Some go for the money and prestige, becoming executive chefs. Some reach for rock star glory, stomping the spotlight. Some want it all, and a few can actually manage that. (Can we please bottle their blood for the rest of us?)

And some . . . some choose cooking. They will forsake all else in their pursuit of perfection within the culinary art. For these select few, there is a distinct fork in the river, just for them . . . swimming upstream the entire way.

For some fish, there is only one way home.

The Salmon Run

Twelve of us took the CMC examination in 2001. As the ten days marched along, we lost a few candidates. When we began the final day, there were eight of us. When day ten was over, only one chef passed the examination. In the past classes, the top chef scoring would get the Crystal Chef Award, and of course, Roland got that award for his class. When I was the only one that passed, the first thing Roland asked me was where was my Crystal Chef? Before I could get upset with him or request, How about congratulations? it dawned on me that he expected me to pass. He expected me to finish first, so "congratulations" was already displayed in all those practice sessions.

Chef had perfect penmanship and handwrote everything in his notepads—hours upon hours, he would write critiques of the Olympic practices and observations. He would send these to us after he arrived back home. These were critiques, not encouragement messages; the encouragement was the fact that he took the time to write these for us, took the time to send them to us and cared enough to continue this practice for the entire time we met as a team. Somewhere in my boxes of trophies, photos, and medals, I have these letters.

–Lawrence McFadden, CMC,
CEO at Sunrice GlobalChef Academy

Over ninety years ago in France, excellence was born. In 1924, a contest of sorts was created. Those awarded were given the title of *Un Des Meilleurs Ouvriers de France*, shortened to MOF: One of the Best Craftsmen of France. The MOF represents perfection in practice. One area of craftsmanship awarded is in the culinary arts. In a country where culinary arts were regarded as the best of the best, the culinary MOF shone like a three-star Michelin:

> In this competition, the candidate is given a certain amount of time and basic materials not only to create a masterpiece, but to do so with a goal of approaching perfection. The chosen method, the organization, the act, the speed, the knowhow and the respect for the rules of the trade are verified by a jury just as much as is the final result. The winning candidates retain their title for life, with the indication of the specialty, the year following the one in which they obtain the title. This prestigious title is equally recognized by professionals and the greater public in France, particularly among artisan-merchants such as pastrymakers, hairdressers, butchers, jewelers, and others whose trades are recognized, particularly those for more luxurious goods.
>
> This competition requires months, sometimes years, of preparation. Technical skills, innovation, respect for traditions and other aspects are all practiced repeatedly to a level of refinement and excellence, effectiveness and quickness to succeed and be crowned by the jury, which makes its decision according to the distribution of points awarded during the entire process.[2]

A few years after Roland Henin crossed the ocean into America, the MOF followed suit. In 1980, Ferdinand Metz went to Germany and adopted the CMC program. He brought it back to America and adapted it, adding Supervisory Development, Nutrition, and Sanitation. As a way to honor the young European chefs who had spent their lives as culinary craftsmen, but who had forsaken their homeland, the idea took hold. In 1981, the United States unveiled their version of the MOF: the Certified Master Chef (CMC). The title of Certified Master Chef, presented solely by the American Culinary Federation in the United States, is the highest level of certification a chef can receive. It represents the

---

2 Wikipedia contributors, "Meilleur Ouvrier de France," *Wikipedia, The Free Encyclopedia,* https://en.wikipedia.org/w/index.php?title=Meilleur_Ouvrier_de_France&oldid=761396351 (accessed May 26, 2017).

pinnacle of professionalism and skill. Today, there are only sixty-eight CMCs and eleven Certified Master Pastry Chefs in the nation.

What does it take to become a Certified Master Chef? Technically, it is the successful completion of eight days and 130 hours of practical and written examination; however, it is so much more than that. The CMC exam is the culmination of one's life work, mastering culinary foundations and classical techniques. Without romanticizing the notion, the CMC is a stamp of excellence upon the soul.

Over eight days of the CMC examination, Practical tests are administered in major segments:

1. Healthy Cooking
2. Buffet Catering
3. Classical Cuisine
4. Freestyle Cooking
5. Global Cuisine
6. Baking and Pastry
7. Continental and Northern Europe Cuisines
8. Market Basket

A perfect score is 100 points and a minimum passing score per segment is 70 points. The minimum passing final cumulative score of the entire exam is 75 points. Since each scoring segment can have one to five judges, a candidate's grade is determined by the average of the judge's scores. The minimum passing score (the combined average of the kitchen skill, and presentation and tasting scores) for each segment is 70 points. And, here is the kicker: the last day counts the most. A candidate must have a cumulative passing score of 75 percent during the first seven days of the exam in order to participate in the last day of the exam.

A candidate may continue with the examination, even if they fail one segment, but *must maintain a cumulative average of 75 percent*. The failure of two segments (less than 70 points) results in an automatic withdrawal from the examination.

What does it take to earn the right to participate? Mastering culinary foundations of cooking is the beginning, the assumption. The CMC exam also requires mastery of ego.

Roland Henin received his CMC title in 1983. At the time, he received the highest cumulative score, an 83.4, which earned him the Crystal Chef Award. Henin's success relied on embracing a *triangle* system of Mind, Body, and Skills.

All must be in top form, akin to running a marathon. These things feed off each other, for good or bad. As Henin preaches, "The worst enemy is the mind. A bad day can kill you."

While one does not "train" for the CMC, there may still be gap areas needing to be addressed. This would be the difference between adding a decorative vase on a dining room table to building the entire house. Henin knew he had gaps in the areas that were added to the MOF, so he audited classes at the CIA, while he was an instructor there.

What Cost, a God?

I did get married once, but as you know, with the time demands of our business, it didn't work too well. . . . Oh well. C'est la vie.

—RGH

The CMC path is not for everyone; indeed, it is barely for anyone. In almost forty years, there have been fewer than 70 chefs who have earned the right to be called Certified Master Chefs.

What does it take to become a Certified Master Chef? Technically, it is the successful completion of eight grueling days and 130 intense hours, but it is so much more than that. The CMC exam is the culmination of one's life work, mastering culinary foundations and classical techniques. The CMC title is a symbol of recognition, rather than assessment. It is the badge of honor.

The CMC path is similar to a PhD program. PhD programs were originally intended to be the organic culmination of years in scholarly pursuit. You work, learn, and grow. In the process, you discover gaps, which lead to questions. It's as if you, alone, were meant to answer these questions. You become insatiably curious, and you develop a passionate inquiry, which becomes the foundation of your research. Research is discovery; pursuing one's research is, in a sense, self-discovery. It leads you to who you will become in life, fulfilling your purpose.

By the time you enter your PhD program, you are already an expert. Earning the degree simply acknowledges years of education, experience, and dauntless pursuit.

AMBARISH LULAY: We had another one of those learning moments at one time, when Chef pulls out a pen and paper and explains something. He explained the progression of a cook in the kitchen. If you hold a title, you should know what the title demands. If you have a title, such as Chef de Cuisine, then you are expected to know what a chef de cuisine should know, meaning you are as good or better than all the sous-chefs who work for you. You're a mentor. You're a trainer. If you're a sous-chef, you're better than the line cooks in the kitchen. You know every station like the back of your hand and can fill in. The traditional brigade is evident, and that's where this conversation was headed.

Chef pulls out a piece of paper and says, "This is how the progression works. We have building blocks in our business. The cook starts out, whether he is a dishwasher or a prep cook. Every step teaches you something. If you're a dishwasher, it teaches you speed. It teaches you about cleanliness. If you're a prep cook, it teaches you about being organized, working fast, and learning how to prioritize." You learn, and I quote Chef when saying this, "We're not in the business of creating waste. We're in the business of creating food." When you're a prep cook, this is the time you learn that. You learn not to waste the onion, as you cut the onion . . . how much to trim off. Who knows how much to trim off the onion? Well, Chef does! They teach you that in culinary school, but as you go through, you learn all these good habits, and those can only happen in a good kitchen with somebody like him.

Chef continues, "Then you make it to the pantry, as a salad cook. You learn how to get used to the lifestyle of the line cook without even touching hot food, yet. You learn how to organize your time, how to put up orders fast, and how to utilize stuff. You learn how to utilize leftovers, when you work in garde-manger. There is a team quality in a garde-manger chef.

Once you've learned that, then you may be allowed on the hot line as a basic appetizer cook, an *entremetier,* or a vegetable cook. You make your way up the hot line: roast, sauté, fry, and grill. You work the stations, and you run this whole gamut. And then, you are responsible for your own station. You may become chef de partie, so not only have you learned your station, but you are learning responsibility for somebody else. You are not only performing, you now are also *training.* You're passing on what you've learned to somebody else and are responsible for that person.

Once you do those things well, that's when you get to be the sous-chef." (He drew this plan, with months and years attached to it, mind you. There's a certain amount of time needed to spend at each of these stations to make it worthwhile.) "When you have done your time as a sous-chef, whether it is three, four, five years—learning all aspects of the kitchen, working hours and hours and hours—then, *and only then,* when the opportunity presents, you get to become the executive chef or chef de cuisine. All these things combined are what give you a solid foundation to be a chef. If *any* one of those things is missing, the foundation is not complete and will be a rocky foundation. Any time you jump before it's time or you miss a rung of the ladder, you are going to miss out on some learning opportunities. If you follow the progression, there is no reason why a chef de cuisine should not know how to poach sweetbreads properly or how to turn a carrot properly. If that happens, that means there is a hole in the training somewhere. Sure, the theme of the restaurant might change, but nonetheless, the fundamentals are the fundamentals. They are building blocks. When you get to the position of executive chef, you deserve it."

It was a moment of clarity for me, knowing that if there is a hole in the game, it needs to be filled. How I get it filled is my problem, but it needs to be done. At that point in time it was important, because if I'm going to mentor young cooks, this is the road I'm going to take: put them through the rotation of things, make sure they do well, and then, give them the next step.

*   *   *

Many chefs possess the backbone, but still not every chef earns this CMC title. What kind of person becomes a CMC? Why do they purse this title when there are other titles worthy of prestige and value, such as the ProChef III or Executive Chef?

What is the cost of becoming a god? What is sacrificed? Some chefs might say everything: family, friends, social life, sleep, and health. Do you enjoy television? If so, kiss the CMC title good-bye. Chef Henin does not own a television and never has. During dinner about midway through the CMC exam week, Henin brought up the subject of "downtime." Some chefs choose to zone out in front of the television. Some choose to practice a deficit skill area. It's all he said, but the gentle change in the tenor of his voice spoke volumes.

Roland Henin left his home as a child, left his family and relatives, left France and Europe. He left his customs, culture, and traditions. He left stable jobs, security, and money. He had no home life, flying over two hundred days per year. His downtime came in the form of fishing, which saved his soul. "I did get married once, but as you know, with the time demands of our business, it didn't work too well . . . Oh well. *C'est la vie*. I have a son who is about forty and doing well in Australia."

Roland is Zeus . . . but at what cost? Why did he sacrifice to become the god of cooking? Or, perhaps the question we must ask: was it worth it?

RGH: I wonder: *What's my value?* I had a feeling that I was "not much." I started running to keep my sanity. Exercise was good. I started in Florida. The weather was good. It was a good way to keep in shape. Then, I began to take it seriously, running half-marathons. I wanted to test myself, to see if I am capable. At almost forty years old, I was wondering and running . . .

Teaching at the CIA allowed me to do that—not working twelve or fourteen hours, I had time to research and reflect. Running cleared my head, relieved stress and tension. When under pressure, some go to drugs and alcohol. I got high from running. You lose weight, function better, and get to think about things. Teaching is hard. American kids can see through you. They knew more, but in the head, not in the way they needed, not with experience. I had lots of energy for the CMC test and to teach the kids. I could work doubles in the E-Room and graduation. Running gave me the energy to think about taking the CMC. It would have never come to me to take the CMC, otherwise.

In 1981, the Certified Master Chef Exam was too new to get involved. But I still wonder: *Who am I? What's my value?* In 1982, I had developed a bad knee from running and spent time recuperating. By 1983, I had the right knee fixed. It was the right place and the right time to take the CMC exam. I needed to know where I fit, where I was. I needed to improve some areas for the exam. I signed up for garde-manger, to learn the new techniques, and audited sanitation class and supervisory development. My foundation was there. I had my backbone. There were twelve candidates taking the CMC exam. I received the Crystal Chef Award for the highest score in the CMC examination.

This was a big turn in my life: passed the CMC; ran a marathon. I was more professional. I stopped questioning myself and had a better feeling of who I was. I did not know where I was going, but I had the foundation and values. I didn't have "people" in my life. I had to find them myself. I knew I was good, but against whose standards? When I found out, I accomplished more. I became a better chef, a better human being.

Death of the Master Chef?

Achieving mastery is not what you do the last six months before the test. It is what you do for those twenty years, learning your craft. It is a way of life.

—RGH

The ACF instituted the Master Chef Certification in 1981. The CMC originally began as the US equivalent of the MOF, validating the European chefs who had immigrated—chefs like Roland Henin and Fritz Sonnenschmidt. In the late eighties and nineties, these original Master Chefs mentored young Europeans and a few American counterparts, sharing their secrets of the craft and forming the next wave of Master Chefs. Chefs such as Ron DeSantis and Raimund Hofmeister joined the CMC ranks. From the twenty-first century, CMCs like Rich Rosendale represent the next generation of chefs, trained not only in a variety of venues, but by a variety of trainers, creating a more diversified level, a kind of "Old versus New Testament" values-meshing.

"Values-meshing" is good, but values *clashing* . . . not so much. Between the years 1981 and 1990, approximately fifty chefs earned the CMC title. Between 1990 and 2016, only eighteen chefs earned the title. In the 1980s, approximately 70 percent would pass, averaging ten CMCs per examination. Nowadays, approximately 15 percent pass. Furthermore, the exam's rigor has decreased since its inception. For instance, the exam is now an eight-day event, compared to its original ten-day schedule. Fewer tests are given in both written and practical areas. Despite its modifications, the CMC exam, in Henin's opinion, is the best international test, even better than the MOF; in fact, Germany adopted the CMC format for its certification.

The Certified Master Chef is the highest and most demanding level of all ACF certification levels. It is the pinnacle of culinary achievement. Interestingly, the CMC exam is a *cooking* test, plain and simple—not *easy*, but simple. While the US CMC examination is the best, its success rate might be the worst. Based on the diminishing number of chefs who pass, the question must be raised: why?

As more chefs enter the industry, fewer seem qualified to earn this title. On the surface, the logic is reversed . . . or is it? Has their training diminished? Has their motivation waned? Is the CMC exam still valid in today's culinary culture? Is the Certified Master Chef a dying breed?

Roland Henin has struggled with these tough questions throughout his life, as have all the Master Chefs. As the man who holds the record for one of the highest cumulative CMC scores, someone who has devoted his life to implementing certification and has personally coached hundreds of chefs through various certification tests, Henin sees little light at the end of the tunnel.

Chef believes it goes back to the backbone. The typical US chef attends culinary school and is hired into the system with the elevated label of "chef," skipping the gradual progression of line cook and then sous-chef and then finally achieving chef status. More and more executive chefs start in their twenties. Chef Henin and his CMC colleagues advocate pacing and respecting growth. Premature advancement is steroidal; without proper support, the candidate is a house of cards and will collapse.

It's not only backbone; the entire landscape of culinary arts has changed. Culinary arts is no longer a cook's game, as Randy Torres discussed: "What is culinary school for, now? Are we teaching people about working in a restaurant, or are we teaching people about cooking? It may sound funny, but those are two different worlds."

Despite these changes and obstacles, about a dozen candidates arrive from each CMC examination. How on earth are they getting there? How does the CMC value survive?

To answer these questions, you'd have to ask those candidates who make it through, who endure the eight days and 130 hours of examination, plus the thousands of hours, days, *years* of preparation . . . the ones who master, not only their techniques, but also their bodies, and the biggest obstacle of all . . . they master their minds. There may be little light at the end of the tunnel, but the light shines brightly for those who insist on swimming upstream.

Certified Master Chefs

Dan Hugelier, CMC

Owner, Wildseason

Wow, I'm in chef heaven! Henin, Sonnenschmidt, Elmer, Corky—all those guys, they were the Culinary Institute. They wove the fabric of cooking in America into these kids.

DAN: I've always had a level of respect for Roland that comes from admiration. He's one of those European chefs that came to America and helped enrich our culinary scene.

I met him at the CIA when I was first trying out for the Culinary Olympic team. It was around 1980, and he was an instructor at the institute. I was on three national teams, flying from Michigan to New York twice a month for like, twelve years. I would see Roland at lunch or in his classroom. He would always visit and interact with the team while we practiced.

Roland was always viewed by other chefs at the school for his expertise. His culinary genetic makeup is such that he was a Farm-to-Table guy long before it became our industry's latest buzzword. Farm-to-Table is not a fad; it's simply what good chefs do—take the best ingredients from the earth when it's time, at prime seasonal harvest. The franchises in the restaurant industry, the bistros and the bars, are claiming to do this Farm-to-Table thing as if it's brand-new. [Laughs]

If you go to Alain DuCasse's website, he says clearly up front, 60 percent of what we do as chefs is dependent on the raw product, and 40 percent is what we do with it. That attitude has been ingrained in Roland throughout his cooking experience. For instance, someone will ask him: What's the proper, classical way to cook a breast of veal? It might be another judge during the Master Chef's exam. Roland will say, "Well, what type? Is it *Parisienne* or *Alsatian*-style? What is the time of year, a winter braise or lighter version with spring vegetable?" He understands little pocket regions of culinary influence that escape the notice of most! I mean, not just in Europe and in our country, but globally, too. Most

American chefs are only looking from one perspective: "Oh, I gotta cook the breast of veal." There are hundreds of ways you could cook that breast of veal. Which style? Which method? We're only limited by our experience.

Ferdinand Metz was our team manager. Metz promoted this "whole new concept" called American Cuisine. He promoted food and wine in America much like Escoffier did in France. Metz is a German-born chef at the helm of an American institute with around 120 chefs from every background you can imagine—heavy European influence—teaching thousands of American kids, trying to put a mindset, a school of thought as a seed that they might grow in the right way. Roland was part of that history. He's French, so he's a passionate perfectionist, to say the least, about everything he does.

SUSAN: *I had him in Fish Kitchen in '83, so would agree.*

DAN: So you were a student there? Awesome. Well that's nice; you know what you're writing about.

SUSAN: *A little bit. [We laugh]*

DAN: I was the Detroit Athletic Club chef for twelve years and had carte blanche. We had the three big auto companies and other executives when the industry was in its heyday. Tax write-offs were the norm, so we did fine cooking there, in different styles, in different venues. That was the biggest part of my education: having those years to exercise my craft and discover. I continued my study of Escoffier and Alain DuCasse and following Frédy Girardet, Daniel Boulud, and Joël Robuchon. These guys know how to cook! I thought, *That's how I want to cook, what I want to do.*

During that time of my career, Roland was always someone with whom I could ask questions about food, our conversations taking endless pleasant detours as we both displayed our curiosity and knowledge with each other. We became friends over the years through those exchanges. When Roland is in charge of something, he fills the room. He melts back into a statesman's mold among his colleagues and has a quiet presence. Everyone knows he has wisdom and answers and that this man would state them.

We did a Master Chefs' dinner . . . we did them all over the country, but we did several of them over the years at Hartmut Handke's place in Columbus, Ohio. Hartmut's a fellow team member and Master Chef. Tim Ryan might be doing a course, or Victor Gielisse, or Peter Timmins, myself . . . we would have like ten or twelve Master Chefs. We would converge on Columbus, and we would do a kick-butt dinner, to help Hartmut, to see each other, and I guess to make an excuse to have a grand event. They were wonderful.

I'll give you an example about Roland in this scenario. One year, he did beautiful poached baby turbot filets in a fish *consommé*, with Beluga caviar, and little *pluches de cerfeuil*. The poached filet lay right in the middle in the rich fish *consommé*. Simple. It was a fish and soup course served simultaneously. The poached fish fit on a bouillon spoon, the piece of filet. I don't recall what the starch element was; he may have had a pastry *fleuron* at the service time. He asked me to taste it when he was plating during service.

We often offer each other a taste as we're going. When Roland was doing the fish course, he handed me a bouillon spoon. I tasted it. "Roland, did you use veal stock for the fumé?"

And he just smiled, didn't say anything.

After he finished dishing up, he approached me. "Why did you ask that?"

I replied, "Your fish consommé has rich viscosity and adheres to the palette. There are not enough glutinous qualities in the fish alone, especially in baby turbot bones, to yield that gelatinous element. Besides, you're French. I know a lot of the old French classical dishes. Escoffier describes putting a ribbon or a border of *glace de viande* around *Paupiettes* of Dover sole, or dipping a slice of black truffle into *glacé* and butter to glaze or adorn fish dishes. I just figured that when I prepare it that way and when I taste it that way, it makes sense to make a veal stock for the fumé."

Roland smiled and he said, "I did. Not too many people understand or can taste that."

At that dinner, I made a ballotine of wild Scottish wood pigeon with foie gras and figs . . . he loved the course. Those birds were shot in Scotland by hunters and dog-retrieved, aged, and shipped over to me. They were small pigeons, and I boned the entire bird, then put inside a fig, with cognac, minced shallots, lemon rind, and fine herbs. That was cut, as I served it open partway. I had a crisp potato *galette*, fresh duck foie gras, and red wine *Jus Lié* with that course.

Another year I did a mushroom garnish inspired by my friend Fritz Gitschner, CMC. He did a version of this for the Bocuse d'Or completion, a few years earlier. It looked like a wild cep mushroom, but it was a baby onion filled with mushroom quiche with a mushroom cap from a shiitake, a golden oak mushroom sautéed with lemon, seasonings, and Madeira wine. This was put on top of a bulging onion. Then I did a calf's sweetbread and duck foie gras with *Zingara garniture*—smoked tongue, ham, truffle, and white mushroom cut real fine, as a garnish. Helmut's restaurant was a German *Ratskeller*-type environment. It looked like a Hobbit might peek out from behind that mushroom.

Roland Henin is, without question, a foundationally solid cook. I don't like these chefs who are always overly-promoting themselves as the next guru of cuisine. They say, "This is my presentation of food"—*Chef So-and-so's* food, like they invented it. Right? Everything we do at a higher level is technically correct. It's not my food or Roland's food. It's the right way to do it.

I spent twenty-two years at Schoolcraft College. I wrote the curriculum for Butchery Charcuterie and oversaw Savory Cooking. Over the years, we served our students with the help of so many friends, past team members, and associates. I am so thankful. We always had great graduation speakers! I used to line up Noble Masi, Fritz Sonnenschmidt, and Ferdinand Metz. We had Charles Carroll . . . I could go down a long list. In my last year, we invited Roland Henin to be our guest speaker.

We plate service for the graduates and their guests, hundreds of people. Each kitchen and chef wants to create outstanding plates, and it was in the springtime, so everybody put on the dog. I had a plate with a wild mushroom variety, wild mushroom ravioli, some veal *jus* and one dish of duck foie gras sautéed throughout the service. Brian did a charcuterie. Jeff baked his best breads. Everybody wants to do well when you bring in chefs of that caliber to speak, right? It was outstanding—one of the best displays of food our faculty and students ever did.

Roland calls us out to this big granite bar in the dining room. "Dan, can you get all of these faculty members together? The food, the food's fantastic."

And I said, "Sure, Roland. Thanks."

I got everybody together and he said, "I thought before we speak to the students toward the end of their education, we could talk about our basic cooking thing, among ourselves, for fun."

Everybody says, "Oh, sure, Roland."

He asks, "Can you name the basic sauces—the proper mother sauces for classical cuisine?"

You learned that when you were a student, Susan?

SUSAN: *Yes, and I think I know where you're going with this story. Chef doesn't believe that espagnole sauce is one of them. He thinks that there's just the four, right? [Full disclosure: I had only just learned that days before, when interviewing Chef Jill Bosich. Thanks and good timing, Chef Jill!]*

DAN: Exactly. We all got that wrong. I said, "No way, Roland!" So I go into the office, I pop open Escoffier, LaRousse, and Herings . . . Son of a gun, he's right. *Espagnole* is a component of braising. It can yield a demi-like sauce, but it is not a mother sauce. I still, today, make my demi with *espagnole* as part of the process.

I don't simply just reduce the stock; I clear it of its impurities as it reduces, replenishing sometimes with water so it doesn't get too meaty, too out of balance. I spent several years as *saucier*, so I love that part of it. I like flavor that's left behind in the demi even after it's clear. It's a different type of taste.

Author's note: *After consulting with Chef Henin, he declared that there are four Mother Sauces: Demi-glace; Béchamel; Tomato; Veloute.*

RGH: *Those old giants of cooking developed the mother sauces out of necessity and practicality. Old kitchens were in the basement, and space was limited on the stove. Certain sauces take a long time, so they needed to make a large quantity at once. These sauces have a roux binder and are therefore stable. They maintain their quality for seven to ten days, sometimes longer. They were also the base sauce for compound sauces. These stable, long-cooking, high-quality building sauces were named the mother sauces.*

Mother sauces have both the quality and quantity. These guys would make a sauce and put it in the cooler, and a week later, it was the same quality as when they put it in. To use, they simply remove some from the cooler and bring to a boil. These sauces take a long time to prepare. Béchamel is the quickest, taking approximately three hours. You don't make these sauces á la minute. You can't, by their very nature. These guys would make a big amount and also stagger the sauces: Béchamel on Monday; velouté on Tuesday; and so on.

Hollandaise, being an emulsion sauce, is not stable . . . it breaks easily. It is not thickened with roux; it is emulsified with egg. It doesn't take a long time to make, so it should be made in small batches. There are only a few compound sauces made from it. For all these reasons, Hollandaise is not a mother sauce.

DAN: But we had a great time. We changed our curriculum. The ProChef, if you noticed, changed their curriculum, and it's because of Roland. If you want to aspire to the highest levels working for food science and want to consider yourself professional at the level of a doctor, these types of refined debates are a step, all so basic, compared to brain surgery.

If I see a chef from Johnson & Wales, I know he's a great manager. He'll be number one with the accountants. If I have a serious student from the Culinary Institute, especially back in the day when you went, I know they've been taught right. I know Jim Heywood, and Corky and all those guys; they did it right and brought finesse to cooking in America.

SUSAN: *Looking back, it was an amazing time to be at the CIA.*

DAN: Absolutely. I think I was twenty-four, Susan, the first time I tried out for the Culinary Olympic team. We had our first practice competition in Bruno Ellmer's kitchen. We were to do a crab-stuffed chicken breast. I was wet behind the ears. I never went to school there. I was not in the group. I didn't know anybody—Metz or any of those guys—when I started. I did a double supreme and removed that little bit of cartilage to peel without splitting the supreme. I ordered baby chickens, these little *poussin*. I did a lump crabmeat filling, but maintained the lump with spinach and shallot, and some toasted *mie de pain*. Mine was the last one to be tasted. Sonnenschmidt tasted it and threw the fork down. It slid down the side and hit the back of the table.

I went, *Uh oh. Maybe he got a shell or something.*

He tasted it with Elmer and they said, "This is the best one."

I didn't know what to do; I turned beet red. I was very introverted.

The other chefs, including Metz, were in there. Each one did their own version and were like [clears throat], "Ahem, ahem, okay then, ahem, we use that one."

And it's like, *Oh man. I'm happy to hang with you guys. I'm not trying to . . .*

But then, Elmer wanted to know, "Why was yours so juicy? Everyone pounded the shit out of their breast, and yours stood, it was juicy."

I said, "I like to pick the young chicken."

Everybody laughed after the practice.

There were still Robot Coupe parts in the sink, so I stayed. It took about a half hour to finish cleaning the kitchen. I didn't know Chef Elmer was still in the building and he came by, had been watching me. "Dan, are you hungry?"

I said, "A little bit, Chef."

He said, "How about if we have a little goulash soup?"

He went to his region and heated up goulash soup and sautéed some spaetzles. I still do it the same way. I cook them like hash browns, let them get a crust and butter and flip the whole thing. But I got to have goulash soup with Chef Elmer.

Whenever I go to the school and meet these guys, I'm like, *Wow, I'm in chef heaven! I have people! I have brilliant people that I can ask questions, who themselves are embroiled in discovery all the time because they love to cook!* That was a great place to be anyhow, but it was a great place to meet Roland. Roland Henin, Sonnenschmidt, Elmer, Corky—all those guys, they *were* the Culinary Institute. They wove the fabric of cooking in America into these kids. And then, I followed their curriculum that I helped them with to deploy at Schoolcraft College.

Back in the day, we weren't just competing for gold medals; we were competing for each other's respect. On my first trip to Germany, I couldn't believe it.

Oh my God. I can get a better meal at the train station in Frankfurt than any restaurant in America! Our food sucks! We don't even have good bread. What the hell are they doing to our sausage and hot dogs that makes them so pink? Weird pink. We were all caught up at a time when we could effect change in cooking in America. It wasn't our goal, but it was just happening, and it was great fun.

One other quick story is when we had tryouts for the '88 team . . . it would have been in '86. They didn't have enough apprentices, so Mark Erickson and I had to share an apprentice for the tryouts. That's huge. But we're guys, we'd read that book.

Roland was a floor judge. He kept coming by and looking in my garbage can. I'd sneak up behind him and pretend that I was gonna nudge him into that garbage can.

He said, "What are you doing, Chef Dan?"

"Listen, Roland, I'm not putting anything in there. You think I'm crazy?" I said, "Go get a job as a garbage man. That's not where the food is, it's up here on the table."

"Now, you need to be respectful, Chef."

"I love you, Roland. You're not going to find nothing in there."

SUSAN: *You sound more like his colleague than his mentee. You've earned that status.*

DAN: I enjoy spending time with Roland. He's a fisherman. He didn't go to our last Master Chefs' meeting because he wanted to go salmon fishing. It was the peak of the season and I just love that he did that. I'm a hunter, and I've made my own long bows and arrows. I have to have my freedom. Roland and I connect in that way. We spent so many years in kitchens, on quarter tile floor, wet slippery knives, and crazy people, right? Around people, kids, and students who should be doing anything else except cooking . . . we did that for fifty years. It's good to get your feet in the dirt, on the earth, or in a boat, and just breathe the air. He earned it.

I cherish anything I can get from earth. I took a doe last week, a nice fat doe. I still have three more tags actually, so I'm still deer hunting, but we eat mostly wild deer, turkey, and wild boar. We forage our own mushrooms and dry 'em. Go crazy on asparagus. In the spring, harvest ramps and wild garlic. We have chickens, so we've always got eggs, and if I could do it over again, I probably would be a homesteader-type farmer. But then I never would have learned to cook well from all the wonderful people who shared ideas with me.

SUSAN: *Where did you receive your culinary training?*

DAN: I always wanted to be a student at the institute, but couldn't afford it. I started cooking. I started working in restaurants when I was thirteen, as a bus-boy and a dishwasher. Watching the short-order cooks amazed me, so I got in there, and one thing led to another. I was cooking when I was fourteen—flipping six-egg pans and throwing down for the bar crowd on Saturdays at two in the morning. I would feed two hundred people by myself. It was cool. I just love the dance, if you will, of line work. And there were waitresses! Where else would I want to be, right?

The people who knew the restaurant owner were chefs around town, running the Polish Center Club and other clubs. They came in to help open this restaurant. They'd take me on the weekends, and I'd learn how to cook prime rib for five hundred people: how to season 'em and start 'em upside down; how to check them with a metal skewer; and how far that fat cap is gonna shrink from bones when they're done. Then another chef would take me on Saturday mornings. I would make spaghetti sauce—six hundred to eight hundred gallons, in these huge kettles for Bella Mia Spaghetti Sauce, Lipari Foods. Then, I got the opportunity to work for Milos Cihelka, who was in the first group of Master Chefs; he tested with Metz in that group. One week before I was married, I left a good-paying job to work for him at the London Chop House, as a saucier. That restaurant was happening, back then! We had all dried meats and aging boxes. We made our own vinegars in huge wine barrels. It was a neat place and my first taste of fine cooking.

Then I went to the Detroit Athletic Club as chef de cuisine. The chef there was a Scottish fella who was a con artist. Six months later, they promoted him to executive chef, and I wasn't ready for that. I was just a kid, so I moved into the chef's office. There was one old book, with a pink-brown cover, I think. It was the smaller version of Escoffier. I skimmed through the book briefly and took it home that night and looked at it. *This guy writes about cooking like a warrior poet! This book makes me crazy! If I want to make something, I got to go from one end of the book to the other.*

I decided I'd make everything in that book, since the Athletic Club had several venues: a formal dining room; the grill room; the lady's dining room, with all Ming china; a men's grill room; and a bowling alley. We had all the athletic squash courts and the foodservice up there, too. I had a place for a club sandwich, chicken liver pâté, oxtail consommé . . . whatever I wanted to make in that book, I had a place to put it. It took about twelve years, and I made almost everything.

In 1988, I took my Master Chef Certification. I was all streetwise and self-studied. I got to write curriculum for your school with Tim Rodgers, and gosh,

Ron DeSantis. I worked on creating butchery and charcuterie videos. I had always wanted to go to school there and ended up helping them with curriculum as well as writing curriculum for other colleges! I learned ass-backward.

Roland does have a sense of humor and a good heart. If he sees someone cooking who is serious, yet they're stumbling—they're lighting themselves on fire—he'll help them. If he thinks they're sincere, he reaches out. He did that with me when I was young. I learned to do that with others.

The hero of the story here is Roland. He shares ideas. He has affected many elements of cooking in America today. Everyone who knows him thinks the world of him. He's a good guy. He's fun to be with. He's a great chef. I'm lucky to have known him and worked with him a little.

That's my story and I'm sticking to it.

Steve Giunta, CMC

Culinary Director, Cargill Inc.

*The fact that we won had nothing to do with our culinary talent and
had everything to do with his leadership.*

I was fortunate to have met Chef Henin early on in my career. I decided to go
to the CIA right out of high school. Luckily for me, I was an a.m. student.
Chef Henin taught the p.m., so I didn't have him as an instructor right off
the bat. Legend quickly grew at the CIA where he taught Fish Kitchen, and
that's where I first met him. He ran his p.m. class differently than the a.m. instructor . . . a bit like a boot camp. He speaks fast, has a French accent, and—
pardon the expression—he's hell on wheels in the kitchen. He quickly had this
bravado about him that he was not going to put up with mediocrity, and he
wanted all the students to know that.

I continued my career at the CIA at the American Bounty restaurant as a
part-time waiter. I befriended Tim Ryan, the American Bounty chef. I graduated
and was offered a fellowship position, which is kind of a junior chef, reporting to Tim Ryan. Fellowships have a bit of an elevated status. We're still looked
down upon because we're not full-fledged chefs, but we were half a step above
the students, so that was a good place to be—in the limbo of where you don't
have the pressure of a chef but are better than a student.

Roland Henin was the young brusque French chef at the Escoffier French
restaurant, and Tim was a young brash American chef. He and Chef Henin became fast friends. They would spend time together on the weekend nights, and
I, being a student groupie, would hang around them trying to gain culinary tidbits. It was awesome to see the interaction between chefs Henin and Ryan because they had both worked in France. They had so much common ground and
appreciation for classic French cooking, so at twenty years old, I got introduced
into real cooking by two *real* chefs.

Shortly after that, Chef Ryan became part of the 1984 Culinary Olympic
Team in Frankfurt, Germany. One of the events leading up to the Olympics
was this "Dinner of the Century," held at the Palmer House Hotel in Chicago.
Chef Henin assisted, coaching the younger apprentices and sous-chefs. Being
Tim Ryan's assistant chef, I flew to Chicago and participated. We were serving
about three hundred people. Chef Ryan had the fish course, and part of that

dish was a caviar beurre blanc. Something went amiss with the beurre blanc, and it separated. Chef Ryan yelled over at me to start dicing eighteen pounds of butter, so that we could make more beurre blanc, but Chef Henin dove into the range, literally swooped down, and with a few strokes, fixed the situation and repaired the sauce. I don't know what he did, but I heard him and Chef Ryan laughing and clapping each other on the back, so I took that as a sign to stop dicing butter.

A year later, I was part of the CIA Alumni Team that competed in a Junior Culinary Competition, an apprentice competition held in George Brown College in Toronto, Canada. I was working for Bradley Ogden in San Francisco. Chef Henin was the mentor/coach and asked if I wanted to try out. I flew to New York, put a platter and a hot dish together, and was chosen along with four other young chefs to be part of the team. They held practices at the Hyde Park facility, but I was busy out in California, so wasn't able to make these. Remember, this is before email, smartphones, and all that stuff. Just through conversations on the phone, I was given a turkey platter to put together and help with the lamb main course we were going to serve as part of the hot food competition.

We arrive in Toronto. There were five of us . . . and it was supposed to be a four-person team. I'm doing the math in my head. *Okay . . . five young chefs are here, and four people are allowed on each team . . . something's not right.*

I went to Chef Henin and asked, "Chef, do we have an extra chef?"

He looks at me, and says, "Yeah. You."

"Oh. Okay."

I had asked for vacation time and spent my own money flying to Toronto and realized that I was the *apprentice* to this apprenticeship competition. I said to Chef, "I don't know what happened, or how we got off the target here, but I want to be one of the four teammate members here. I don't want to be the *commis* to the *commis*."

Chef goes and talks to the group, comes back and says, "Well, you're the Team Captain now."

I went from not being on the team and being the pot washer to Team Captain. I don't know what happened. The downside to Chef Henin is that he's not always the greatest, most clear communicator. Right? He takes a lot of input, but he does things his way. This was a great example of him just trying to do the right thing and not hurt anybody's feelings. He's got a big heart, but in the middle of all this, he said yes to everything and wound up with a five-person team. The four were from New York, and I could see a kind of *out-of-sight, out-of-mind* thing where he might have forgotten about me. But when I approached him, I think he realized—I had many conversations about this with Tim Ryan, after this competition—I think Chef realized: *Oh, this is Tim's guy.* Tim is now the president of the CIA. At some point, Chef Henin realized, *I cannot make this guy fly all this way and not give him a spot on the team.*

It gets better. We're in the middle of this competition. I had not done any practices with the team, so I didn't know the system they had put into place for the cold food—what platters they were using, etc.—so I'm just doing what I normally do with my experience on the Culinary Olympic Team and put together a turkey platter. I'm standing there, ready: everything glazed in aspic; all my *tourneyed* vegetables cooked, glazed, and beautiful; all the garnishes and the dough pieces. I'm ready to lay out my platter. Chef Henin looks around and doesn't see any other food ready or any other junior chefs there, so he starts screaming. It's just his way of showing love, but he's upset that the "new guy who just got promoted" is ready, while nobody else was. He asked me to put my food back in the cooler and go help the others. Now I've become the bad guy. I get to be the intermediary, going around saying, "Hey. You guys are running late. You have to get our food ready." Chef Henin is *losing it.* As he was judging other teams, and since he was our mentor/coach, he was not allowed to physically *do* anything. He was not allowed to pick up a knife. I've never seen someone so uncomfortable with their hands tied behind their back. He couldn't help the young chefs get their food ready, and he was like a caged animal. We put our cold platters out, and the next day, we did our hot food competition.

If you looked at the hour it took to get our cold platters together, you might have said, "This team will finish dead last." We were just running around like crazy. The story I tell is, it's like the football-catch game with the ball that vibrates . . . all the players stand on the field, and the ball kind of vibrates, and they move around in different circles, and they look like they're lost? That was us.

At some point, Chef took a deep breath. He went from purple to a light-red in the face, and then he brought us together. To be able to cook as well as he does, but also to problem-solve at such a high level was amazing. He quickly realized who was in trouble and who wasn't, and he paired the weak and strong together. Without his leadership, we wouldn't have gotten the food out at all. The fact that we won had nothing to do with our culinary talent and had everything to do with his leadership. The way he got us—through fear, mainly—but how he got us together at crunch time. . . . We won the 1985 international competition.

Chef Ryan was a newly-found culinary team member and Chef Henin was an up-and-coming chef at the CIA. Tim had spent his time in French roots, but is now trying to be an American Chef. So, Chef Ryan was making a seafood sausage, with pike as a forcemeat. Chef Henin asked him if he was interested in using a *panada* in the forcemeat, for the sausage. We soaked some bread and milk and added it to the pike as we ground it up. You forget about the roots of French cooking when trying to make something that sounds "American." But, the minute we added the *panada* into the mixture, it was elevated.

I'll never forget Chef Henin making pike quenelles, a ground pike *mousseline* forcemeat mixed with *pâte à choux*. The ratio is important: 2/3 *mousseline* and 1/3 *pâte à choux*, shaped into these large quenelles, poached, and then coated in *Sauce Americaine*. It was a dish in the Escoffier Room. I probably would have poached the quenelle and served it with the sauce separately, but true with Chef Henin's style, coating the quenelle with the lobster sauce gave it a depth of flavor and silkiness that it hadn't had before. I went on to work with Georges Perrier at Le Bec-Fin, and we made that exact same dish the exact same way. It was not only eye-opening when Chef Henin showed me, but it was confirmed by another French master.

The finishing technique with braise is an example of the elevated cooking needed to happen at the Master Chef's exam. Young chefs learn to braise: take a piece of beef; make sure it's dry; season it; brown it in a clear fat; and build flavors from there. Use wine, stock, and a thickened stock like a sauce *espagnole*, and then braise it. The liquid should come halfway up the product. You cook it covered in a moderate oven until it's fork-tender. That's all well and good. You create something beautiful.

But Chef Henin taught me how to *finish* that—unlike anything I had ever seen up to that point. He would take the braised meat and put it on a rack, like a baking sheet tray, put it in a moderate oven, and baste it once or twice with the braising liquid, while the sauce is finishing. What happens is, the seared crust was brought back. You would get this deep, rich, brown crust on the meat, glazing it dry in an oven like that. After watching him, I studied that section in Escoffier's *Le Guide Culinaire* and the same reference was there. Chef Henin learned that growing up: you take it 90 percent of the way there, braising it the way we're taught, but the final 10 percent makes all the difference in the world. To taste a braise that's been glazed like that, in the oven on a rack . . . it's unbelievably magnified beef flavor. It creates great food from good food.

Chefs Henin and Ryan would talk about three-star Michelin restaurants in France and the differences in those kinds of restaurants: their attention to detail and level of service. Wait staff were journeymen. It was their career and passion to serve food at the highest level. I noticed that the underlying theme of these discussions was a little frustration that the students weren't willing to understand the dedication it took to be part of a three-star Michelin restaurant. Tim Ryan talked about climbing a ladder and putting your chin over the next rung. He says you'll never understand that viewpoint unless you've seen—you've struggled to climb and see from a different vantage point—what excellence is all about. Chef Tim was fortunate to get that and it meant so much to him, because he no longer had a ceiling for his view of excellence. It was never unattainable, but higher than he would have anticipated before seeing it—the absolute preciseness of *à la minute* cooking—cooking things perfectly, precisely together, and serving them immediately. Everyone harmonized around serving something of perfection at the optimum time. Chef Henin confirmed this: that sense of urgency was compromised, over and over again, as our business grew bigger and has more people working in it. The ideal of a three-star restaurant meant the world to both of them.

Chef recently wrote me a four-page letter in this incredible French script, almost like calligraphy. Who writes a four-page letter anymore? I'm gonna buy him a tablet or something that he can type on (but he probably won't use it). The four-page letter is about preparation for the CMC exam. He goes back to the basics. What he sees in young chefs is that they don't spend enough time developing a plan, making sure that the plan works, and then executing it within the timeframe. That's the way he runs his organization. That's the way he mentors people, and that's the way he conducts his life: you start from the beginning; you make sure that you master the fundamentals, and you can build on top of that. *Don't go too far too fast.* The fundamentals are so important that you can't go anywhere without them. He honors excellent technique, which is the soul of French cooking.

Raimund Hofmeister, CMC

University Director, School of Culinary Arts and Hospitality Management, Stratford University

We don't like to talk about this in our business, but there is sensitivity in those kinds of people. You go deep, fine-tuning into every fiber of your body and connect with the food. You connect with the environment. It was one of the most spectacular things I have seen.

RAIMUND: I was born and raised in Germany and apprenticed in Baden-Baden, which is near the French border. I graduated at the top of my class and spent a lot of time in the Alsace region and went to some nice places in Switzerland. I spent a couple years in South Africa, joined Westin hotels in Johannesburg in 1972, and then moved with Westin Hotels to the US, in Kansas City. Opened up the Beach Plaza Hotel, the Detroit Renaissance Center, and then moved to Hawaii. From there, went to Tulsa, Oklahoma to open the Williams Plaza. I got the flagship of the company, the Century Plaza Hotel, and became executive chef there, in 1979. That was a rather incredible milestone in my career: I was twenty-nine years old and got this big monster hotel. The Century Plaza became the headquarters for Ronald Reagan away from home, hosting all the events and functions for the president, officially and unofficially. I tried out for US Culinary team and became a member in 1982, and then went for my CMC in 1986.

It was in about 1982, in my assignment to the US Culinary team with Ian Bender, where Roland and I first connected. Not that we recognized each other on a personal basis, but it started a relationship during my CMC exam in Hyde Park, New York, where he was the judge for the classical part of the test. I think this was the first time we made a lasting impression on each other, with the famous Wiener schnitzel episode.

During the exam in the International category, I got a rather complicated Italian menu, while my counterpart got a Wiener schnitzel. I was kind of laughing, because I didn't see the comparison of the challenge. The chef who got the Wiener schnitzel was pooling sweat, in a panic.

I asked him, "What's the problem?" I've done thousands of Wiener schnitzels in my apprenticeship and all through my career and never thought it was a challenge.

He said, "You don't know what I've gotten myself into. It's the worst I could imagine."

I watched him make the Wiener schnitzel. It was a wonderful Wiener schnitzel . . . and he just barely made it. He squeaked by with 3/10 of a point, and I thought to myself, *My God, what's going on here?*

On the final day of my exam, in the general basket, where you pick your assignment . . . guess what? I got the Wiener schnitzel! So, I was now in desperation . . . the last day counts as 50 percent of your grade. After several days of cruel examination, everything you have accomplished is still in jeopardy. You do stupid things when you are desperate and tired. I looked at the Wiener schnitzel and thought, *He did a wonderful Wiener schnitzel. I don't know why he got such a low score. What can I do?*

I scored the breading, marking it. It's something you just don't do, but I did it. Of course, as I fried it in the pan, it came out kind of bubbly, nice . . . but the breading kind of broke, because I cut into it. As it went in to the judges, they didn't come out of the room. That wasn't a good sign. I'm pacing up and down and I saw all this nightmarish news . . . *Chef Hofmeister didn't make the CMC exam,* this and that. I was in a suicidal mood there. The doors open and somebody screams out of the room, "HofmeistEHR! Come in!"

I got in there, and I still see it in my head, just like yesterday. There's this big table. And there's this one mean chef in the middle who has my Wiener schnitzel on his fork. He kind of threw it down on the table. The breading just . . . went *everywhere.*

He looked at me and he said, "What do you call this? A Wiener schnitzel?!"

I mean, my world's just finished, at that moment. I said, "Is this it?"

It was Bruno Ellmer. He looked at all the Master Chefs behind him. He kind of, in a dominant way, influenced the other chefs.

"What do you think? This qualifies as absolutely nothing!"

He went down the line, one by one, to ask them what they thought. The first four judges were absolutely negative; they agreed with him.

Then they come to Roland Henin.

And Roland . . . I just love him. He looks at Bruno, and deep down, I'm still convinced that somehow, Roland must have gone through a similar kind of a torture, and this is his chance to get even. He just looks at Bruno Ellmer and he says, "I don't know what you have with this Wiener schnitzel. To me, it looks perfectly fine."

It was kind of the icebreaker! After that, yes, I slipped by. I just barely made it—of course, not with Bruno who was concerned, but with the rest of the other Master Chefs.

Later on, I was so mad, and that night it was Mystery Basket for ten people, and Roland kind of was scouting around, watching every move I made. I was so upset, and I just cooked my heart out. *Put him in the ground,* you know, this is not sitting well, so he came to me and said, "Raimund, you mustn't be angry. Small potato. Wiener schnitzel is not a culinary thunderstorm." He looked at me and he says, "Your classic examination was one of the best, and that is all that counts." I had one of the highest scores in the classical French cuisine, and that laid the foundation of our relationship. I have the utmost respect that he stood up for me, and he knew there was more in my life than cooking a Wiener schnitzel, or maybe messing up on a Wiener schnitzel. Ever since then, I would never let anything bad happen to Mr. Roland Henin. [Laughs]

After I passed the exam, of course I don't have to tell you how drunk I got, but it was quite an ordeal. My friends picked me up, and we had the celebration at Windows on the World in the World Trade Center. Ever since then, Roland and I have had a great relationship. After winning the Culinary Olympics and during the world championship in 1986, I had the task to put the first original ACF Culinary team together. We asked Roland if he wanted to come in as the team captain for the ACF Western Regional culinary team, which he then accepted. Those were two wonderful years. We developed an incredible concept.

I received my CMC in April 1986, and we put the team together a few months later. We went to the Culinary Olympics with the Western Regional team in 1988, and we did the America's Cup in Chicago, which we won. It was a good endorsement to compete in Frankfurt, because the establishment didn't want to have regional teams. We were self-funded and not officially endorsed by the ACF. We ran against the establishment, but were instrumental. You don't have to win in order to leave your lasting impression. In those two years, we forced the ACF to think differently and allow regional teams, allowing more people to participate in the various aspects of Culinary Olympics. We don't interfere with the national team, but we compete in different categories for different honors. We actually supplied national team members out of that team for the next four years. Our long-range fighting against the odds was pretty good.

SUSAN: *Being allowed to compete in this way sounds pioneering—it hadn't been done before?*

RAIMUND: Not on such a large scale independent organization. We covered the entire ACF Western Region. We went out there and scouted for the chefs to get on the team. It was a rough two years. We worked extremely hard. It's nice to have a budget and sponsors; we didn't have that, so we started from scratch.

We got a few donations and made chapter presentations to get a little money. At the end, we had a wonderful setup, a nicely put-together machine. We went to Frankfurt with almost thirty people. I love every minute of the memory of that, especially the finish. Roland never forgives me for what I did that day, but that's what friends are for. [Laughs]

We were competing all through, and of course, when you finish with all that, you're pretty tired, so we decided on the last day that we were gonna go and have dinner. We went to a nice restaurant in our hotel, we were having a good time, and Roland fell asleep. He was so exhausted. He sat at the table with his eyes open, just snoring away. Everybody made his own little token comment. *Let's set him up here.* We tell the maître d' that we're going to go outside, and when we're outside, he should wake him up and give him the bill. He didn't know what to think. I said, Be insistent. Force the issue. Threaten to call the police or something. And sure enough, we were all outside, and we look in the great windows of the restaurant, watching the whole scene. The maître d' woke him up. Roland became confused and then disturbed to find he was all by himself in that restaurant. The maître d', of course, speaks German, and Roland doesn't. If you could have seen that, it would have been a classic comic. He was so confused. He argued back and forth, and finally, *finally*, the maître d' let him go, and Roland stormed out the restaurant. We were maybe a few steps down and were all outside cheering at him. He was so mad. He didn't speak with us for two whole days. [Laughs]

SUSAN: *I thought he let things slide, like a duck with water rolling off his back . . . we don't have to talk about the "table dance" . . .*

RAIMUND: [Laughs] No no no. I mean, really, what are the rumors about that?

SUSAN: *Just a line in an email I caught . . .*

RAIMUND: After a few drinks anything is possible.

SUSAN: *We'll get off the table and back into the kitchen. I thought of you both as equal mentors to other people, but did you have some kind of mentoring relationship with him? Did you work with him in kitchens or just in competitions?*

RAIMUND: We worked those two years in training sessions, and we'd meet in Practical exams and other food competitions. We have not worked one-on-one in the same kitchen. He had one of the most spectacular food displays in

Frankfurt, in the 1988 Olympics. He did get a gold medal. What he did there was borderline perfection. When you develop those kind of things, practice session after practice session, you get in contact with the man's inner commitment. We don't like to talk about this in our business, but there *is* sensitivity in those kinds of people. You go deep, fine-tuning into every fiber of your body and connect with the food. You connect with the environment. It was one of the most spectacular things I have seen. If he had been representing the US national team, the notoriety would have come so much bigger and stronger for what he did. If he had been part of *any* national team, it would have been a sensational display.

I always hate to say *better than me*, but . . . yes, he was definitely better than me, in that competition. I can say, "Well, I was team manager, I had a million things to do, I couldn't really concentrate." Those are only excuses. He just was better. I thought it was the most downplayed display, and I never have seen such an in-depth commitment from anybody on one single expression—to bring out the Pacific Northwest: the barnacles; the unique seafood; the unique plates of color combinations and compositions. He's a fisherman, and all of that reflected into that display. He must have spent I don't know how much time to research what is unique to the region. I had seen him, week after week, working on the same thing, little by little, picking the ingredients, making sure they're all perfect, cooked together perfect. Your respect for a man grows when you see those kinds of things. The outcome was spectacular. I fell in love with it. I couldn't see enough of what he did, and the whole team benefited from that corner display. People were constantly marching around that section of the table, looking at it. We all felt spectacular. When you think back in history, when those things happen, you don't connect all the dots. You have to grow up in life and go through a certain period to know it better than you knew it at that time.

SUSAN: *Yes, we live in strange, polarized times . . . more people are connecting with food locally, while globally, mono-cropped food is becoming horrifyingly industrialized.*

RAIMUND: Food—is it safe or is it not safe? Here we are. We talk about organically grown foods and this and that, but this is what people like me and Roland grew up with. You have a whole different connection. There's so much talk about genetically engineered foods and what a bad future we all have. All this happens because we let it happen. As long as we let it happen, a disaster somewhere down the road is going to come.

When I ask a student, *Describe to me how an asparagus is grown?* They have no clue. If they would see an asparagus field, they wouldn't even recognize that they grow the asparagus there, okay? I mean, you have CMC exams, and half of the chefs never recognize an artichoke! Yeah, it's a challenge to anyone, because who wants to grow fresh artichokes? Who wants to do some of the more complicated stuff? When you see it, it's shocking.

Roland and I have a similar thought about this: if you get a beef tenderloin on your certification exam, it assures that you've passed. You can't screw it up. It's tender. It doesn't take rocket science. But give them something they have to work on, use skills of slow cooking—simmering, braising, etc., what good cooking is all about—and watch what happens. That is what is missing, and that is what he knows. A lot of what makes Roland Henin so great and powerful in this trade is his connection with food: the way the food is grown, the way the food is appreciated.

His weak habit, I tease him of it, could nearly be German . . . he's so organized and particular in everything he does. I refer to him as one of the last dinosaurs because of the level he is. There are not many chefs out there who still have this, this old precious value. It just does not exist anymore. We have conversations while watching Master Chef exams. We've done a lot of judging together and this and that, and the conversations always boil down to the basic principles of good work ethics, the work procedures, and the professional pride of people. If I would have been a student and had him as my teacher, I would be lucky.

Roland has been most criticized about his style in critiquing. You have to take it at face value. Whatever he says is true. Sometimes when you speak different languages, things come out in a different meaning. What weighs heavy in one language isn't always heavy in the other language. His critiques are *always*, always right on the button. I love to listen to it . . . very often, I couldn't say it any better. He put a lot of effort in for young chefs to help them develop properly, to give the advice. These days, it's not always taken the way it should be, because people don't give the time anymore for proper development. They think it has to be overnight and that doesn't happen in our business. Unfortunately, the whole trade suffers.

If I ever want to bring up an example to my students, I bring up Roland. I say, "You have to connect with food. If you want to become an exceptional chef, all the fibers in your body have to connect with it. Everything you touch. Everything you do. The way you pick it, the way you're looking at food, the way you display your food. You have to nurse it, babysit the steps of preparation. You just have to be in love with it." Roland Henin can do that. I have seen it.

What he is even better at is the everyday application of his trade. I can tell you what I think, how lucky the people are who work with him on an everyday basis. It has to rub off. People, if they are around him for a while, exact his style, his mannerisms, all aspects, they learn hard to treasure it. When I talk to people who have the privilege of working with him, they think the same way as I do. He's one of the best out there, and there's no question in my mind about that.

Ron DeSantis, CMC

Director of Culinary Excellence, Yale University and State University of New York Empire State College; Chef Consultant, Cancer Nutrition Consortium

Those forty minutes helped me for the rest of my career.

RON: I learned to cook in the United States Marine Corps. I was chef of the quarter Marine Corps Recruit Depot, San Diego. I won many awards and had emeritus promotions. Our dining hall in Okinawa, Japan, was the best dining facility for small category West Pacific. I was the chief cook there. After there, I went to school at the CIA. After graduation, there was one country in Europe that was working visas. The CIA faculty thought you had to go to Europe to be a good chef, so I went to Germany for five years and then got a job as a CIA faculty member. In a short period of time, I ended up in the Escoffier Restaurant, their four-star restaurant that, a couple of years before me, was the domain of Chef Roland Henin. He left the CIA about a year before I got there. I had heard of Roland Henin, but hadn't met him. So, I was working in the E-Room, as we affectionately called it, and the Certified Master Chef exam was under way. The exam coordinator, Chef Noble Masi, approached me and said he'd like me to be an expert judge in Classical Cuisine. I had no idea what this guy was talking about in terms of the exam and hadn't been back in the United States long enough to get information about it, but of course I was young and full of myself, and I figured, *Yeah, let me do this thing.*

I walked in, and they put me down in this judges' room next to Master Chef Byron Bardy.

"What's going on?"

"You'll be fine. Just enjoy the food, eat it, and give your feedback."

So, I did. Thankfully, I was asked my opinion about classical preparations, which is what I was teaching.

Somewhere along the line, my evaluation caught the attention of Chef Henin. The tasting was over, and we had to evaluate the station of the chefs to see how they had left it and their leftovers. Henin came over and said, "Chef, you're coming with me." Naturally, I jumped up and entered the kitchen with him. I was pretty sure about attention of detail and prided myself about that, but in that period of forty minutes, we went through these different stations.

He demonstrated to me what was valid, what things they shouldn't have done, why things were leftover, what things should have been used, product utilization or lack thereof. It was an unbelievable learning experience. Those forty minutes helped me for the rest of my career. That was my first time meeting Roland.

SUSAN: *You were in Germany for five years?*

RON: I was in Germany from 1981 to 1986. I was only going for one year, but I met this girl, and it took me four more years to convince her to move to America. For most of my final years, I lived in Bamberg, Germany, in Northern Bavaria. Bamberg was founded in 973. It's an old city, and, actually, to digress for one moment, Bamberg was the center of the Roman Catholic Religion. The Vatican moved to Bamberg, because Pope Clement II wanted to have his papal office there. The cathedral in Bamberg is where the Roman Catholic Church resided during his reign, and he is the only pope buried outside of Rome. How's that for some trivia origin history?

Roland and I wanted to know the traditions leading up to this thing, because they were more important than the raw ingredients. For example, during my Master Chef test, I drew a mussel dish to prepare, probably some Belgian dish. Having traveled to Germany and the Belgian border, I knew that when you serve mussels in Europe, you always take one clean mussel shell after they were steamed, because invariably there's one empty shell, and you slide it to the edge of the bowl. The whole shell clips on to the edge of the bowl, as it's still hinged. You use that one shell as tweezers to extract mussel meat from inside the other shells. I know these things, because I lived there for five years and made a point of experiencing and understanding these traditions and what these things meant. When I went for my CMC test, the judges put it on my critique, saying it was a nonfunctional garnish. I said, "That's good, because it's not a garnish; this is a function of this dish. This is the mussel shell you use to eat all the other mussel meat." I saw three pencils flip around to eraser, erase numbers, and put fresh numbers down. Had I not known these origins, then I wouldn't have been able to have that conversation.

That's the kind of connection Roland and I have. It's about good, excellent, wonderful cooking and great ingredients, but the other part of it is, where does the food come from, what are the traditions and origins of these different foodstuffs? I love these conversations with him. If you were not talking with a Belgian and understanding its origins, you might think that *beef flamande* would be a chuck cut, portioned into steaks and braised, where in reality, it is a stew. These kinds of things were in the Master Chef exam, so when it came up, I passed it. A couple of tests later, it comes up again, and somebody cuts the chuck into steaks. Roland said, "This is interesting, but this is not how it's done." During the Master Chef test, we ate that, together. The two of us could go on and on about *beef flamande* all night, about what this food is and what it represents: what size of the cut is used; what are the ingredients; how much onion goes in; what type of beer? You can't use a Budweiser. You need dark ale, because it will give a rich flavor to it, instead of being too bright or bitter. He and I can have that kind of conversation: him understanding precisely what this dish is and my visiting that area and having an Old-School Belgian colleague. Those conversations are rewarded when you understand the origins.

Roland speaks from the heart, which is fine, but if you don't know him, you may interpret that as harsh. He's not being harsh; he's being honest. There's nothing personal in what he's saying. People can be so thin-skinned that when they get real feedback, it might not be pleasant to hear. Roland doesn't filter what he says. He's not going to get caught up in the pleasantries of it. His feedback is factual, measurable, and objective. Sadly, people think, *Oh gosh, did you hear what he had to say?* I'm like, "Yeah, I heard it. He was spot-on." That's one of the things I absolutely admire about him. If you're not ready for professional, honest feedback, then boo-hoo on you. My feedback is exactly like his. I don't beat around the bush; I give it straight like he does.

In Michael Ruhlman's book, *The Soul of a Chef*, numerous people say he portrays me as the villain, because I leaned menacingly into CMC candidate Brian Polcyn's face saying, "Your knife skills have to be good, all the time."

Author's note: *The exact quote is as follows:*
"The major thing is your knife skills." He looks Polcyn dead in the eye and says, "You really need to have good knife skills."

"Yes, Chef." Polcyn swallows at the insult and cannot hold his tongue. "Actually Chef, I do have the knife skills. It's just that sometimes they don't come out."

DeSantis leans into Polcyn's face, and with quiet menace says, "During these ten days they have to come out."

"Yes, Chef."

RON: I was not menacing; I was being matter-of-fact and giving straightforward advice. Someone saw it as *I'm being a villain*, and that's what people don't understand. You hacked off a hunk of this terrine and your knife skills were horrible. They were sloppy, and I told you your knife skills have to be exceptional, especially during this exam, and the author saw me as being a menace. How I said it to that chef was exactly how Roland would have delivered it. So, I think our mentorship styles are extremely close.

When you are part of my mentor circle, you're in for life. When Roland works with people, he's always available for them. Probably the most rewarding project we've worked on together is the Cancer Nutrition Consortium (CNC). CNC is an extremely rewarding part of my life. I'm one of the founding members on the board. One of the biggest benefactors has been Delaware North. Roland and I developed a team of chefs and nearly 100 recipes to benefit patients undergoing chemotherapy. Cooking videos are primarily from some of Roland's chefs, such as Percy Whatley and Kevin Doherty. On the website are all these things that CNC has provided for cancer patients, under Roland's leadership—recipes, photographs, and videos: see www.cancernutrition.org.

For the last three years, he bugs me to go salmon fishing with him, sending pictures of the salmon he catches and his boat. I'm optimistic that 2017 will be the year. It's not such an unusual thing, because if you understand what we do in our craft, the natural thing is to know where the food comes from and go from there. Most of us grow vegetables and herbs and support farmers markets. His going to the sea—going to the source, catching that fish and having people join him—is his way of saying, "If you really want quality food, let's go out and catch that fish. It's going to be the most delicious fish you can ever imagine, because you're going to catch it and eat it as fresh as possible. You're going to be part of the entire process where you're getting up early, going out against the sea, and dropping and hauling the line."

It's just an obvious thing that he would ask. We've gotten together over the years and had fellowship of the table so many times. It's so rewarding and such a great way to exchange ideas. You talk about things like the Master Chef test and how to strengthen it, mentoring others, and how to drive things forward that are good for our industry. Those are valuable conversations, but taking that bigger step of going to the source and catching the food is so Roland Henin. That is exactly the right kind of thing to do.

Rich Rosendale, CMC

Chef & Entrepreneur, Rosendale Collective; Advisor, Bocuse d'Or USA 2017; Star of Emmy-nominated *Recipe Rehab* on Zliving

You never know who you're training—
you may be training the next Thomas Keller.

RICH: The first time I met Chef Henin was in 1998, as an apprentice working at Hartmut Handke's restaurant, in Columbus, Ohio, where we were hosting a CMC dinner. This is something they would do once or twice a year—all the Master Chefs would come together and each of them would prepare a different course. Chef Henin, being one of the CMCs, would do one of the courses. I had heard about him, obviously being Thomas Keller's mentor, for one thing. Roland Henin had an ominous, legendary reputation, one that would command respect.

SUSAN: *What led you to apprentice with Hartmut Handke?*

RICH: The culinary world is this big ecosystem. There is a lot of crossover, a lot of relationships that run parallel to each other. You may not have worked with somebody but feel like you know them because of the lineage of chefs who came through these kitchens. There is a lot of cross-pollination of cooks and chefs who worked with each other's mentor. When I finally met Thomas Keller, I felt like I already knew him well, because of my working closely with Chef Henin all these years.

I was a young apprentice at the Greenbrier resort. The Greenbrier has an old apprenticeship program—founded in 1957, it is the oldest program in the United States. You could be a young chef working with Chef Henin and may not understand his degree of training and the world he is coming from, but the Greenbrier program runs in the manner of Escoffier and the classical kitchen brigade, a European-style apprenticeship. I used to wear a starched chef hat and neckerchief; that's the way the Greenbrier was. Many CMCs have passed through that kitchen. An amazing depth of talent came through there. You would hear Roland Henin's name muttered many times, as a way for other chefs to motivate you. The apprenticeship season ran from April through November. In November, you had the opportunity to work during off-season and return in the spring. I decided to work with Hartmut Handke, a CMC who also used to be the executive chef at the Greenbrier, and who was also good friends with Roland Henin—again, a lot of crossover. You're a few degrees away from every other chef; it's a big sprawling network.

Chef Henin has been in both worlds: out there in the public restaurant and Michelin world, but also coming from that CMC/European training. It's almost like two different worlds. Chef Henin touched both of these groups, like a bridge between different sectors of the industry. And also, he's touched the competition world; Chef Henin understands and participates in the entire culinary spectrum.

You don't see Thomas Keller and Daniel Boulud taking the CMC exam, but the cooking principles are the same. It's why I get along with them; we understand and appreciate each other. There are not a lot of places where you can get this kind of training anymore. You'd have to go to Europe, to these old brigades with Escoffier-style training, and that's just not common. It used to be part of a chef's upbringing: work with a chef, through all of the disciplines in the kitchen: charcuterie, saucier, etc. This form of education, the apprenticeship, is becoming a lost art.

In the Michelin world of restaurants and restaurants in general, competition hasn't been something you see a lot of—that is, up until now, with Thomas Keller and Daniel Boulud very much involved in the Bocuse d'Or world culinary competition, in Lyon, France. Hartmut Handke also competed in the Bocuse d'Or. At the Greenbrier, culinary competitions were a large part of your training program. Their legacy is now passed down to me, as the next generation of chefs. I have a restaurant in Virginia and am also in the Bocuse world. I go out to the French Laundry in January to mentor the next competing team.

The origins of so many of these relationships, these seeds, were planted through people like Chef Henin. Think about what he started and what has manifested; it's remarkable, a ripple effect. You couldn't possibly imagine the reach that it had: the chef who took somebody like Thomas Keller under his wing and shaped him, and look how many people Chef Thomas has trained and influenced. And now, here I am—a different generation, talking about Chef Henin who has influenced me, flying out to the French Laundry next month to give feedback and critique to the next team competing at the Bocuse d'Or. It's layers of an onion, all connected and traced back to someone like Chef Henin. Chef Thomas and I didn't know anything about culinary competitions and the Bocuse d'Or until somebody like him exposed us to it.

I tried out for the Bocuse d'Or in 2008, the first time that Keller, Boulud, and Henin all had gotten involved. At the time, I was team captain for the

Culinary Olympic team, and I was opening a second restaurant, plus having a child. My wife was not thrilled when I decided to try out, because it's such a consuming endeavor. But I said, "Hey, all these people are involved in this; I've just *got* to throw my hat in the ring."

They announced the tryouts, and I went through the process. Eventually, you make it to the final cook-off in Orlando. I was the first chef out of twelve to put my food up. I thought I did well; in the end, Timothy Hollingsworth from the French Laundry was selected. I got second place and Michael Rotondo from Charlie Trotter's restaurant placed third. When they put the medal around my neck, I said I would be back. I wanted to compete again and I did . . . in 2013, I was selected to represent the US.

Before I was selected, Chef Henin was probably the most important person in helping me prepare. It's one thing to say you want to do the Bocuse d'Or, but you must earn the right to compete. Chef Henin essentially created the framework for me to be selected, and I followed diligently. He coached me one-on-one. I would fly out to other cities to meet with him. I didn't think there was anybody else but him who understood what it was going to take. He was the best person in the country to talk to. It must have been a good decision, because I got selected.

I stayed in touch with him from time to time, emailing him, and letting him know that I eventually wanted to do the Bocuse d'Or. I also was heavily involved with international competitions all over the world: Germany, Switzerland, Luxembourg, and France. Being someone who was also passionate about culinary competition, I would see him at these events. If he would ever tell me to call him anything other than Chef Henin, I would still call him that, because I had so much respect for him. I *still* call him Chef Henin. Whenever we meet, he asks about my career and my culinary team. He would ask me a lot of questions about how it was going at the Greenbrier. Early on, he had a soft spot for me. He liked that I was getting similar training to his. Anything I talk to him about—whether the CMC exam or the Bocuse d'Or or my experience on the Olympic team—whatever it is, he wants to improve the person, system, or process. He is not standing on the outside looking in, complaining about it. He always gives a solution.

He puts so much thought into an email and a conversation. Nowadays, you try to get somebody to send you just a text; they misspell half the words and it's like a partial sentence. This guy writes an email like it is a letter, *and*, by the way, he still writes handwritten letters, which I think is so refreshing and thoughtful: somebody who would take the time to write a handwritten letter or send several paragraphs in an email, with proper etiquette. It's just uncommon.

SUSAN: *What qualities attracted you to each other?*

RICH: I'm a disciplined person. Some might say intense, but I think of it as passionate, and he could see that. He's always going to help people and offer his feedback. People like him see qualities in someone that the person may not fully realize or may not see in themselves. He will try to bring out the best in you. Who knows . . . maybe if some of those emails had never come across to me, I might have taken a different route in my career. Maybe I wouldn't have tried out for the Bocuse d'Or.

We take the journey for granted: *no matter what, the outcome is always going to be the same.* Subtle or seemingly insignificant interactions with somebody may end up having a profound impact on the trajectory of your life. Conversations with him were meaningful and heavily influenced my decisions. A lot of people will point to circumstances in life as being what drives where you're going to end up or what you're going to accomplish. I don't think that's the case. I believe what we're going to achieve is based on decisions, and your decisions are heavily influenced by the people you surround yourself with. I feel fortunate to have met him and to have maintained our relationship.

The CMC exam needs to live and have a more relevant position in our profession. We need more people to take it. A lot of chefs are scared to death to take that exam, because it's pretty likely they're going to fail. The fail rate is about 90 percent. I think he saw, in me, somebody who could pass it, and so he pushed me. He also believed I was someone who could complete in the Bocuse d'Or, and so he pushed me. I'm glad he didn't just shoot off a two-line email, because who knows how things would have turned out? Maybe there were some parallels in his career that he saw in my experience. You look at Thomas Keller. If he had not met Chef Henin, who knows . . . maybe the French Laundry wouldn't exist. You think about the ripple effect that he has had on American cooking, and how many lives have been touched—not just the chefs, but the cooks who work for the chefs, and the people who work in these restaurants, and the customers who eat in these establishments, and buy the products, and share their passions with more people. It all starts with Chef Henin meeting someone and having that initial dialog.

SUSAN: *Describe a few Henin stories that represent the man.*

RICH: In preparation for the 2013 Bocuse tryouts, I decided to contact Chef Henin for his advice. This is a year before the tryouts. I had not yet taken the CMC. I was executive chef at the Greenbrier, which is a huge property: 750-room hotel; 15 kitchens and 200 chefs. The Greenbrier is a massive operation and still, I wanted to compete. I reached out to him, asking "What do you suggest?" He sent me this email back. Wow. I just reached out for suggestions on how to plan and prepare, and his response was like . . . it was like he was waiting for the question.

Basically, Chef sent me a blueprint. It was everything from: what would you expect; creating a training kitchen; talking to my employer about the commitment required; talking to my family; talking to my employees about what it's going to take; fund-raising and having the capital necessary to fund doing it right, to be ready; getting an isolated training kitchen, solely dedicated for my training; maintaining my role in my personal family life. As executive chef of this property and overseeing the apprenticeship program, he suggested hiring a trainer to develop my stamina, making sure I wouldn't fatigue. His being a runner, I'm not surprised that he would factor fitness into the training regimen. He also suggested taking the CMC (which I did), as part of my training for the Bocuse d'Or.

Most who would read this, their heads would be spinning. They'd be like, WOW. *You're talking about taking a year of 100 percent relentless sacrifice while you're working a full-time job, and you also have all your normal personal commitments with roles as husband and father.* A lot of people would have thought, *this is crazy,* but for me, I knew, *This is it. This is what it's gonna take. He's 100 percent right.* I took that and used it as my framework—The Plan.

I took that email, printed it off, and highlighted it. I used the topics as bullet points for what I was going to do that year, leading up to the tryouts. Mind you, this was just for selection to be able to *compete.* I went so over-the-top for preparing and finally getting selected. Then, I used a lot of his principles and training again, for being focused in the actual competition. When he said, *get a training kitchen* . . . when I was at the Greenbrier, I discovered a nuclear fallout shelter built during the cold war, a decommissioned bunker. I commissioned the maintenance team to go in there and jackhammer out the floor in the cafeteria, and we built an exact replica of the kitchen I was going to compete in, in Lyon, France. That's where I trained—behind a twenty-eight-ton glass door. People would look at me and they were like, *Does it really take all this to get ready to compete in a culinary competition?* Chef Henin understood. His emails would talk about how *everything had to be exactly as it was, in France.* Your muscle memory for reaching for something and dropping something off should also be pulling something *back; no* motion could be wasted during the competition. He was probably the only person I knew who got it. There was nobody else who spoke that same language. It may be one of the reasons he had this relationship with me. He knew I understood what he was saying and that I was going to do it. And I did. I did everything he said.

I'll tell you one story that is funny . . . and kind of embarrassing. Because I am so organized and so is he . . . You have these two organized, on-the-ball people, but really, we are also very busy. I was traveling and training and getting ready and also running the Greenbrier kitchens. We were building a casino at the Greenbrier, plus building and opening five new restaurants . . . all kinds of stuff.

This one time, we were scheduled to meet in one of the Delaware North stadiums. It was going to be a quick meeting: we were going to fly into this stadium, meet, and fly back. It was just kind of a *fill-him-in-on-how-my-training-and-everything-was-going* type of meeting.

I'm in, I think it was New Jersey, and he's inside the stadium, telling me where to go. I'm talking to him on the phone, saying, "Chef, I do not see the entrance you're talking about." I keep going around this ballpark, over and over again, and he's explaining where to go, while I'm with my taxi driver. We're looking at the street names, and Chef is right on the phone, explaining, "Turn down this street, turn down this street . . ."

I'm like, "Chef, I can't even *find* that street."

I'm trying to tell the taxi driver and he's looking at me like I'm crazy. It's been like forty-five minutes, and it finally gets to the point where I'm thinking, *I'm not going to have time to meet with him and get back in the car and drive back to the airport. I may actually miss my flight.*

Finally, we put two and two together.

"Chef Henin, I know this may sound strange, but . . . where exactly are you? What stadium are you in?"

He was at another city, at a different ballpark. I think it was in Buffalo or something like that. Here I am, in New Jersey. When we figured it out, I was like, "Chef, I am at . . . the Meadowlands."

"Ooh. Okay."

We had talked for almost an hour on the phone, trying to find each other. Even at that point, he was still, "Okay. Well, how long would it take to get on a train?" He was relentless, still trying to make it happen.

"Chef, let's just reschedule. This trip clearly did not work."

It was so embarrassing. I told my wife, I said, "Laura, so the meeting I was at? I don't even know how to tell you this."

She looked at me like, *You whaaat?*

We scheduled this meeting, and we were in two completely different cities . . . the biggest total goof of a travel issue I've ever had. I've never had anything like that ever happen. I mean, maybe get the wrong street or the wrong building, but I never . . . completely wrong city altogether. Not even in the same *state*. To this day, I don't know who would ever say whose fault it was. [Laughs] I thought I had the right city and the right stadium. It's ironic, though, especially for two people who are so organized. To this day, I travel so much, and this has never happened to me again.

SUSAN: *That's definitely going into the book! Would you tell me more about your CMC experience?*

RICH: Taking the CMC exam is extremely stressful—eight days and 130 hours of cooking examination. There is a consistently high fail rate. You don't sleep. You lose weight. There are different people coming in and out the entire week. Every day, you are being timed: you get four hours and twenty-eight ingredients; now go cook a five-course meal. They throw all kinds of curveballs at you . . .

It was the last day (which counts for 50 percent of the entire score). There was this one moment: I was full-throttle, face down, looking at the cutting board, just chop-chop-chop, getting the stoves full of stuff. You get consumed with it. At this one point, this *hand* comes into the picture. It grabs one of my knives, a cleaver, in a joking way, like they were getting ready to chop my fingers off. I looked up . . . it was Chef Henin. He's smiling.

It was a calming moment, in all this noise. There are so many people watching you, and so many cameras and people in the glass, looking in. And, here's the *man*. He just walks right in, during the exam. There are all these people around and other CMCs judging. "I'm going over to see Rich." It was just a smile . . . he winked and walked away. Sometimes, something like that, in the midst of all that chaos, can be enough to get you across the finish line. We didn't say anything. He put a smile on my face, and I got back to cooking.

The last day, you are cooking Continental Cuisine—different dishes, from around the world. You are already fatigued from the days prior. At the end of *that* section, you get a thirty-minute break. And by the way, within that thirty-minute period, also they present to you twenty-eight random ingredients to incorporate into another five-course menu. After your break, you go right back into the kitchen and begin cooking again. It is a dizzying amount of work and requires an intense concentration. You've got to be really good, at many different things, for a long time, to survive.

It's a great exam, yet I can understand why a lot of people opt to not take it. For some people, there is probably more to lose than there is to gain. I mean, if you're an accomplished chef, why put yourself through that? But I wanted to take it, to see if I could. People like him are guiding you along through the years, not saying, *Hey, go take it*, but rather, referencing it in conversations. It puts you on a course to feel compelled. That's a prestigious group, mainly because of people like Chef Henin. Plus, I thought it would be good training for Bocuse d'Or, which it certainly was!

SUSAN: *Final thoughts?*

RICH: What reveals the most about him isn't necessarily about him; it's the people he's influenced. That's always impressive, when you see how many people somebody has influenced. That has influenced me to take on more of a role and be patient with people. You never know who you're training—you may be training the next Thomas Keller. You just don't know. He's always done that in a selfless way. He just wants to help people. It's just fascinating to see what that effort has blossomed into, in so many ways. Even for me, I point to him as somebody who has been an influencer in my career, so it's an honor to contribute in any way I can.

Guarding the Eggs: The Legacy of Roland G. Henin

I saw it, but nothing I can do. I can't get in the way. I can't fix it. Let them continue to make their mistakes, and learn.

—RGH

SUSAN: *Now that you're retiring, you are creating a legacy here at Delaware North with Chefs Kevin Doherty and Percy Whatley, mentoring them through their CMC exam.*

RGH: If I leave today, I have no legacy; if I haven't trained chefs to become Master Chefs, to start thinking the way that I am thinking and acting, then between three weeks and three months from now, everything that I've done—*everything*—will be back down to the ground, will disappear, will melt away. I guarantee you that. I guarantee you that it will revert. If I leave, who's going to take over and carry on these kinds of things? I do it for the preservation in the company.

There are two guys—one on the east coast, one on the west coast—two strong operations, two strong chefs (well, sort of strong) developing. They are going to be able to carry on quite a bit of my legacy. I get into some argument with them, because they are . . . well, it's a new generation, and they are culinary school-trained. They haven't gone through apprenticeships. It's a different lifestyle.

Sometimes I shake them up a little bit, because they are too easy, or too soft, or too lenient . . . too acceptable. I said, "No, guys. You need to stand up. You need to validate your rights, what you preserve. It's a profession. You cannot just pass it under the carpet. It's a *craft*." You cannot let them just push you around. Middle management, it's not their fault, because they are trained to cut corners, protect the bottom line. *What's the return on investment?* It's their job, but you have your job, too. Those guys, if you let them do it just once, they will do it forever. You have to stand up for that. That's why you're the chef.

We determined who would be most appropriate out of five candidates. Four have potentials, and two are the best. Better to have two to carry the legacy, to strengthen the values. One traveled from the east, one from the west: Chef Kevin Doherty, executive chef from TD Garden, Boston, Massachusetts; Chef Percy Whatley, executive chef for the Ahwahnee Resort, Yosemite, California (now vice president, Food & Beverage, Delaware North Parks & Resorts). Both are involved in different dimension than just executive chef. They had the willingness to step out. No shoving down throat. You can't force them to want it. They stuck it out, and here they are. You can meet them halfway, like horse to water. Can't make them want it or convince them that it is worthwhile value. You can't make a plow horse a racehorse, *but*, you can expose a racehorse to the track.

* * *

Since receiving his CMC title in 1983, Roland Henin has remained directly involved in the CMC certification process, as are all CMC title holders. Henin served in an advisory capacity to chefs John Fisher, Lawrence McFadden, and Mark Erickson and less formally to several other candidates. For chefs Kevin and Percy, the CMC training took place primarily at the Niagara Falls Culinary Institute (NFCI), a spectacularly equipped culinary school in the heart of Niagara Falls.

Four Months Before the CMC Exam:

Excerpts from the CMC Training Session Journals

Percy Whatley; Boston, Massachusetts: June 15–20, 2014

June 16: Rented truck and moved kitchen equipment from casino to NFCI. Set up respective kitchens and drew assignments and kitchen rotations for the following day. I drew *Coq au Vin* and *Rouladen*. Kevin drew *Goulash* and *Hasenpfeffer*. On day two, we would switch items.

June 17: 7:30 a.m. departure to NFCI. I had station #1 with a 12:00 p.m. service time. I struggled to get going . . . *commis* was not available until 9:30 a.m., which set me back a little and forced me into doing some items normally accomplished by the *commis*. The only good thing of the day was my biscuit. Shabby day altogether. I should have fired the capon an hour earlier than I did and the butchery of the veal top round was HORRENDOUS! I am not thinking before acting upon some tasks and being STUPID! Had to pound thick slabs of veal where I should have sliced thinner and only had to pound lightly to flatten them out. Garnish was not well thought-out. *Pommes Purée* was watery, extra mushrooms redundant, etc. *Rouladen* a disaster overall . . . time to regret this day altogether, but chalk it up to a learning experience. At least I had my pants around my ankles. . . . Disappointed in myself is an understatement.

June 18: With my tail between my legs, breakfast at 7:00 a.m. with a 7:30 a.m. departure. I had to rebound today with a level of redemption necessary. I was much happier with the quality of end product, but there is still work to be done with the thought processes of *garniture*. Using vegetables as containers to stuff (tomatoes, eggplant *roulade*, stuffed peppers, etc.) is an *AHA* moment that must become the norm in practice. Proteins were cooked well. Two hours of braised cabbage and still *al dente*?! MUST BE MORE FOCUSED ON MULTITASKING throughout the cooking window: blanch all veg at one time; don't do one thing at a time on the stove; there should be three or four things . . . WORK SMARTER . . . start by doing the things I DON'T LIKE TO DO FIRST. . . .

June 20: Went to TD Garden to get all the items (food, equipment, etc.) and loaded up for the two-hour drive to Amherst, Massachusetts. We arrived at 8:00 a.m. and set up the kitchens. Being a large institutional bake shop, there were some equipment challenges, but nothing too serious. Since we had MEP (*mise en place*) scaled out, we did our items in four hours with no *commis* (five hours in the exam). Chef Tom and Noble critiqued us with the following pointers:

- Soak *Joconde* in Calvados simple syrup to provide moisture and to tie in flavors of pumpkin mousse and apple *gelée*.
- White chocolate ice cream is too sweet; reduce from 12 oz. to 8 oz.
- Instead of ice cream quenelle, do a shiny ball with a Zerolon scoop. It will fit better in the *tuile* cup, as well as tie into the shapes existent on the plate.
- Focaccia should be 75 percent hydration dough, where my recipe is about 50 percent. Should be much wetter. I should find an interesting shape, such as a rectangle, so that I can slice it like a true focaccia is sliced in Italy.
- I should lightly *lié* the compote, so that it has a more "saucy" consistency.
- A little powdered sugar sprinkled on the streusel topping will give it a little bit of added elegance.

Departed UMASS at 4:00 p.m. Nice homemade dinner at Chef Kevin's house with his wonderful family. Thanks for the hospitality. Bed at a little after 9:00 p.m. and a 4:00 a.m. departure for the airport. Unfortunately, a nine and a half hour delay with a plane cancellation. Didn't get back to California until 7:30 p.m. . . . long day.

* * *

Kevin Doherty; Niagara Falls, New York: July 20–25, 2014

July 21: Rented minivan from National, picked up chefs Percy and Henin. Percy rented U-Haul to gather equipment from Hamburg. Unpacked and set up kitchen. Small fire alarm issue, with the building being evacuated for about twenty minutes. Picked numbers out of the hat to cook the next day. I picked *Coulibiac* and *Chicken Kiev*. And Chef Percy had *Paella* and *Osso Buco*. Chef Roland took inventory of items in freezer, and we pulled a few things out to thaw as needed. Wrote a shopping list for our day(s) of cooking and went shopping. Homework until about 10:15 p.m.

July 22: Depart for NFCI at 7:30 a.m. with 8:00 a.m. arrival. I set up kitchen from 8:30 to 9:00 a.m. Began cooking with good sense of urgency, since we did not have *commis* assigned. We solicited Chef Scott Green to provide assistants. They arrived at about 10:30 a.m. and that was good, but these cooks who have worked for Chef Scott for three years have little to no skill. This is good training for us, as no idea of who will be helping during exam. My *Coulibiac* was okay, need to straighten lines, pour butter into chimneys. *Kiev*, I should know better than to use raw garlic . . . should have been boiled or roasted for maximum sweet flavor. Cleaned up and departed the school. Homework in hotel room in preparation of Day Two. Bed around 11:00 p.m.

July 23: Assistants arrived on time ready to work. I don't know as I did not take these two main dishes seriously as they were not executed to the level of mastery. *Paella* was not good, rice was undercooked on the smaller one, chicken was undercooked, and I put the shellfish in way too early and it overcooked. *Osso* was good, but could have been tighter. It was marinated for thirty minutes, seared. Risotto was good. Broccoli stems needed to be trimmed or removed for another dish. After cleanup we were able to build a menu from existing proteins and ingredients for a Freestyle menu session. We were given a small budget to supplement the ingredients of $3 per person or $60 total, between us. We came in at $53 for the shopping trip. Did homework until about 10:30 p.m.

July 24: Breakfast at 6:00 a.m. and arrive to NFCI at 7:00 a.m. Started stocks with a gentle reminder from Chef Roland. *Commis* showed up on time, ready to work. *Commis* had a good sense of speed today, had to ask him to pick up the pace at one point during tomato peeling. I think this is where Chef Henin notes I become gruff . . . looking at this every day, as I do not wish to be labeled as losing control etc. This seems to be a weakness that shows itself now and again, not all the time. Making note on it. I cannot say it's an East Coast thing . . . Service needs to be a bit more organized, tighter, making my table cleaner as the spectators noticed my cluttered table.

One Month Before The CMC Exam

Kevin Doherty, CMC Training Session Interview, Niagara Falls, New York: September 30, 2014

SUSAN: *How's the training going?*

KEVIN: Back to the three-sided triangle. You've got to be in sync, or at some point it will fall off. Your best ally or your worst enemy is your mind. Chef reminds us, "We have a good day; we have a bad day. If we have a good day, we should be able to have two good days. If you can cook good two days, you should be able to be a good cook four days." You look forward to the trip (to Buffalo) all the time. Getting on the plane, it's stress-free. I have an easier flight than the two of them—fifty minutes nonstop, from Boston. I did my mental *mise en place* and checked a bag with all the stuff I've been lugging back and forth. When we were given our proteins yesterday, it wasn't a daunting piece. When everybody's talking about the Classical Cuisine, it's still just cooking; that's the approach I took. I wasn't freaking myself out about Escoffier. Cooking is cooking. I'm just following a recipe and some old principles.

I would have had a good day if I had used a little more salt. That's going to kick me in the butt, all night long. My artichokes could have been a little whiter, but my vinaigrette was there and had some spring in it. It was a fun salad. I was missing salt on my fish. With the exception of the lemon and the salt, it would have been there. For day two going in, I'm looking forward to the Mystery. It's all the mental preparation. You saw the homework that we do and how we physically walk through the cooking of the dish, and what the *commis* are going to do. Ideally, I'm done fabricating something by the time he has the *mirepoix* done, so we went to the pan together. It's the dance.

Up until when I had the five recipes for my baking pieces, it was like I was in quicksand. I couldn't get out. Chef has a different view, but I know I didn't freak out about the oven. It was the recipes that got me overwhelmed . . . simple three-four-ingredient recipes. It's like, wow. That's when you just try to breathe through it. You see the dishes, and you see the colleague's dishes knocked out, and it doesn't matter. If everybody else jumps off the bridge, I'm not. It goes back to what they say in school but just taking it all in and hopefully making the corrections. As Chef says, "The devil's in the details now." Really. *Salt.* Salt is going to send me home.

SUSAN: *After all those years and all that work.*

KEVIN: Right. Or what else? My asparagus. Why didn't I make a little soft *purée* with the rest of it to put in the tartlet? I know better than that. For whatever reason, whatever my mind messed with me a month ago, I didn't brown my *mirepoix* for the braise. It's like one of the cardinal sins. I thought he was going to rip my arms off. Why? I looked at him. I didn't have an answer. Just drew a blank. Knowing that you're caramelizing for flavor, because it only makes the finished product better.

SUSAN: *Knowing something is right but also executing it precisely, in that moment.*

KEVIN: Exactly. In that moment. Pull it together. See what's going on . . . it just seems incredible . . . again, yes, you get the *commis*, but it's just one man orchestrating everything that would normally be five or ten frickin' brigades, putting out a meal like that, for ten people. If you work smarter, that's one of the pieces we try to ask for the platter service. How are you going to orchestrate the plate if you have only thirty minutes?

A good example was something like rainbow chard: you blanch it and you line a *timbale* and you put some type of *purée*, vegetable, grain. Even if your grain was in a mold, you can leave the lid on until service. That's one less step, because you're dealing with five books as you cook. You have forty-five separate components between all those dishes and even though you have the pictures, your brain goes, *That goes on course two,* even though you have it in your hand and you want to put it on course one. *No, that doesn't go on course one.* It's prioritizing when you read your list and sticking to your list, because when you read your list you have a clear head, if that makes sense. There's no pressure sitting in the hotel room. Or you do things so you're not reinventing the wheel every time. Cook with what you're comfortable with. I'm not going to frost a cake for my dessert. That's not one of my strong points. So yes, acknowledging that it's a weakness, but why am I going to expose it if I don't need to? Cook good honest food.

SUSAN: *When you were first approached about this a few years back, how you were vetted?*

KEVIN: In late 2006, we were in Las Vegas for a conference and I was asked if I'd be part of the team that was going to Germany. I just said, "Okay, yeah,

I'm down with anything, all right." I had no idea what I was getting myself into. We practiced at the Balsams. It took me eighty minutes to peel nine pieces of asparagus correctly. My family would go away for long weekends and holidays at a vacation home, and here I am practicing. I think what hurt the most was during this practice, I learned every possible scenario that can go wrong with lobster tandoori when making my platter, because I never had the same negative results. I think through it, adapt my next run. I'm going to fix it. Well, it wound up being too high. I overcompensated. Finally, I send Chef a letter. *I don't know why I'm doing this. I'm full of myself. I work thirty hours in three days, and I've got worse results.* I'm prepared until you have the ten issues that could go wrong, and all of a sudden you have an eleventh issue, and "Oh my God, how can this happen?"

But it all did come through, in the end. The last practice wasn't terrible, and we went back to our own units and got ready to go. If you don't do something for a couple days you get antsy. You need to get back into it. I was ready, so I think the components that I made there were not terrible. It was enough to get me a bronze, and I think I missed a silver by a couple peas on a platter.

Now, training for the CMC, Chef looks at my work and goes, "You had a better platter five years ago in Germany."

"But I don't do it every day, Chef."

You look through the pictures and your brain goes, *I know how to do that. Yeah, yeah, yeah.* You get rusty. You miss. You get out of sync doing it.

Percy had to jettison a lot of things, and maybe it might be better to under-promise and then over-deliver. Less is more, but if you expect A and B, and I give you A, B, *and* C, you say, "Ooh, what a nice surprise that is." *Mmhmm . . . Look, he made that extra thing.* Dessert wasn't required, but it was factored into my schedule. Then, I put out an incomplete product, because I was missing a component. I would have been better off not doing that and then focusing my energy on the salt factors of the other dishes! Those are the pieces that keep you up at night.

SUSAN: *Chef Henin was saying, "Today is a perfect day for commis, because the Master Chef candidate is responsible for everything."*

KEVIN: During the prep time, we talk about the plan. At any point during the day, we stop for the demo. *Let me show you what I'm doing.* You're taking the time, even though you're putting yourself behind. It makes good points with the judges. You're teaching, which is mentoring that other person. You gotta keep your cool. They're trying to do their best. He was saying sometimes the judges would kick you out if you lose your patience with the *commis*. After all that work, it comes down to just a moment, just like that. It's incredible.

SUSAN: *Any advice to yourself for tomorrow?*

KEVIN: Just review notes and . . . then write the notes to myself. And take a nice long bath.

SUSAN: *You guys are going to be here for a while, tonight?*

KEVIN: Yeah.

* * *

Percy Whatley, CMC Training Session Interview, Niagara Falls, New York: September 30, 2014

SUSAN: *How'd it go, today? You were just talking about the scrapping or "eighty-sixing" of menu items.*

PERCY: Yes, if I'm going to eighty-six something, then make sure that the other things are to an acceptable level and then move on. Even though in this particular day, there were too many things I had to end up scrapping. As far as planning, I need to not over-promise and under-deliver. That's a hospitality-focused statement. I'd rather under-promise on my menu and then over-deliver if possible. At the Master Chef's level, when you have something soft like my fish plate— a soft custard, a soft texture with the fish, plus a soft and thick texture with the sauce *Americaine* lobster chunks—it needed a "Crunchy." I shouldn't have let that slip by. Same with the soup. There were a lot of incompletes. Chef Henin would agree that everything I did was seasoned properly. Maybe there were some bad decisions with regard to the finished product, but everything had the cooking level that was expected. Still, when you put something that's 80 percent complete together, that's all you can hope for, from the score.

It's the finishing details. He's like, "Put the finishing touches on your food." It's the difference between, say, a 75 score and an 83 score . . . just a little more. Today's (score of) 85 can be the buffer for the next day. The math continues with regard to the aggregate score. The cumulative score that you need to pass the exam is 75 while 70 passes the segment; if you pass the day at 70, you're already climbing uphill, even when you pass the day. You have to bring a new attitude, a refreshed look, and it has to be complete. Chef has mentioned many times before: all the physical stuff is there; our setup is there. It's the four hours of the day that matter most, when you can fall apart, but if you don't do the fundamental stuff the night before, then you are not set up for success in the first place.

With his mentorship and pushing us to the brink, mentally, we're a hundred times better than we were two years ago. We're a thousand times better than we were three years ago. Kevin and I did nine months by ourselves without his direct involvement. We were just spinning on a wheel. It is him. Henin is an incredible mentor. The sixteen years that I've been working with him from being a junior sous-chef to where I am now certainly has a lot to do with him, about his leaning on me in a positive way, as a mentor should.

Mentor/mentee relationships in the culinary world are so important, beyond the ACF or the certification part of things. Thomas Keller is a perfect example, of course. Keller learned that mentorship legacy from Henin, and he carries it on in his own gigantic world-class company. They inspire me and Kevin to do the same thing—take people, and it's almost a good cop/bad cop kind of thing, where you have to break down walls and say, seriously, it's a time for honesty. There are days when he says, "If you do this, you don't have a chance in the world." It may hurt sometimes, but that's not the point. The point is improvement and continuing forward. No soft bunnies floating around. It has to be honest. Kevin and I have to be honest with ourselves. Without his brutal honesty, we wouldn't be able to see any kind of light at the end of the tunnel.

SUSAN: *I want to give you a chance to respond, because Chef Henin will say, "Today the commis is perfect, because everything is a reflection of the CMC candidate." You could extend that logic and say, "Okay, if the CMC candidate is not ready, wouldn't that be a reflection of the coach (Chef Henin)?"*

PERCY: I'm sure he does ask that question to himself. He's like, "So, is there something wrong with me?" I'm sure he's asked it many times, "What's going on? Why can't I get these guys out of this muddy ditch, with their feet stuck in it?"

SUSAN: *As amazing as he is, he is a human and so is the system. If there's going to be training in the future, for instance, if you and Chef Kevin are the ones with the baton, might you change how the CMC preparation happens?*

PERCY: I wouldn't change a thing. I wouldn't change the method of taking two people, unless they're in real close proximity to each other. We're on both coasts, so we need to find neutral ground that is as distraction-less as possible and be able to cook together and bang our heads against the wall—or whatever you want to call it, where it's a frustrating day—or celebrate a day where we all feel good about it. The stakes are going to happen in the exam. That's normal, we're going to have days like that. Out of the eight days, we're going to have days of, hopefully, knock on wood, just skating by because of our weaknesses.

Our weaknesses are glaringly different from each other. How do we overcome our weaknesses, going into any given day of the exam? Mine is the transition from cooking into service: *Let's scrap the Crunchy; let's scrap the dessert; let's make my window.* My service window was less cluttered than it's been in the past. There's a little more focus, but not to the level of, *Wow. He's got his stuff together.*

You can't be a bull in a china shop, in the kitchen. It needs to be a seamless kind of flow. My sense of urgency generally can ebb and flow; it may start strong out of the gate, ebb midway, and then somehow into the fourth hour, kick back into gear. Urgency needs to be steady in the first, second, and third hour, then hit third gear and rev up for the next forty-five minutes, and then fourth gear all the way through service. Just like a car's transmission, you're getting onto a seventy-five-mile-per-hour freeway.

SUSAN: *Chef Henin in the beginning was talking about communication with the commis as being one of your challenges. How did that go today?*

PERCY: Ahh . . .it was okay. There were a couple of commands that I did not execute well or he wasn't clear with me, and there were some miscommunications. I asked for large diced onions and he quartered them, but that's going to happen. The physical distance in this kitchen made it a little challenging, but that's part of the game.

SUSAN: *Right. You have to make anything work.*

PERCY: Days one and two of the CMC exam are going to be the same way. It would be nice to be acclimated within the first fifteen minutes of cooking, but that's not how it goes, just from a human nature standpoint—maybe it's just me. A kitchen is a kitchen is a kitchen, sure, but we all like our home bases. There's no orientation day. You walk in the kitchen, make sure the workstations look right, see where the refrigeration is, or the dish room. You see it right before you cook in it.

The mastery of anything is still rooted in fundamental knowledge: Can you communicate properly with a *commis*? Can you show them what you expect and follow through, without his making a bad decision? Can you think in complete sentences from a cooking standpoint? *Okay, for* Blanquette de Veau, *I need this much roux. I need this much veal.* "Complete sentences" is the best analogy I can put to it. Can you think in complete sentences when you're cooking, all the way to the "period"?

SUSAN: *Any advice to yourself?*

PERCY: The only thing now is the homestretch. I need to perform well the next couple of days and then go home. I have a few weeks planned out of pretty solid cooking. Cooking at home is a little bit different, obviously. Then, just keep my head up. Take the last six or seven days off before Kevin arrives and head down, get settled in, and almost meditate on it for a week. We're going to head down to L.A. on the twenty-second and have a few days to figure out some logistics. *Where is a good dry cleaner? What's the most traffic-less way to get to the school?* [Laughs]

* * *

Roland Henin, CMC Coach, two weeks before the CMC exam:
October 13, 2014

Susie,

I need to be careful as to what I'll say here . . .
   The CMC Exam is a little like a fishing trip . . .
   You plan for the best tides . . .
   You get all your gears in a row, fully ready . . .
   You do your "homework and research" as to where the fish are and what they are biting on . . . thru all your contacts . . .
   You check what the weather forecast is going to be . . .
   You get the best baits available . . .
   You check all the boats details . . . Tags, Plugs, Gaz, Oil level, Battery, PSF jackets, etc. . . .
   You get to bed early in order to get up "earlier" . . .
   You review your LIST over & over again not forgetting lunch or the ice (just in case you get some fish) . . .
   Now that you've done all that is under your control . . . and wonder if you could have possibly done MORE . . . ?? You just GO . . . and hope for the best possible situation . . . focusing on the darn fish . . . !!! With absolutely NO GUARANTY that they will meet you halfway . . .

C'est la vie . . . At least we've made an honest effort doing our "HOME-WORK" for the past few years, which is definitely a lot more than what a lot of others people have done . . . BUT . . . this is NOT a "Guaranty of anything," either . . . Always keep in mind the consistent small percentage that makes it thru . . .

It's quite a bit like the swimmers who cross the Channel between England and France or the other way around, France to England . . . When you jump in at the start, you never know when or if you are going to make it to the other side at all . . . You just hope for the best!!!!

IT'S a REAL BITCH . . . R.G.H.

2014 CMC Examination: Le Cordon Bleu College of Culinary Arts, Pasadena, California

**Kevin Doherty, CMC Candidate, Exam Journal,
October 26–November 2, 2014**
There were a few things I had said long before going to take the test:

1. They will have to fail me. I will not quit, no matter what.
2. I will be better for doing this . . . no matter what.
3. What are you afraid of? I only need to cook for this test. My dad ran into burning buildings, as a fireman . . . now *that's* tough.
4. Never walk out of a room with your head down in shame. If you did your best, then stand up, because you tried and that takes courage.

Pre-Day One: Meeting with judges and other candidates finally came, we were told the ins and outs of what the time was going to be. Took the healthy test—twenty-five questions, come to find out later our scores were all over the board. I think I did fairly well on this. The judges went over the duties of the *commis*. The *commis* cannot do as much as we had practiced in the past. To sum up what they can do: peel vegetables, chop *mirepoix*, clean and chop herbs, wash vegetables/lettuce. Otherwise they are the "gopher" to wash a pot or pan and bring it back, get a lemon/lime, etc. Another gigantic obstacle to overcome. We were given our basket of ingredients and had to have menu, requisitions, and dietary stamp complete and emailed off by 6:00 a.m., which is when we were due at school as well.

Day One, Healthy Cuisine: Arrive at 6:00 a.m. for my 7:30 a.m. starting time. The reflections become a little diluted as this four-and-a-half hour cooking window and thirty-minute service window became one flash of time in the memory. I was introduced to the *commis* about one hour prior to cooking. We took this time to review the status of what we are going to do for the next four hours. Day one is the first turning point for me. I thought I did a pretty good job at putting the req and menu together, things were going as planned, then BAM, hit the wall. Chef Buchner brought my cart with the req . . . upon quick review I said, "Chef, there seems to be a problem."

"What is that, Chef?"

"There are no proteins on my cart."

He replied, "You did not order them."

"Oh my God, they gave me a basket, but required me to req the ingredients. . . ." So, there was what seemed like a forever silence.

He said to me, "What are you going to cook?"

I had to think for a second as, at this point in my life, I was scared, I wanted to curl up into a ball and start rocking . . . but something said, *Cook vegetarian.*

"Chef, I will cook vegetarian."

He left, which left me frantic: *What do I do now? Ah crap, I am screwed!! I am going home . . .* This lasted a few seconds, and then I started to put items into the cooler. Twenty-three minutes later, Chef returned. He asked me what my basket was, and I replied quickly and politely. Chef handed me my baskets of proteins, but I did not see the fruits, lettuce, etc. I did cook okay from a time point of view. I moved like my ass was on fire, butchering lamb, putting stock on, scaling fish, and proper butchery. I believe my *commis* was obsessive-compulsive; he was alphabetizing the items on our table as well on the common table . . . another *Oh My God.* I did make my service window on time.

Upon the group critique, we were handed envelopes with our score. I could not open my envelope, until we were home. I knew for sure I was going home for my lack of mastery on Day One. We get home and Chef Percy says, "Are you going to open it?" 76.30!! Holy crap, a gift from the gods! Okay, this lights me up again. We start the long haul of menu planning, as it's due in a few hours.

Day Two, Garde-Manger Setup: I was kinda ready for this, as I had done a twelve-hour cold production in Chicago a few years back for Team USA tryouts. I wrote my list of priorities as to what I thought was good, I broke down the pork and started browning right away in the pan, also had a brine on to use with pork and tongue, broke down a pheasant for *galantine*, which would be cooked in a stock later in the day . . . the tongue was going to be *en gelée*, lined with Savoy cabbage. I was in my zone, pouring *chemise* by 5:15 p.m. and we were told a 7:00 p.m. departure. At the end of this day, we were assigned our Classical Cuisine assignments. A menu and requisition was due by 6:00 a.m. the next day. We had the ability to pick the recipes from *Le Guide.* This took some calculated time. Then, we needed to write the requisition and menu and send it via email by 6:00 a.m. This, plus all of the other things needing to be accomplished, put us in bed at 2:30 a.m. Wake-up call was at 4:45 a.m.

Day Three, Garde-Manger Service: At 6:15 a.m., Chef Giunta walks in and makes a statement regarding the chicken *consommé*. Many of us were going to use the ground chicken for the clarification, but he clearly stated that following the recipes is what the segment was all about. The recipe calls for lean ground beef for the raft. This put many of us in a situation where we were climbing out of a hole for the day, mentally. Chef Leonard walks in and gives all of us a stern talking to, that we did not do our research, etc. They did make the concession of making it available; however, we all would lose some kitchen points for not fulfilling the requisition correctly, and making a late "addendum" will be a reduction for the remainder of the exam.

Start of the second Garde-Manger day, I began with my plan: warm my gelatin and begin slicing. Upon unwrapping my pheasant from the cheesecloth that had cooled in the stock all night, it looked nice, tight . . . until the first slice. There was a giant hole. The inlay of the breast had moved . . . OMG bad. I knew I was in trouble by the look on my face. All of the floor judges were now looking as well. I did stay composed, and did my best to have twelve correct facing slices in order. On to the next one, the *en gelée*: the first slice was okay, but upon slice five, the gelatin between the tongue and mushrooms was separating . . . *shit* . . . *shit*, I am thinking, but still in control. Now I know I have to do some major repair, painting this together with gelatin to have it stay and make a forcemeat paste to fill in the holes on the *galantine*. The Tasso-spiced pork loin was good, but brine did not penetrate 100 percent. Craftsmanship of two pieces that were barely hanging on is going to cause me pain. Chef Giunta came over and spoke to me about a hyper-fast curing agent he has used in the past. He also told me to take a deep breath and focus on finishing plating the platter that I had done all the right processes for, the day earlier.

My platter did not make the 70 percent, but my kitchen work overall made my score a 70.2 percent for the day. I scored an overall 69.91—not enough to pass the day . . . still in the game, but now staring down the barrel of Classical Cuisine. Chef Kevin Storm failed Day One and Day Two and is out. The trees start falling in the forest. We knew this would happen, but so soon is hard to swallow. . . .

Day Four, Classical Cuisine: I had a *commis* who was green and nervous, so I made the changes early on as we were told to do: you need to teach, but work them on tasks and push them. I started with the plan for this day and butchery— took off a single filet of sole per side, breaking down the chicken and such to start the stock to have my consommé cooking long enough. I planned to sauté the fish and keep warm, while the tournedos were cooked in my window, but

I rushed the reduction to finish the sauce, the emulsion broke, and my sauce separated on my plate during judging. Consommé had good taste, but a bit of fat on the surface . . . crap.

Upon receiving my kitchen critique, Chef Leonard said, "Do you think you cooked at a mastery level today, Chef?" "No, Chef." He agreed, and we spoke of the errors in the following meal—all things that Chef said over and over, in the years of training . . . ATTENTION to the tiny details. Upon review in the judges' room, I scored 69.89. This was my second fail. I am going home.

* * *

Percy Whatley, CMC Candidate, Exam Journal, October 26–November 2, 2014

Kevin and I drove down to Pasadena on Wednesday, October 22, 2014, from Yosemite. He had never been to Yosemite, and I think it was a good thirty-six hours or so for him to wake up in the serenity of the mountains and be able to breathe high elevation air for a little while. The condominium in Pasadena was close to perfect: plenty of space and a two-car garage for organizing. We shopped at the local supermarket to sustain ourselves without having to go out to eat all the time. This would save in overall expenses and time, as well. The condo had enough room for Chef Roland and also Chef Ambarish, who arrived at the beginning and provided moral support.

The days leading up to the exam were the most intense amount of stress—all of it being mental, as we truly did not know what to expect, although we were constantly reminded of it by Chef Roland. Chef Ambarish joined us on Thursday and stayed until Sunday morning. He assisted in keeping the condo clean and making us coffee and breakfast, when needed. It was a pleasure to have him around as I was constantly spinning in my own mind. He is a calm presence, and this was good to have around.

Pre-Day One: Kevin and I were given our basket of ingredients via email Wednesday evening. This allowed the ability to theme out the menu, write skeleton recipes, and extrapolate the nutritional information. We sent it off to the registered dietitian to use her software, accurately extrapolating nutrition and then signing off on it via letterhead from her company. All of this is needed within twenty-four hours of receipt of the basket.

Day One, Healthy Cuisine: It was both a good day and a bad day, as the adjustment to the slightly different setup made for some fast decisions. I need to adjust the thinking of the timeline to make everything fit. Fifteen minutes' setup at the beginning is taken up by unloading your small equipment and tools, sanitizing the station, setting up the station, gathering the china you need, polishing this china, and putting it away, and gathering your first few pots and pans for your kitchen.

At your cooking window time (chefs begin cooking in staggered fifteen-minute increments), your food cart comes with what you requisitioned, along with your assigned proteins and other ingredients. This needs to be sorted and adjusted. Before you know it, ten minutes is gone from your cooking time, and you need to start hustling and readjusting. Timing has been my nemesis, the biggest hurdle to overcome for all of my days. We were informed early on by Chef Roland that our biggest weaknesses would shine brightly at the exam, and it was ever so true. I was assigned a *commis* from China who could barely speak English, so culinary sign language was used to get the tasks completed. I cooked okay considering all circumstances and received a 76.58 for the day.

Day Two, Garde-Manger Setup: I was assigned yet another "English as a Second Language" student—a polite and professional Iranian, but awful English. I took a deep breath. We began our twelve-hour day at a good pace, getting all the tasks done, yet by the time I was in my gross piece building time, I was already a half hour behind schedule. The added time needed to explain expectations slowly to the *commis* ate away at my time.

I made a couple of very bad mistakes. I should have used the calamari in my *en gelée* piece instead of an inlay in the scallop terrine. When I did the inlay, I did not poach the calamari tube or the small dice of calamari meat that was stuffed inside the tube. The calamari released so much water that the forcemeat did not have the binding effect I had hoped for. I struggled with the gelatin in the avocado mousse and had to reintroduce more aspic into it for the proper setting consistency. Other than these, there were a bunch of other minor mistakes until the end of the night . . . I poured my *chemise* and had a good pour. The box-cover was ready to go. After covering, we got the station nice and tight, cleaned up and put away for the next day. After this, we had to place the platter in the walk-in refrigerator. As I took the box off of the platter, I noticed that the box had "wilted" and an edge had scarred the *chemise*. OH NO! I had to put it away and plan on re-pouring it the next morning in my timeline. I also did not get as much accomplished as I had hoped for, so there was still a lot of work to be done.

Day Three, Garde-Manger Service: Arrived to the candidate room at 5:45 a.m. for preparation to get through this day. I was assigned a different assistant—wow, he spoke English! At 6:15 a.m., Chef Giunta walks in and makes that statement regarding the chicken consommé. I focused on my three-hour window. I was in at 7:30 a.m. again and needed to put that out of my mind for now and concentrate. I jumped into the window on full throttle and had a good sense of urgency through the three hours. However, slicing the scallop terrine was crappy; the inlay was still almost liquid. I should have tempered the mousse and the *en gelée* piece for a half hour prior to doing my platter lay out. The tasting judges were not happy with the outcome. Critique from Master Chefs David Kellaway and Fritz Sonnenschmidt below:

- *Barquettes* were overfilled. They should be level to the crust and not heaping.
- *Tuiles* need a flat surface to sit on when "holding" a garnish.
- *Gelée* and mousse were not tempered long enough; therefore, the mouthfeel was not good.
- Avocado mousse was too acidic.

The platter did not make the 70 percent, but my kitchen work overall made my total score a 70.2%.

I passed this day, but was now in a situation where I needed a decent score to offset this day. When Kevin went in for his critique, I figured he had a much better day than I had. When he came back in with the defeated look on his face and stated he did not pass, I was shaken to the core . . . NO WAY! I thought . . .

Day Four, Classical Cuisine: There is only one word for this day . . . DISASTER.

I had a solid timeline and wrote a "safe" menu, but this day will be the day of reckoning for me and the exam, overall. Time got completely away, and I was in quicksand the entire four hours. I processed the protein pretty well. The judges weren't around for much of it, indicating I was "okay." I marinated the beef and fish pretty quickly, but somehow an hour of my four disappeared completely. At the 1:45 mark, I finally made my raft for the consommé and got it going. Where did the time go? Somehow, I feel like I didn't cook much; it is weird looking back on it. I would like to forget this day. It will plague me for quite some time. . . .

I did not make my service window. I was able to get the consommé and the fish out, but the beef *accoutrements* were incomplete. I did not manage my *commis* with a correct priority, and this left me with some tasks that were not needed. When you miss your window, you go to the back of the line and are given the chance to put the rest of your food out. Since I was three hours away from having the ability to complete it, I had to put all things into the refrigerator for safety. This meant I needed to deal with cold tenderloins, already an obstacle to overcome. We cleaned up our station and walked out of the kitchen to wait.

I found a corner of the candidates' room and had an emotional breakdown. This was something that was too much to bear and hold in. It was enough to make a grown man cry, that is for sure . . . but the release felt good, and I am certain that this is where I turned a corner in the exam process. After going back in and presenting the beef to the judges, I knew I would not pass but would cook stronger and better in the following days.

When I was critiqued and given the 67.5 for the day, I thought this was a gift. I lost five points right off the top for not making my window, but this meant that my food actually passed? I was surprised, honestly . . . and will take that news as a positive thing, which I am certain made it even more plausible that I will continue through the exam . . . but I had a LOT of ground to make up in points. It wasn't going to be easy. We were handed the Global Cuisine assignments at the end of the recap day, requisition due at 6:00 a.m., but the menu was already written, so no need to brainstorm.

Kevin went in for his critique and returned with another defeated look on his face. He was done, he did not pass the day, and two failures meant the exam is complete for him. OH NO!?! I could not let this bother me, but that is easier said than done. We came so far together, and it was hard for me to get it together, especially after the day I had just a couple of hours earlier. We went home with some pretty heavy hearts. Kevin was taking it okay, however. He is a strong person. He was extremely supportive of me and my continued pursuit. I will forever respect him for this show of strength. I did my requisition and gathered all necessary small tools for the next day. Bed at 11:30 p.m.

Day Five, Freestyle Cuisine: After a little more sleep (five hours, versus the three, nights prior), I felt pretty good. Still disheartened that Kevin was not going to be there, I continued to put this out of my mind and prepare to cook. I had a good timeline and was now writing my cooking timeline in for three hours and forty-five minutes rather than four hours, due to what I have learned over the last couple of days. Kevin had coffee ready by the time I came downstairs at 5:00 a.m. We had a cup and gathered all the things I needed for the day. He drove me to the school and said his parting words: "Just cook your food. Don't worry about me." Off I went.

I finally felt the magic of full speed cooking, something I hadn't since the exam began. Although many things were not accomplished with the finesse of a Master Chef, I hit that "gear" in my sense of urgency; it was surreal.

I chose to grill the whole turbot and filet it at service time. It was the biggest mistake of the day, unfortunately, but something I will try again, because it is a neat way to do a big flatfish. The basket was a mix of Asian and Western ingredients, so my theme was *East-meets-West*. I am confident that the flavors were following this theme. The judges were complimentary overall, but the mistakes were glaring:

- Too much garnish in the coconut soup with rabbit and veal tongue.
- Grilling of the fish was not visible, due to the way it was grilled. The poached oyster *cuisson* was not reduced properly or mounted with the appropriate amount of butter.
- The salad was a disaster: just beans, artichokes, endive and poached pears; no color, crunch, or texture difference; all one color and a hurried presentation that looked like crap.

The beef course saved my day: braised bacon and soy-seared flat iron with herb couscous and vegetables, truly at the Mastery Level. This gave me the 73.6 for the day, despite all of the shortcomings. The beef course was truly a winner, in my mind and the judges'. I needed to attack the rest of my menu in the same level of concentration to hit those high marks. It is starting to make sense to my tired, fatigued, sleep-deprived mind . . . do good food, simply and tastefully, and you will pass this exam. We have talked about it so often with Chef Roland: *It is not sorcery. It's not that complicated* . . . all quotes from our mentor stating the true nature of the exam.

Chef David Daniot was eliminated for two failures after this day. Then, there were seven.

Day Six, Global Cuisine:
Menu Assigned:

- Jerk Pork Tenderloin, Cuban-Style Black Beans, Fried Plantains, Pineapple Salsa
- *Paella Valenciana*
- Potato Samosas, Warm Cabbage Salad, Tamarind Chutney, Tomato Relish, Cauliflower Curry

Although there is a lot to do in this four-hour cooking window, I was able to get it all done. Unfortunately, I started my paella a little too late. The rice was inconsistently cooked and the flavors were not entirely homogenous. I nailed the samosas; the judges stated that I hit the authenticity of them the best of the whole group of candidates. The jerk seasoning on the tenderloin was vibrant on its own, but dulled by the meat. Coming out of the oven, I should have basted it with more marinade. All said and done, 73.2 for the day—a pass, yes, but not what I was hoping for. I wanted 78 or 79 for the day. Shake it off, and come out on fire for Baking and Pastry!!!

Chef Tim Recher was eliminated after this day. Then, there were six.

At 9:00 p.m., Chef Randy Torres, Chef Jonathan Moosmiller, and I had a conference call to strategize the menu the three of us were assigned. Although we did not have the same *accoutrements*, we discussed the methodology of the final product in the center of the plate. We wrote our own requisitions and tried to get some sleep. I turned in at 11:00 p.m. Wake up, as usual, at 4:45 a.m.

Day Seven, Baking and Pastry: My *commis*, a strong young man, quickly scaled all of my recipes, accurately. The biggest mistake of the day was dealing with my puff pastry—a school-made product, something I had not dealt with in quite some time. I placed the wire grate too low, and the fluffy rise did not happen. The result was a hockey puck of puff pastry, somewhat disastrous.

The other products were quite good. Small details would have added a point here and there: pumpkin-shaped *tuiles*, a little too big for the dessert overall; quenelles were not beautiful and shiny; *gelée* of apples were not tempered correctly, the texture challenging to cut through cleanly. The focaccia and olive oil quick bread were acceptable, although one judge stated that the basil did not come through in the bread. I ended this day with an 81.7 . . . a good score, and was expected to have a high score for the overall day.

After all critiques were given to the remaining candidates, I was pulled in and given the news that I did not have the 75 percent average score for the combined seven days, which was needed to continue cooking, for Day Eight.

My experience was coming to an end.

The True Legacy
of Roland G. Henin

We learn from our mistakes, ten times more, than from our successes.

—RGH

Out of the eleven CMC candidates originally enrolled in the 2014 CMC Exam, two passed (one chef withdrew before the testing began). The newest Certified Master Chefs are: Jonathan Moosmiller, CMC, executive chef at Southern Hills Country Club, Tulsa, Oklahoma; and Daryl Shular, CMC, director of education/executive chef at Le Cordon Bleu College of Culinary Arts in Atlanta, in Tucker, Georgia.

Does Master Chef Roland Henin's dream die with his failed candidates, or will the legacy continue? Is Roland Henin's legacy having two Certified Master Chefs at Delaware North or is it something more? At the end of the day . . . what does "legacy" mean?

* * *

Chef Kevin Doherty, post-CMC exam, written reflection:
Day Four: I am going home. Well, not home, but I cannot continue. So yes, I am out, but we are a team, and my teammate needs me now. Whatever I can do to assist Chef Percy, I will—cook, drive, give him support, etc.

As I packed my tools, you could see on the faces of your new brothers . . . they were sad as well. We have just spent the last ninety-six hours together, living the same pain and happiness. I shook hands, wished them well, and went on . . . thinking of how I got here, the drive and passion that kept me going, not just for Chef Henin but for me, my family, for DN, and for my staff. They all let me do what I needed, to muster the balls to come and take this exam. I was emotionless, not happy nor sad. I kept hearing those words: *Chef Doherty, you do not have enough points to continue on to the next day. The flavors are enough to pass, and kitchen scores are okay . . . it's just the attention to the details.*

This goes back to the plan: Nail the taste with an okay score and have a good kitchen day, and you can pass this. But your weaknesses come out, just as Chef Henin said.

Someone asked me, "What do I have to prove?" Well, how do I rate? I have ProChef III and my CEC (Certified Executive Chef), but the Certified Master Chef is the top of the grade. I want this. I told my wife, "One day . . ." She says, "Yeah, well go get it."

Chef and I were on the phone last week. He was talking about the Culinary Hospitality Council—Chef Henin, Chef Percy, and a couple of junior chefs, plus members of IT and HR—about fifteen people. He says, "I've voiced my opinion that you and Percy are the only culinary members who need to be on it. It is okay that you didn't pass. You did well."

It felt pretty cool that he said that. It would have been better to have the other result, but he's not mad or disappointed because—and I can't speak for Percy—you know what? I did try. And I didn't place the blame on: *well . . . I'm too fat. I'm too tall.* I have to look in the mirror and say, "You know what? The scores I gave myself going into it is where I landed . . . almost to the T." That's kind of scary. He agreed with those scores, but he still let me go, which is cool.

There is one last closing remark to this entire journal. As we were packing our final things at the condo in Pasadena, Chef Roland wrote down something that will carry me through my remaining days on this earth, and will continue to remind me of just how human I am: "We learn from our mistakes, ten times more, than from our successes."

* * *

Chef Percy Whatley, post-CMC exam:
Day Eight: My internal alarm clock woke me at 4:45 a.m., just like the seven mornings prior. I got up and made coffee and enjoyed the silence and solitude for a couple of hours. I then decided that I needed to touch food. I made eggs, potatoes, and bacon for chefs Kevin and Roland. The smells woke them up, and we enjoyed a simple breakfast together.

Day Nine, and beyond: The trip home was uneventful. After trying to talk Kevin into taking a plane out of the Los Angeles area instead of Fresno, he was being stubborn: *We have journeyed long and hard together, and we would end it together, as promised.* The conversations of the fact that achieving this level of certification is not impossible were a major topic throughout the hours of driving. If you can clear your mind from the first day in, this would play a big role in the success of it, for sure.

Over the course of the next few days, I did my best to settle back into work. I was back in the kitchen on Tuesday morning. By Wednesday morning, I was feeling great. I knew there was plenty of preparation to get accomplished for the 140 people coming to dinner the next day. It is interesting . . . as I hit the cutting board, the magic hit me . . . can't explain what this feeling is exactly, but I had the dance, that thing that hit me in the exam, rocking and rolling. Maybe it is the systems learned over the last two years of development, but the prep just flowed out of my body, fluidly, like it was prepping itself?!?! Meats processed and marinated, stocks simmering, octopus poached in a flavorful *court bouillon*, etc, etc, etc. . . .

By the end of that day, I knew for certain, and without one speck of doubt, that I had made the right decision to pursue this level of certification. Pass or fail, I was cooking at a different level, because of the hard work and effort leading up to the exam. It was now part of my DNA to do right by the food, no shortcuts, no loss of integrity. I pulled the chef team into the office and explained that "I am back." There will be some changes to the current processes. Improving our cooking will be a continued focus of mine, and feelings may get hurt, but it is about the cooking, and nothing else.

* * *

After fifty years, Chef Henin's legacy is simply for the good work to continue. Henin's fear is, "If I go, within weeks, it will all go back to the way it was, eighteen years ago—beer, peanuts, popcorn." Hopefully, DN will continue the legacy that Henin established. Time will tell. Based on some recent emails from Chefs Kevin and Percy, it just might be okay.

Chef Percy . . .
YOU make me so proud, for doing the Turkey "Two ways" . . . Braising the legs ahead of time . . . and roasting the breasts on the day of . . .
Thank you so much . . . have a GR8 day . . . you deserve it . . .
See you soon . . . RGH

Susie,

You will see that Chef Percy is also following up on doing, for all the guests at the Ahwahnee, the process that I developed, Braising the stuffed legs and making the sauce/gravy with the neck/back-bones, etc. a few days ahead and then simply roasting the breast as needed on the day of, just prior to service . . . and NOT several days ahead like it used to be in the "OLD Days." When I brought this up, I was told by every-one . . . It COULDN'T be done! CRAZY FRENCHMAN!!

Susie,

I hope this email finds you well.

I just mailed a small box to Chef. Contents of the box were as follows:

—1 quart container rubber bands—these are used in rigging his stuff for fishing. The purpose is to keep my spot as "Boat Bitch" for next season.

—A bag of sorghum seeds—for chef to cook for dinner.

—A small local selection of beautiful vinegars made just south of Boston, to enhance his salad.

—A small can of Urbani truffle / tomato—as I had these as samples and I thought of his garnish for the asparagus Velouté . . .

—And a crisp 5-dollar bill, to make sure I keep current on my debt.

All of these little trinkets were in an Urbani cooler pouch, which he can reuse for his lunch.

It's the little things that mean the most .keeping chef being the mentor.

Kevin

This book was intended to be Roland Henin's legacy, a documentation of the great chef's life lessons; however, these lessons only serve to illustrate his true legacy. What Chef Henin leaves behind, more than any wild story or culinary skill, is mentoring. His legacy is thousands of great chefs—chefs deeply rooted in the fundamentals while vigorously challenged to embrace their own unique gifts. Chef Henin is the Johnny Appleseed of this industry. Every culinary venue, competition, and federation is associated with this man. Over the course of fifty years, spanning across the globe, Chef Henin has affected the entire contemporary culinary culture . . . one chef at a time.

Are we the salmon, or are we the river?

We are both.

2009 CIA Graduation Speech, Greystone Campus

In 2009, Timothy Hollingsworth, coached by Roland Henin, made "America's first orbit" into the Bocuse d'Or atmosphere, earning sixth place out of twenty-four competing chefs. Until that time, ever since the Bocuse d'Or began in 1987, the United States had never come close to the podium.

The Bocuse d'Or is the most rigorous culinary competition in the world, held every two years in Lyon, France. In 2013, Rich Rosendale reached the podium, placing third. And then, in 2017, in the Bocuse d'Or's thirtieth year, Team USA won the competition.

If you are reading this book, you have an interest in Culinary Arts. As someone who has an interest, you are a culinary student. You are learning about the art, growing in your own skill, and igniting your passion. As a student, you carry a weight—an obligation of sorts, to be an advocate for these fine chefs who choose integrity over everything else. You have an obligation to be the voice for these unassuming heroes who mostly find themselves in the back of the restaurant, in the kitchen, fighting the fight, and always working when others are playing. Honor these fine people and share their message. Most importantly, model their integrity. Live your life as if you are preparing a meal for Roland Henin.

To honor that momentous year, 2009, we include a speech given by Roland Henin to the CIA graduates at Greystone Campus, in St. Helena, California, in the heart of beautiful Napa Valley.

* * *

Dr. Ryan, distinguished guests, and members of the first graduating class of 2009: as a professional chef, it is my privilege and a great honor to be with you on such a momentous occasion.

As you just heard, this is not my first encounter with the Culinary Institute of America. I was a member of the faculty from 1981 until 1985—some of the best years of my life, as a matter of fact. As a result of my teaching experience, I believe I have a thorough understanding, not just of this fine institution, but of culinary students and recent graduates, in general.

Actually, it was my mission in life to "shape up" near-graduates, just before they enter their last class of the program—the American Bounty—where a good friend of mine was the chef instructor. . . .

Once there were two students at Hyde Park who were taking a course in sauces. They were pretty good students. In fact, they had solid As going into the final exam, but they were also a little arrogant (it is par for the course). So the weekend before finals, they decided to get a head start and go to Johnson & Wales, up the road a bit, to party with some friends, and of course, commiserate on their particular chef instructor. Suffice it to say, they had a good time, and as you can image, didn't make it back to the CIA on time.

They were more than a little nervous by now. They found their instructor and apologized for missing the exam, saying they went off-campus to prepare for the exam, and on the way back, they encountered a flat tire. They were impoverished culinary students, so they had no spare and had to wait a long time for help to come to the rescue. This made them so late, they missed the final test.

The instructor, being such a nice and understanding guy, thought it over and agreed they could make up the final on the following day. The two guys were relieved. They studied hard that night and reported for the exam early the next morning.

The instructor placed them in separate rooms and handed each of them a test booklet. They looked at the first question. It was worth five points and pertained to Carême's four mother sauces. "Cool," they thought. This was going to be a piece of cake. They answered the question and turned the page. They were unprepared, however, for what they saw on the next page. It said—for 95 points— "Which tire?"

An A.O.S. CIA culinary degree is quite an accomplishment. For the rest of your career, it will capture attention and will get your foot in the door. But it will be your job and your responsibility to live up to your credentials. And keep in mind that you also bear the burden of representing many, many successful and prominent chefs who came before you. So . . . screwing up is not an option.

Right now, however, you're probably thinking about getting out (I'm sure a few of you just can't wait) and trying things on your own. One thing for sure that I can tell you now . . . there has never ever been, in the history of the world, a better place, and a better time, to be in the culinary arts.

I'd like to offer you a glimpse of what the future is going to be like for you. Allow me to put it in terms that we chefs can understand. See your career as a seven-course meal. . . .

You might feel today like this is the end of a long hard course of study. But in reality, it is just the beginning. You have just completed the **hors d'oeuvres** course—the little tidbits of this and that. Perhaps some of you are even still in the middle of it. Either way, you've had a taste, just a taste, of what being a chef is all about and, of course, you are hungry for more. Your appetite has been whetted.

That is the purpose of the hors d'oeuvres. They are designed to be a teaser, to make you want more. And from what I've seen, they have done their job.

Soon after this, you will move to the **fish course**, the very beginning of your career. Here it's important to be careful. Fish is delicate and can easily be done incorrectly or even ruined. Don't get carried away. Stick to the fundamentals and what you've been taught, and be open-minded to what others have to teach you. Resist telling others what to do, especially those who are more experienced than you. I have heard many graduates say, "That is not how we do it at the CIA." You may be right, but this kind of attitude will not allow you to win friends. So get used to the taste of your own tongue, because you'll need to develop a habit of biting it, rather than appearing like a know-it-all smart-aleck . . . and I am being polite! Remember that you will be judged harshly on this first course. It's important to do it right, so you can gracefully move into the next phase of your career.

If your fish course is successful, and I am confident that it will be, you'll soon be ready to move into the **main course** phase. Now, you're really cooking. This will be the time from about age thirty to forty, or roughly ten to fifteen years or so after culinary school. The demands on your time and talent will be significant. You'll be working long hours, perhaps moving around quite a bit and finding your way and hopefully advancing at a rapid pace. There will be challenges—both personal and professional. Stay focused. Your plate shouldn't be heaped with everything in your repertoire. You'll have to make choices about what you want to serve, or in other words, about the kind of chef you want to be and the kind of life you want to lead. This will demonstrate the core of who you are and what you are made of!!

The seed you sow in those first three courses will begin to bear much fruit that you will be able to start harvesting during the **salad and cheese** courses. Like the salad, your career will now have a lighter and more refreshing feeling . . . your reward for having worked so long and so hard to get to this point. At the same time, it will be characterized by the strong and powerful flavor and aroma of the cheeses, coated with some of its creaminess. You will have earned a reputation that will precede and follow you. During these years, you will be serving as a mentor to other chefs and perhaps guiding and teaching. You will definitely be making your mark in your very own kitchen or serving as a leader in a culinary association or organization. Whatever path you are on, you will be building a legacy that you will one day leave to others.

Then, someday, you will wake up, look around and realize it is time for **dessert**—the sweet times. First you will wonder if the meal could have been any better, but when you taste how sweet and good this course is, you'll have your answer. Now, you're ready to relax a bit—lecture, coach, give speeches, even write a book. In your quiet time, you can sit back and reflect on how you might have tweaked some of the courses along the way and changed a menu item here or there. But overall, if you've done things the *right* way, you'll be able to realize it has been the kind of meal you always dreamed of.

Then, finally, you'll pour yourself a small glass of the perfect, fine digestif, raising your glass in a toast to all of those who have helped you along the way. Yes, even the lowly assistant and the last *commis*, as all of these people have been instrumental in your success. And honestly, you couldn't have done it so well without each and every one of them on your side.

For the past twenty-one months, you have worked hard, and you deserve to be congratulated. In fact, may I invite everyone to give you a full round of applause?

Ladies and gentlemen . . . to the graduates.

And now, it is my honor to thank you, my fellow chefs, for joining me for dinner. May your meal be fulfilling and flavorful, and may you savor every bite.

Bon appétit.

What's Wrong with This Picture?

For fifty years, Master Chef Roland G. Henin's accomplishments spanned the globe, beginning with a humble stint at the 1967 World Expo in Montreal, Canada:

- Canadian Federation Chefs de Cuisine
- Keltic Lodge at Highlands, Cape Breton, Nova Scotia
- Digby Pines Resort, Nova Scotia
- Hôtels des Gouverneur, Quebec City
- Everglades Club, Palm Beach, Florida
- Grand Bahamas Beach Hotel
- Le Grand Lodge Mont-Tremblant, Quebec
- The Chanticleer Restaurant & Gardens, Nantucket, Massachusetts
- The Dunes Club, Narragansett, Rhode Island
- Johnson & Wales, Chef Instructor
- Textbook Author, *A Practical Understanding of Fonds de Cuisine and Sauces*
- Chef de Cuisine, Breakers Hotel, Palm Beach, Florida
- Executive Chef, Rancho Bernardo Inn, San Diego, California
- Culinary Institute of America Educator:
  - The Stage
  - The Escoffier Room
  - Seafood Kitchen
  - Student Advisor
  - Competition Coach
- American Culinary Federation member:
  - Certified Culinary Educator
  - Approved Culinary Judge
  - Certified Executive Chef
  - Certified Master Chef
  - First National ACF Chef Professionalism Award
  - ACF Certified Master Chef Exam Judge
- Food Editor, *The Art and Science of Culinary Preparation*
- US Western Regional Culinary Team Captain
- US Culinary Olympic Team USA Coach
- World Association of Chef's Societies
- American Academy of Chefs

- Affiliations/Consultant:
  - The Greenbrier, West Virginia
  - Balsams Grand Resort Hotel, New Hampshire
  - The French Laundry, Yountville, California
- Executive Chef, OSF International
- Culinary Research and Development, Truitt Bros, Oregon
- Oregon Certification Chairman
- National Culinary Arts Committee
- Gold Medal, World Cup Winner, Luxembourg
- Director, Art Institute of Seattle
- Delaware North Companies
  - Ahwahnee Resort Hotel, Yosemite
  - Culinary & Hospitality Council
  - Bracebridge Christmas pageant
  - Chef's Summit, CIA Greystone Campus
  - Food Editor, DN Cookbook, *Pathways to Plate*
  - Food Editor, DN Cookbook, *Home Plate*
  - Super Bowl, NFL
  - All-Stars Games, NBA
  - Democratic National Convention
  - Graduation Speaker, CIA, Greystone Campus
- Bocuse d'Or Coach, Lyon, France
- World Association of Chefs
- Global Master Chef
- Fisherman

In 2014, Roland Henin transitioned to working one week per month. Some of his commitments included overseeing the transition of his retirement, continuing the training of chefs Kevin and Percy for the CMC exam, and completing his mentorship of company chefs who were preparing for their next professional certification goal.

Although he enjoyed the idea of freedom in working one week a month . . . Roland Henin is not a "one week a month" kind of guy. Work continued at a "slightly modified full throttle" pace, and his jar remained full. Back in 2014, in a late night conversation during a CMC training session, Henin reflected:

I bought a beautiful boat—25-foot aluminum wonderful Deep V ocean fishing boat. After three years, I have been on this boat for four hours. . . .

I also have this Airstream. My Airstream is the same length of the big boat . . . I never took it on the road. I took it out of the dealership in Seattle and drove straight thru to Chinook and put it in the campground for a couple of weeks . . . sleep in there a few nights . . . never connected the water, only the electricity . . . .with all of the electronics, radio, stereo, TV, and what have you . . . Here again, never "played" and the refrigerator never used . . . or the bathroom or the shower, as there was a great setup in the camp . . . and then I took it to my storage where all my boats were, and it has been there ever since . . . I realize that it is about three or maybe four years old, but it has never been used . . .

What's wrong with this picture???

During the four years of creating this book, Roland Henin continued working his "slightly modified full throttle" schedule until January 2017, when he finally, officially retired from Delaware North Corporation. Chef Henin is now dedicated to spending more time with his first love.

I love to fish, simply because it is total relaxation. There is no telephone, fax, or internet . . . or politics! Our jobs have a lot of distractions, and you try to cope with them and do your recipes. You cope with the long hours. When you are fishing, it's just you and the fish, no deadlines, no schedules. Catching fish is the bonus, not the reason. Fishing is just a healthy outlet for me, balancing the hectic life of a chef.

My aspirations are and have always been to become a good cook, not really famous or rich . . . and if, in the process, I can help my colleagues, especially the young ones, then so much the better. I am happy simply going fishing, growing a small garden, and best utilizing the products of these activities and sharing them with friends.

Someday, when I move to the coast, I hope to raise a few chickens, a few rabbits and maybe a goat or two to do the "mowing" (more time to fish) . . . Now that I am "officially" retired, I bought some cork sheets and am going to make a big board and take everybody's picture with all their "catches!" Hundreds of pictures . . . on the "Wall of Shame" . . .

I consider myself to be lucky, as I am fairly healthy and "almost" wealthy, as when I came into this country, I had a CAP (Certificate of Aptitudes Professional) and $60 in my pocket. And today, I have so much more!!

Roland Henin has a fish camp on the lower Columbia River near Astoria, Oregon. He is always inviting friends onto his boat. Think you got what it takes? Email him and book your spot. Chef would love your company . . . just make sure your lures shine like army belt buckles.

As we were winding up this project, Chef sent me a "memory package" of photos, speeches, and articles, including the CIA graduation speech. Also included was a cardboard box containing a mountain of his name tags and press passes from previous events. In an uncharacteristic presentation, the tags arrived all tangled up in a mass, as if (shudder) Roland Henin had just *thrown them into the box*, haphazardly! I slowly and methodically extracted one lanyard from the bunch—the 2009 Bocuse d'Or Coach pass—and I wore it around my neck, all day. Hey, a girl can dream.

Chef also sent a 2003 article, "The Accidental Master Chef," from *Nation's Restaurant News*. In the article, the then-middle-aged Roland Henin discussed his retirement:

"At some point in the future, I will have to step back. It will be interesting to see all the young bucks positioning for my job." He pauses, allowing himself a slight smile, before adding, "They will be better than me."

Afterword

Certified Master Chef Raimund Hofmeister

I like to bring up Roland Henin with my students. "I know this crazy French chef. He's a good friend of mine. If you haven't heard of him yet, you will sometime in the future. He is a culinary powerhouse and one I respect the most, anywhere in this country. The way Roland Henin chooses to live his craft . . . *This is what you need to do.*" I get silence in my classroom.

It's not just respect. I mean, I love the guy. It's something you can only explain through the life experience you have with that person He has devoted his life to helping others to achieve better results. How many people do you find nowadays who are still that committed? Not many.

We don't like to talk about this in our business, but there *is* sensitivity in certain kinds of people. You go deep, fine-tuning into every fiber of your body and connecting with the food. You connect with the environment. If you want to become an exceptional chef, all the fibers in your body *have* to connect with it . . . everything you touch . . . everything you do . . . the way you look at food . . . the way you select it . . . the way you display it, and the way you serve it. You have to nurse it and babysit every step of preparation. You have to be in love with it. Roland Henin can do that. I have seen it.

Roland and I are different, but not that different. Our essence is the same. How you express your passion, of course we're all different in that, but the *essence* of what we want to do and how we commit is the same. Growing up in kitchens in Germany and France, the chain of command was clearly identified. You worked hard to be recognized. You outshined your competition. It was more hands-on than anything else. In an apprenticeship, the ultimate person is the Chef. Whatever he says is law, and you do it.

Our essence . . . is the same. We grew up in an apprenticeship program. An apprenticeship is different than a degree program. You have to do everything from scratch, the old-fashioned way. We didn't have convenience food. You grew up on the farm and saw animals. You were involved in the cultural part of growing food. We didn't have vacations. No. The school district came by, and they said, "Always pick your 'apprenticeship vacations' from the summer to the fall, because we need all your kids to go to the field and pick the potatoes, or pick the asparagus, or pick the grapes or this and that." At the age of twelve, we knew more about life and the way food is grown and what food is all about than a lot of chefs in this country ever will know! You see? That is the difference. You were connected to Mother Nature in a different way. In cooking, that is an important connection.

Nowadays, we live in a degree society, and in Europe, a similar thing is happening. It's a worldwide trend. The future chef's generation will have to learn to deal with that. Roland is trying to relate the old values to the younger generation because he knows how important they are. He stresses the importance that hard work still gets you ahead in this business. It is not so much what you know when you start out in the career, but where your skill set is, at that point. That is more important than knowing things they tell you from school that you don't know how to apply yet. It takes a 1-2-3 step to build a career, and he is desperately trying to relate this to the younger generation. He is absolutely right, and the few who listen to what he has to say are pretty lucky.

Roland Henin is a dinosaur. He is on the list of extinction. The younger generation of chefs is not aware of what they are missing out by not being around him. He should be much more challenged to be in the limelight. He wants his retirement life, but he's got so much to give. Our doing this story on him is such a gift to whoever comes after, to remember that people like him do exist.

Epilogue

Standing on the Shoulders of Giants

A message, from Roland Henin:

America got where it is today because people invested in their future generations. When I joined the 1967 Montreal Expo and Master Chef Ferdinand Metz started to develop a US Culinary Olympic Team, the American chef didn't exist. So America started to develop culinary schools. We put in effort, money, and energy to the next wave of young cooks . . . developing that spirit of the American chef.

The funny thing is, it wasn't "America" developing American chefs. It wasn't just me or Master Chef Metz. It was *all* those guys, the old giants who left their homes, made a better life for themselves, and then gave back to their new home. Ferdinand Metz and, before him, all the chefs in restaurants, clubs, and instructors . . . they developed the young American kids who were interested in cooking. Thanks to *those* guys, we have chefs today, American-born and American-raised. They hired the American kids, groomed them, and developed them for the future. The next generation should eclipse you—they are like your kids. These giants provided the opportunity for these kids to eclipse.

Nowadays, you don't have many European chefs in the United States. You don't need to, because there are American chefs like Rich Rosendale and David Burke. They were not developed overnight. Even Thomas Keller, who is at the top, the one who has the most integrity with the fundamentals, still gets people like me and others to come back and do workshop. Some cooks are still "sleeping" and he wants to get them on track. We love it. We work it, tutoring these young US chefs. When I ask those guys, what kind of cooking is this? *Is it fusion? Or is it confusion?* They don't know. They shoot from the hip. American cooks were not born into food—not raised on farms, with families who make their own food, not homesteading or foraging. America was the Sahara for cooking. When I came here, you couldn't get fresh tarragon, thyme. . . . When I was a kid growing up in Europe, cooking in America was hot dog and hamburger! Regardless of where the chefs came from—Asia, Europe, etc.—all those mentors, they all play their part.

In the old days, recipes were *sacred*. Now in America, it is the opposite. These culinary giants were interested in *sharing*—knowledge, recipe, technique, so those young American kids could prosper. We need to say thank you to all these giants! As far as I know, nobody has thanked them for their work! They didn't do it for their own benefit; they did it for the future, the American chefs. Look at them, now.

This book is not about me. I am just an instrument at the right time, right place . . . this is a celebration of *all these chefs*. Let it be a tribute, a dedication to all those giants for giving their life and sharing their knowledge and secrets, so that America could be what it is now—a force in the industry, Farm-to-Table, artisan . . . and now . . . winners of the 2017 Bocuse d'Or World Competition! Team USA 2017 brings home the Bocuse d'Or Gold, for the first time ever!

Kindly join me in a THANK-YOU for that whole group of giants, from around the 1950s–1980s. This list is incomplete, and we are surely forgetting some names, but the spirit remains: America owes its culinary identity, its pride and passion, to *all* these men and women who gave everything to our country. America stands on the shoulders of giants. We are forever in their debt.

Adam Balogh	Arnym Solomon	Eugene Bernard
Alain Chapel	Bernard Rosenstein	Eugenie Brazier
Alain Sailhac	Bruno Ellmer	Eugene Szollosi
Alain Senderens	Charles Camerano	Ferdinand Metz
Albert Kumin	Christian Delouvrier	Fred Welt
Aldo Graziotin	Claude Guermont	Franz Lemoine
Alfred Portale	Claudio Papini	Frederic (Fritz) Sonnen-
Alice Waters	Clement Grangier	schmidt
Andre Bertin	Dieter Faulkner	Frédy Girardet
André Soltner	Ella Brennan	Gaston Lenôtre
Anne Willan	Elliott Sharron	Geh-Yah Yin
Anton Flory	Eric Saucy	Georges Perrier
Arnaldo Bagna	Erik Kristensen	Gérard Pangaud
Arno Schmidt	Erwin Ceppok	Gilbert Le Coze

Gunther Heiland
Hans Schadler
Hanz Paetzold
Hartmut Handke
Hartmut Kuntze
Heinz Dubow
Heinz Holtmann
Helmut Loibl
Henri Soule
Hermann G. Rusch
Hugo Bua
Ingo Lange
Italo Norman Peduzzi
Ivan Salgovic
Jacques F. De Chante-
    loup
Jacques Pépin
Jacques Pic
James Beard
Jamie Oliver
Jean Banchet
Jean Henri Salomon
Jean Joho
Jean Marc Loustaunau
Jean Nicolas
Jean Paul Combettes
Jean-Jacques Rachou

Jean-Louis Palladin
Joachim Splichal
Joël Robuchon
Johannes Van Der
    Horst
John Dodig
John Kinsella
Joseph Amendola
Joseph Aranda
Joseph Sheess
Joyce Goldstein
Julia Child
Kurt Schnyder
Leon Dhaenens
Leopold Damm
Leopold K Schaeli
Louis Szathmary
Luc Brondel
Lucien Birkler
Lyde Buchtenkirch
Marcella Hazan
Martin Frei
Maurice Bonfils
Maurice Helou
Michael Bully
Michael Cardena
Michel Richard

Milos Cihelka
Nick Matheos
Noble Masi
Patrick Healy
Paul Prosperi
Paul Prudhomme
Peter Chang
Peter Van Erp
Piero Selvaggio
Pierre Franey
Pierre Latuberne
Pierre Pollin
René Verdon
Rudolf Lang
Rudolph Speckamp
Seppi Renggli
Stanley Slomski
Tsing Pai
Uwe Hestnar
Victor Gielisse
Walter Schreyer
Walter Staib
William Kohl
William Marino
Zoltan Szollosi